RETHINKING WRITING

Rethinking Writing

ROY HARRIS

INDIANA UNIVERSITY PRESS
Bloomington and Indianapolis

Manufactured in Great Britain

Library of Congress Cataloging in Publication Data
A catalog record for this book is available from the Library of Congress.

ISBN 0–253–33776–3 (cloth)

1 2 3 4 5   04 03 02 01 00

Contents

Preface

A profitable Invention for continuing the memory of time past, and the conjunction of mankind, dispersed into so many and distant regions of the Earth; and with all difficult, as proceeding from a watchfull observation of the divers motions of the Tongue, Palat, Lips, and other organs of Speech; whereby to make as many differences of characters, to remember them.

Thomas Hobbes

Hobbes's matter-of-fact description summarizes centuries of traditional wisdom concerning writing. More specifically, the kind of writing in question was that which has formed the basis of European education since Graeco-Roman antiquity: that is, alphabetic writing. Hobbes does not mention writing of any other kind. That alone bears witness to the tyrannical hold that the alphabet has exercised over Western thinking on the subject. An alternative title for this book might have been: *The Tyranny of the Alphabet and How to Escape from it.*

Escaping from it has never been easy for anyone educated from childhood onwards in European schools. For the traditional wisdom about alphabetic writing is deeply embedded in elementary pedagogic practice. This, being based on teaching the alphabet in one or other of its several European versions, varied little over time. It has varied little since Hobbes's day either. Many of us were taught our 'ABC' by methods that are not far removed from those described by Quintilian in the first century AD.[1]

The traditional wisdom is based on certain assumptions about the relationship between speech and writing. Throughout the Western tradition, original contributions to analytic reflection on those assumptions have been few and far between. Two of the most important, one ancient and one modern, will be considered in some detail in this book. They form an essential background to any attempt at rethinking writing today.

Why should there be any need to rethink writing at all? Anyone as satisfied as Hobbes was with the traditional wisdom will presumably see no reason whatever. But the more closely the traditional account is examined, the clearer it becomes that there are basic questions that have been left unanswered or dodged. So trying to answer those questions is one reason for a new attempt to rethink writing. Another reason is that modern technology makes available resources for reading and writing that have never been available before. But perhaps a more important reason than either of these is that how people think about writing is bound up in many subtle ways with how they think about their fellow human beings. There is more to rethinking writing than just looking for a more satisfactory intellectual analysis of particular communicational practices.

Before developing this point further, a fundamental point about alphabetic writing itself needs to be made clear. Alphabetic writing is one form of language-based, or 'glottic' writing. Reading this sentence aloud would be a trivially easy task for millions of people; but impossible for anyone – even if literate – who knew no English. Similarly, anyone who knows no Thai will be hard put to it to read a Thai newspaper (either aloud or silently), even though Thai writing is also alphabetic. These disparities are diagnostic indicators of glottic writing. However, the alphabet as such is not a

---

[1] *Institutio Oratoria*, I.i.21ff.

glottic system. Furthermore, glottic writing is not the only kind of writing human ingenuity has devised. Musical and mathematical notation do not require any knowledge of English (or Thai); but they do require an understanding of the principles on which the notation is based. These principles, however, are quite different from those of glottic writing. Which is why you do not read a musical score or a mathematical table in the same way as you read this page (or any other page of glottic writing in any other language). Forms of non-glottic writing will occasionally be mentioned in this book, but only for purposes of comparison with glottic writing.[2]

Those of us who have learnt to read and write on the basis of using at least one glottic system are usually counted 'literate'. This is not primarily a book about literacy (nowadays a highly controversial concept) but about the concept of glottic writing underlying it. So anyone looking for literacy statistics or discussion of teaching methods will be disappointed. Unless, like the author, they think that arguing about literacy is likely to be unproductive until glottic writing itself is better understood.

Literacy does nevertheless come into consideration, since it affects ways of thinking about writing.[3] In other words, how literate people view writing is often coloured by their opinions concerning literacy and their own status as literate members of the human race. So much so that the very suggestion that there might be any need to rethink writing may seem almost heretical in such an 'advanced' literate society as ours is usually deemed to be. That kind of complacency is itself one symptom of the kind of

---

[2] For more on non-glottic writing in general, see R. Harris, *Signs of Writing*, London, Routledge, 1995. Like all distinctions in this area, that between glottic and non-glottic writing can be problematic. The question of the limits of glottic writing comes up for discussion in the final chapter.

[3] It would be tedious to keep repeating 'glottic'. So from this point on the reader should take it that the term *writing* refers to glottic writing unless there are contextual indications to the contrary.

difficulty involved in trying to reconsider the question of writing objectively.

In a society which invests so much in literacy it is reasonable to expect that the topic of writing might be considered of some importance. So it is. But chiefly because parents are nowadays concerned that their children are not being trained adequately in the relevant skills. Teachers are concerned because they are blamed for this. Governments are concerned because they are urged to improve matters and worry about their electoral popularity and their education budgets. There, however, public concern with writing often ends. Wider issues are rarely raised, and it is rarer still for anyone to ask whether the traditional assumptions commonly taken for granted about writing are sound. These assumptions are among those that have to come under scrutiny in any serious attempt at rethinking writing today.

People commonly measure the level of literacy in a society by estimating what proportion of the population can read and/or write. Exactly how that should be measured is itself controversial. But there is a quite different way of looking at the question. What people think writing is must be counted a no less important aspect of literacy than counting how many of them have mastered the practice. That kind of thinking is the aspect of literacy that this book addresses.

As regards understanding what writing is, societies may be seen as going through three stages from the point at which writing is recognized as something different from drawing pictures and other ways of marking surfaces. The first of these stages, which may be called for convenience 'crypto-literacy', is one in which everything surrounding writing is still regarded as a form of magic or secret knowledge, reinforced by various superstitions and shibboleths. These include myths about the origin of writing (such as its invention by gods or animals).[4] The second stage – with which this book is mainly concerned – might be called 'utilitarian literacy'. It begins when writing is no longer regarded with mystical

---

[4] R. Harris, *The Origin of Writing*, London, Duckworth, 1986, Ch.1.

awe, but as a practical tool or technique for doing what would otherwise have to be done by means of speech, or left undone. Hobbes's statement about alphabetic writing is a typical product of a society at the stage of utilitarian literacy. The third stage, 'full literacy', which arguably no society has yet quite reached, is one in which writing is no longer regarded just as a 'profitable Invention for continuing the memory of time past, and the conjunction of mankind', but as a particular mode of operation of the human mind and the key to a new concept of language.

Chronologically, these three stages are by no means well separated. The first clear indications that writing is regarded as something more than a utilitarian technology, useful to bureaucrat, teacher and poet alike, begin to emerge in the nineteenth century. On the other hand, long after typically utilitarian improvements like the invention of printing, European scholars were still discussing whether the alphabet their printers were using had been designed by God – an idea which clearly belongs to the stage of crypto-literacy. Nowadays much nonsense about runes is popular with adherents to some kinds of 'New Age' lifestyle. Survivals and revivals of primitive beliefs, however, do not alter the general picture. The kind of literacy that has predominated throughout the Western tradition, and still does, is utilitarian literacy. In the Western perspective alphabetic writing is regarded as the *nec plus ultra* among systems of writing because, as Giovanni Lussu has recently put it, we have a conceptual model in which, implicitly or explicitly, writing is regarded as 'nothing more than an ingenious technical device for representing spoken language, the latter being the primary vehicle of human communication'.[5] It is this conceptual model that needs rethinking.

For as long as that model prevails, writing will be valued chiefly for the ways it offers of replacing speech in dealing with and disseminating the kinds of information that are regarded as important. It is essentially a surrogational model; that is, writing is viewed as a surrogate or substitute for speech. The particular

---

[5] G. Lussu, *La lettera uccide*, Viterbo, Nuovi Equilibri, 1999, p.11.

utility of the substitution is seen as being that writing can transmit a verbal message in circumstances where vocal communication would be difficult or impossible. In this sense the written surrogate provides a convenient extension of the spoken word.

The old notion that writing is 'but a substitute for the art of speaking'[6] goes hand in hand with the idea that the basic function of the marks used in writing is phonoptic: i.e. serving to make sound 'visible'.[7] For Voltaire, writing was a 'portrayal of the voice' (*la peinture de la voix*). This seemed so obvious in the mid-nineteenth century to R.C. Trench that he declared it to be an 'unquestionable fact that the written word was intended to picture to the eye what the spoken word sounded in the ear.'[8] The phonoptic thesis is sometime summed up even more succinctly in the phrase 'visible speech'.[9] This curious oxymoron still survives as a reminder of the assumptions underlying the surrogational perspective on writing.

The comparatively recent introduction of communication by telephone, radio and television, together with various electronic forms of recording, have to some extent compensated for the 'disadvantages' of speech as compared with its phonoptic

---

[6] Joseph Priestley, *A Course of Lectures on the Theory of Language and Universal Grammar*, Warrington, 1762, p.22.

[7] Optophonic devices convert light into sound, rendering what was visible audible: phonoptic devices do the reverse.

[8] R.C. Trench, *English Past and Present*, London, Parker, 1855, Lecture V. (Everyman edition, London, Dent, 1927, pp.135–6.)

[9] The term 'visible speech' was applied by Alexander Melville Bell to his own system of phonetic writing (1867), which he regarded as 'self-interpreting physiological letters, for the writing of all languages in one alphabet' – a kind of apotheosis of glottic writing. It was later the title of a well-known book on sound spectrography (R.K. Potter, G.A. Kopp and H.C. Green, *Visible Speech*, New York, Van Nostrand, 1947). More recently, it has been reapplied to traditional writing systems (John DeFrancis, *Visible Speech. The Diverse Oneness of Writing Systems*, Honolulu, University of Hawaii Press, 1989). But the notion that writing makes speech visible goes back a long way in the Western tradition.

counterpart. But that has not as yet undermined the standing or the indispensability of writing as a utilitarian device, in spite of alarmist latter-day prophecies of its impending demise.

The kind of thinking which seems characteristic of utilitarian literacy belongs to a stage in cultural evolution where those who have learnt to read and write are still congratulating themselves on not being 'illiterate'. It is *not* knowing how to substitute writing for speech and, conversely, substitute speech for writing which, for them, epitomizes the state of ignorance they have just left behind. Thus, for all their sophisticated acquaintance with books, documents and records of various kinds, their reflection on such topics is still backward-looking. They think of literacy as an unnatural but beneficial state of affairs which has quite late in human history (within the last few thousand years) begun to supersede the natural orality of the human race. In short, writing is viewed as an artificial superimposition on speech, which still provides its foundation and to which it can still be held accountable. (Hence, for example, periodic outbursts of zeal for 'spelling reform', in which the reformers mainly want to persuade us to do things like write *tough* as *tuff* 'because that is how it's pronounced'.)

A society can remain in this stage for a very long time. People can fail to understand how writing has entirely reshaped their understanding of the world, because they still hark back to the old assumption that writing is just a useful alternative to or, at best, improvement on vocal communication. That is the stage we are still in today, and will remain in for as long as we continue to pat ourselves on the back for progress in eradicating 'illiteracy', regard reading the right books as the basis of all education, and postpone the rethinking of writing that is long overdue.

* * *

Anyone who can both read this sentence aloud and copy it out in a notebook realizes that writing and speech are quite different biomechanical activities. One involves the hand and the other involves the mouth. Hand and mouth engage quite different sensory motor programmes. These can be independently studied as such by physiologists and psychologists. Reading aloud and reading silently are also biomechanically different. It would be possible to read (and understand) this sentence silently without having any idea of how to read it aloud. It might even be possible to read it aloud without understanding what it meant. But if a society is to progress beyond utilitarian literacy to full literacy, writing and reading must be viewed not just as biomechanical activities but as biomechanical activities involving signs. In order to distinguish this kind of thinking about writing from the various other ways of regarding it, the term used in this book will be 'semiological'.[10] A theory of writing without a theory of signs is like a theory of eclipses without a theory of the solar system.

The first important thinkers in the Western tradition to think about writing semiologically were Plato and Aristotle. Aristotle was the first to describe writing explicitly as requiring 'symbols' (*symbola*). His view of the relationship between speech and writing – or simplified versions of his view – became part and parcel of received scholarly opinion on the subject. It was not challenged in any significant way until the twentieth century. The challenge came from one of the founders of the intellectual movement subsequently known as 'structuralism': Ferdinand de Saussure. It was also Saussure who introduced the term *semiology* (*sémiologie*) into the vocabulary of modern cultural studies. This explains why there is so much discussion of Saussure in *Rethinking Writing*. Saussure tried to rethink writing at a basic level for the first time since Aristotle and put it into a wider semiological framework. But at the same time he tried to provide a better theoretical foundation for essentially the same view of the alphabet that Aristotle had taken. Whether Saussure succeeded in what he attempted to do is open

---

[10] To those who find the term *semiological* rebarbative, the author offers no apology, since he did not invent it. Those who find it pretentious into the bargain are invited to stay the course and then judge for themselves whether what was presented as 'semiological' was, in this instance, pretentious or not. Those who wonder why *semiological* was chosen in preference to *semiotic* will find that question dealt with later.

to question. If he did not, it seems important to understand his failure. His work is in any case the starting point for subsequent theorists. Whichever way we look at it, Saussure's thinking about writing is pivotal and commands attention from anyone interested in the subject.

* * *

Those who are content with the traditional wisdom about writing may well ask what is the point of questioning it, unless so doing can be shown to lead forward to practical pedagogic or remedial advances of some kind. These are demands characteristic of utilitarian literacy. But this book does not promise any dramatic improvement in students' spelling or new insights into the treatment of dyslexia. Nevertheless, the Foreword tries to indicate why we should not be happy just to go along with the traditional utilitarian wisdom for ever and a day. Perhaps the most immediate worries have to do with the fact that the traditional wisdom is nowadays being revamped as a 'scientific' basis for all kinds of projects: and *that* it certainly is not. Unfortunately, it is often invoked also to justify linguistic policies and attitudes that should be considered unacceptable in a society of the twenty-first century.

The reader does not have to share the author's worries on this score in order to follow the argument. For the argument is based independently on two strategies. One is pointing out the internal contradictions in earlier views (as judged by their own criteria). The other is pointing out that an alternative approach to writing is available which does not fall into these contradictions. Anyone prepared both to examine the contradictions and look for available alternatives is already committed to rethinking the assumptions underlying traditional utilitarian literacy. That is exactly the kind of rethinking the author had in mind.

* * *

Most of the chapters began life as lectures given at the Sorbonne in the academic year 1991–2. An edited version of those lectures was published in Paris by the Centre National de la Recherche Scientifique in 1993 under the title *La Sémiologie de l'écriture*. Since then I have frequently been told that it was a pity no English version had been made available. However, there was no English version, since the original lectures were in French. Furthermore, when I came to look at the possibility of translating them, I was struck by how odd certain aspects of them might seem to an English readership. I also felt unhappy with the way certain points had been dealt with. So *Rethinking Writing* is not a translation of *La Sémiologie de l'écriture*, but an updated re-writing in English of some of the same topics, often illustrated with different examples. It incorporates both condensations and expansions of the original material, as well as certain changes of emphasis.

I should like here to reiterate my thanks to Marine Valette, Colette Sirat and Rita Harris, all of whom gave invaluable assistance at various stages with the preparation of the French publication, to Sylvain Auroux, to M. Marcassou at CNRS Éditions, and to my former colleagues at the École Pratique des Hautes Études, where I was privileged to spend the year during which these ideas first took shape. For the development of my ideas on integrationism I am indebted, as usual, to Daniel Davis, Hayley Davis, Chris Hutton, Nigel Love, Talbot Taylor, Michael Toolan and George Wolf. Rita Harris read the whole of the present book in draft form and made many excellent suggestions.

R.H.
Oxford, June 1999

Writing and Civilization

When Boswell objected to Johnson's calling the Chinese 'barbarians', Johnson replied curtly: 'Sir, they have not an alphabet.' Eric Havelock reminds us of this anecdote in his original and challenging book on literacy in Classical antiquity.[1] The reminder is a timely one, since the study of writing has been beset in the past – and doubtless still is – by many misconceptions and prejudices. None of these is more pernicious than the persistent belief that writing, and particular forms of writing, are somehow to be taken as diagnostic indicators of levels of civilization or mental progress among the peoples of the world.

Johnson's reply to Boswell is, on the face of it, puzzling. One might have been less worried if he had said: 'Sir, they have no democratic government.' Or even: 'Sir, they have no knives and forks.' But why should a particular *method of writing* be taken as marking a dividing line between civilization and barbarism?

Johnson was not alone in the eighteenth century in holding such a view. Rousseau distinguishes three general types of writing in his *Essai sur l'origine des langues*. The first of these types involves the depiction of objects, the second the use of conventional

---

[1] E.A. Havelock, *The Literate Revolution in Greece and Its Cultural Consequences*, Princeton N.J., Princeton University Press, 1982, p.2

characters to stand for words and sentences, while the third is alphabetic writing.

These three ways of writing correspond almost exactly to three different stages according to which one can consider men gathered into a nation. The depicting of objects is appropriate to a savage people; signs of words and propositions to a barbaric people, and the alphabet to civilized peoples [*peuples policés*].[2]

Rousseau's example of the writing of a barbaric people is Chinese. But although he is rather more explicit than Johnson in his correlations between forms of writing and forms of society, it is still far from clear how these correlations are established. Or why the order of superiority should be as Rousseau evidently takes it to be. But it may be worth pointing out that by Rousseau's day the French term for a person unable to read or write was already *analphabète*: which by implication equates literacy with mastery of alphabetic writing.

Although it is not explicitly invoked either by Johnson or by Rousseau, there was a religious controversy lurking behind attitudes to the alphabet in the eighteenth century. Many people held there was Biblical authority for believing that the alphabet had been invented by God. Joseph Priestley, who rejected this view, nevertheless acknowledged that:

The transition from speaking to writing is so far from being thought easy and natural by many persons, that some of the greatest men this nation ever produced [...] have had recourse to supernatural interposition to account for it, and suppose that the first alphabetical writings were the two tables of stone, which were written by the finger of God himself. And it must be acknowledged, that the oldest accounts we have concerning the use of letters in *Asia* and *Greece* is so circumstanced, as by no means to clash with this hypothesis.[3]

---

[2] J-J. Rousseau, *Essay on the Origin of Languages*, trans. J.H. Moran, Chicago, University of Chicago Press, 1966, p.17.
[3] Priestley, op. cit., pp.23–4.

Priestley himself came to the conclusion that 'the imperfection of all alphabets, the Hebrew by no means excepted, seems to argue them not to have been the product of divine skill . . .'[4] But he also thought that alphabetic writing, for all its imperfections, was superior to that of the Chinese:

> we are told that it is, in fact, the business of half the life of a *Chinese* philosopher to learn barely to read a sufficient variety of books in their language: and the difficulty of inventing, and establishing the use of new characters (without which they could have no way of expressing new ideas) must itself prevent the growth of arts and sciences in that nation.[5]

This kind of *a priori* reasoning about writing systems is by no means extinct even today.

* * *

Underlying the notion that links the invention of writing to the dawn of civilization we can detect at least two supporting theses. Both are plausible, widely held and misleading. One thesis is that the practice of writing requires of the practitioner feats of mental discipline and agility that are beyond the powers of immature minds. Thus the observation that children commonly learn to speak before they learn to write feeds the equation between the pre-literate community and social immaturity. The other thesis is that unless individuals can express themselves in writing and enrich their own minds by reading, their lives and personalities will never reach their full potential. Learning to read and write is seen as an achievement which makes it possible in principle to overcome what would otherwise be inescapable limitations of the human condition, and even to overcome human mortality itself.

As Samuel Butler put it:

> The spoken symbol is formed by means of various organs in or about the mouth, appeals to the ear, not the eye, perishes

---

[4] Priestley, op. cit., p.29.
[5] Priestley, op. cit., pp.35–6.

instantly without material trace, and if it lives at all does so only in the minds of those who heard it. The range of its action is no wider than that within which a voice can be heard; and every time a fresh impression is wanted the type must be set up anew.

The written symbol extends infinitely, as regards time and space, the range within which one mind can communicate with another; it gives the writer's mind a life limited by the duration of ink, paper, and readers, as against that of his flesh and blood body.[6]

This in turn leads to the conclusion than when the bonds of communicational contact are not merely between one living individual and another but – through writing – between present, past and future generations, the result is a superior form of social entity.

This seems to have been the conclusion generally accepted by anthropologists of Butler's day, who draw the line between 'primitive' and 'civilized' peoples by using the presence or absence of writing as a yardstick. Edward Burnett Tylor, who became Oxford's first Professor of Anthropology in 1895, wrote:

The invention of writing was the great movement by which mankind rose from barbarism to civilization. How vast its effect was may be best measured by looking at the low condition of tribes still living without it, dependent on memory for their traditions and rules of life, and unable to amass knowledge as we do by keeping records of events, and storing up new observations for the use of future generations Thus it is no doubt right to draw the line between barbarian and civilized where the art of writing comes in, for this gives permanence to history, law and science.[7]

By this criterion, the Chinese are at last upgraded from barbar-

---

[6] S. Butler, *Essays on Life and Science*, ed. R.A. Streatfield, London, Fifield, 1908, p.198.

[7] E.B. Tylor, *Anthropology*, London, Macmillan, 1881, Ch.8.

ism to civilization. (Tylor magnanimously attributes their failure to develop an alphabet to the proliferation of homonyms in spoken Chinese.) And Tylor at least gives a reason for looking to writing as a measure of human progress. But it is a reason which puts the emphasis on the *consequences* of writing, rather than on writing itself. And this in a way makes the rationale even more puzzling. It is rather like taking the invention of the steam engine as a defining moment in modern history. (A case can be made out for the steam engine, to be sure: but it was what the steam engine made possible rather than the invention itself which, retrospectively, makes it seem of importance. As for actually operating a steam engine for some routine task, it may well be within the competence of a nincompoop.)

The notion that human beings did not become civilized until they became literate was perpetuated by historians of writing for generations after Tylor's book appeared. In 1949 a respected authority on the alphabet stated:

> In the growth of the spiritual human advance, that is of civiliza-
> tion, the origin and the development of writing hold a place of
> supreme importance, second only to that of the beginnings of
> speech, as an essential means of communication within human
> society.[8]

This claim appeals to a different rationale from Tylor's. But it raises even more serious problems. For the fact is that this allegedly 'essential means of communication' was for many centuries in the hands of a fairly small elite. Thus it can be argued that for a long time writing did not contribute a great deal to communication 'within human society'. It was 'essential' only for those to whom it brought power and prestige. The social function of writing was *not* like the function of speech: it did not unite the community, but divided it.

That division, it might be said, is intrinsic to the Western concept of literacy in at least the following respect:

---

[8] D. Diringer, *The Alphabet*, 2nd ed., London, Hutchinson, 1949, p.19.

The key factor in the formation of a specialist literate class in the West has been the difference that existed since the beginning of the alphabetic revolution in ancient Greece between the language of the texts used to teach literacy and the language of the people who were to learn it. This difference, which could only increase with time and literary conservatism, created the need for a class of interpreters of the language preserved in the texts – the literary language. It is important to realize that the expertise of this class does not lie simply in being literate. Nor does it lie simply in its linguistic mastery of the language or dialect of the texts used to teach literacy. These are, of course, necessary attributes but not sufficient. The defining feature of the class is its expertise in constructing justifications on the basis of the texts alone for the linguistic features that the texts happen to manifest.[9]

Put more simply, the point is that it would be naive to construe literacy as a mere matter of knowing how to perform some mechanical but complicated task(s) with writing materials and their products. Literacy involves the creation of a social status for initiates, and the acceptance of a scale of values over and above those which the tasks themselves entail. And this has generally required *inter alia* a revision of ideas about language. As the same author observes:

> most of those who wanted to become literate had to assimilate the conceptions of this [sc. literate] class as to what linguistic competence involved.[10]

The views we encounter in histories of writing to this day still reflect the views of the literate class about its own superior status. Thus one authority assures us: 'Writing exists only in a civilization and a civilization cannot exist without writing.' This is little more

---

[9] Bennison Gray, 'Language as knowledge: the concept of style', *Forum Linguisticum*, Vol.3 No.1, 1978, p.30.
[10] Gray, op. cit., p.30.

than a generalization from the same scholar's view of the position of the illiterate individual in contemporary society. He even extends this without hesitation to comparative assessment of backward and more advanced nations in the modern world:

Nowadays an illiterate person cannot expect to participate successfully in human progress, and what is true of individuals is also true of any group of individuals, social strata or ethnic units. This is most apparent in Europe, where nations without any noticeable percentage of illiterates, like the Scandinavians, lead other nations in cultural achievements, while those with a large proportion of illiterates, like some of the Balkan nations, lag in many respects behind their more literate neighbours.[11]

What is questionable here is not simply how 'advanced' the Scandinavian countries are by comparison with other parts of Europe. There is a circularity involved in appealing to notions like 'human progress' and 'cultural achievement' in an argument addressed to readers whose own education has already taught them to identify literacy as the indispensable basis of progress and culture.

*   *   *

One could go on adding to the list of dubious reasons that scholars have advanced in justification of their own treatment of writing (or particular forms thereof) as landmarks in the history of humanity. Some have even divided this history into three great phases: (i) pre-literate, (ii) literate, and – yet to come – (iii) post-literate.[12]

Anticipation of phase (iii) is recorded as early as 1895, when H.G. Wells published one of the original masterpieces of science fiction. In *The Time Machine*, Wells's narrator describes a society of

---

[11] I. J. Gelb, *A Study of Writing*, 2nd ed., Chicago, University of Chicago Press, 1963, p.222.

[12] Ch. Higounet, *L'Écriture*, 7th ed., Paris, Presses Universitaires de France, 1986, pp.3–4.

the future in which writing has long been forgotten. In this society, orality has regained the monopoly of verbal communication. Books are museum exhibits, and even the museums are in ruins. The passage quoted below tells of how the time-traveller discovers that he is now in the post-writing age. He is exploring what remains of a large palace, accompanied by Weena, a young woman of the aristocratic Eloi race, who speak a language of which he has picked up a few words.

> The material of the Palace proved on examination to be indeed porcelain, and along the face of it I saw an inscription in some unknown character. I thought, rather foolishly, that Weena might help me to interpret this, but I only learned that the bare idea of writing had never entered her head.[13]

This is one of the great missed opportunities in English literature. Wells does not tell us whether what Weena failed to understand was the semiological status of the inscription *per se* (i.e. whether it was a sign at all) or whether she misconstrued it as a sign with some different kind of meaning (e.g. as a drawing, as a mark of ownership, etc.). The 'bare idea of writing' is not quite as bare – or innocent – as that casual phrase seems to suggest.

What the 'bare idea of writing' is – or might be – is a question central to this book. It is not a popular topic, because there are so many vested interests concerned to promote ideas of writing that are far from bare. And it might be argued that if there ever was a 'bare idea' of writing people have long since lost sight of it. Nevertheless, the intellectual exercise involved in trying to reconstruct that idea might well be worth the pursuing

* * *

Comment is called for at this point on one of the 'less-than-bare' notions of writing dear to some scholars in the humanities. It impinges on our present concerns because what is assumed is that the worth of a civilization is ultimately to be judged by its 'litera-

---

[13] H.G. Wells, *The Time Machine*, London, 1895, Ch. 8.

ture'. Hence the curious restriction of the term *writing* and the verb *write* to apply to the production of literary compositions. As when Roland Barthes, in a seminar at the École Pratique des Hautes Études, delivered the oracular pronouncement:

On the one hand we have what it is possible to write, and on the other what it is no longer possible to write.

This is one of those truisms of such striking banality that they sound oddly like the result of profound and original thought. For Barthes this truism applied to one culturally privileged activity: that of the writer *qua* author. It is the sense of the verb *write* in which the answer to teacher's question 'What did Balzac write?' is expected to be: 'Balzac wrote *La Comédie Humaine*.' And doubtless everyone agrees that it is no longer possible to write the novels of Balzac. They are already written and Balzac is dead. What he wrote can be republished, imitated, or adapted; but it is no longer possible to *write* it – that is, write it in the sense in which writing is a creative activity and the product is a literary work. It is in this sense that modern universities offer courses in so-called 'creative writing': the students would be surprised and perhaps alarmed if offered instruction in innovative calligraphy. They want to be poets, novelists, playwrights.

Other interpretations of Barthes's equivocal dictum can certainly be proposed; for example, the point might be there are subjects which a writer can tackle today, but others that it is no longer possible to write about; or there are styles of writing that are nowadays acceptable, but others that are quite outmoded. Straight away the proposition become less banal. But in all these cases the activity of the writer is conceived as that of literary composition. When Barthes invented the notion of a 'degree zero' in writing he was thinking not of the illiterate's struggle to master a script but of a certain neutrality of literary expression.[14] His categories of the modes of writing were bourgeois writing, Marxist writing, poetical writing, etc.

---

[14] R. Barthes, *Le degré zéro de l'écriture*, Paris, Seuil, 1953.

Similarly when Ezra Pound, many years before Barthes, pro-
claimed that 'writers as such have a definite social function exactly
proportioned to their ability *as writers*' he did not have in mind the
ability to hold a pen and form legible characters, or to display a
versatile competence in the many writing systems of the world.[15]
A parallel restriction applies to the term *reading*. When I.A.
Richards published a book entitled *How to Read a Page*, he did not
begin with the question of which way up to hold it.[16] His advice
never addresses the problem posed by the fact that different scripts
and different formats require different scanning procedures if we
want to make sense of them. Nor is reading a newspaper treated
differently from reading a legal contract. 'Reading', for Richards,
begins with the assumption that the archetypal experience is dealing with a (Western) literary text. What is interesting about
Pound's emphasis on the ability of writers '*as writers*' is that it
epitomizes a literate society's reverence for the literary text and
hence its tendency to identify 'writing' as the mode of serious
expression *par excellence*. The elevation of 'the writer' to a position
of high cultural prestige is characteristic of a society imbued with
the assumptions of utilitarian literacy. 'The writer' is one whose
works *deserve* to be circulated and preserved for posterity: and only
writing can ensure this. In the Western tradition this attitude goes
back to ancient times: Cicero already uses *scriptor* interchangeably
with *auctor*.

But the writing that writers like Balzac and Cicero do constitutes no more than a minute fraction of writing as understood by
the historian or the anthropologist. Writing in this broader sense
too could, at a pinch, be brought within the scope of Barthes's
dictum. For there are writing systems that have disappeared as
well as writing systems no longer in use, just as there are lost
languages and dead languages. In this wider context, Barthes's
truism recovers its reassuring banality. But underneath this banal-

---

[15] E. Pound, *ABC of Reading*, 1934, Ch. 3.
[16] I.A. Richards, *How to Read a Page*, London, Kegan Paul, Trench, Trubner, 1943.

ity one senses an attempt at definition. The suggestion seems to be that if, for any particular society over any given period of time, we could somehow draw a moving line separating what literate members of that society could write and what they could not, then we would at one stroke have sorted out the history of writing.

This, however, would be a jejune idea. For *what* it is possible to write (either in the broader or the narrower sense) is secondary and adventitious. Before anything can be written at all, writing has to be available. Not so much in the sense that a system of writing has to be in existence before anyone can use it, but in the sense that without the concept of writing the question of *what* to write does not even arise.

As soon as this conceptual priority is given its due, Barthes's pronouncement is no longer the truism it seemed to be, and to take it seriously would be a mistake. The history of writing is not a steady, gradual progression in which some primitive concept of writing is replaced by concepts that become successively more sophisticated or more correct.

Nor should the current popularity of the odd expression *oral literature* be allowed to obscure what is at issue here. What the oxymoron *oral literature* reflects is Western culture's belated and somewhat embarrassed attempt to come to terms with the realization that the production of poetry, narratives and other verbal compositions that engage the intelligence and the imagination is not the exclusive prerogative of literate civilizations. But the downmarket label 'oral literature' makes it clear what is happening here: outsiders are being reluctantly granted a cultural status to which 'literally' they are not entitled. Authors of 'oral literature' are thus automatically branded as second-class citizens in the Republic of Letters.

* * *

There is a certain historical irony in the fact that Wells's prophecy of a post-literate society was addressed to readers who belonged to the first generation to benefit from Disraeli's famous education act of 1876, which laid down that every child in the land should be taught to read and write. In other words, at the very moment when universal literacy is recognized as an achievable ideal (at least, in one country) we find already a forecast of eventual reversion to a state of universal illiteracy. In fact, more than a hundred years later, the number of countries where more or less everyone is taught to read and write as a matter of course remains quite small. It is by no means out of the question that in some parts of the world literacy will simply be bypassed by the advent of new communications technologies which make it unnecessary to teach the skills of reading and writing to the whole population.

This thought should provide us with another reason to reflect on what we mean by a literate society and on the connexion between literate societies and civilization. According to historians of writing, we know nothing that allows us to suppose that there were literate societies before, roughly, the beginning of the third millennium BC. But this is because most historians of writing regard the evidence as beginning with the appearance of the earliest surviving texts (or what are nowadays recognized as such). Is it reasonable, however, to speak of a literate society if we know that the production of such texts remained in the hands of a small, privileged class of professionals? This question reflects back upon the notion that there is some kind of equation between writing and civilization. And in turn raises the question of whether it is only the literate members of a society who are civilized.

From at least the time of Disraeli onwards, it is indeed possible to detect in educational reform the assumption that teaching the illiterate to read and write is a matter of civilizing them, of making them fully participating members of society. This idea is often overlaid and reinforced by the further assumption that literacy brings with it access to an essential religious text: the Bible in the case of most Western educators. Carried to its logical conclusion, this brings us to the notion that literacy not only civilizes but, more importantly, opens up the prospect of spiritual salvation for the individual. That conclusion has been overtly embodied in many programmes of missionary linguistics, and still is. It is no coincidence that in many parts of the world the first writing systems were devised by missionaries and the first published texts were religious texts.

How does the 'bare idea' of writing relate to these far-from-bare enterprises that are seemingly based upon it? Do they have anything to do with it at all? Or is writing itself merely a neutral technology, which can be used for whatever purposes the user decides? And if the latter, why should one continue to insist on the advent of writing – rather than, say, the advent of the steam engine or the advent of electricity – as heralding the dawn of civilization?

The most ambitious answer that theorists have recently proposed as regards the importance of writing in human evolution involves the claim that writing is not 'just' a technology, a means of storing and retrieving information. Writing is said to be something more, and this something more is psychological. Writing, it is held, 'restructures consciousness'.[17] The claim is that when *Homo scribens* eventually succeeded *Homo loquens* a new kind of mentality made its first appearance in the history of the human race.

A deeper understanding of pristine or primary orality enables us better to understand the new world of writing, what it truly is, and what functionally literate human beings really are: beings whose thought processes do not grow out of simply natural powers but out of these powers as structured, directly or indirectly, by the technology of writing. Without writing, the literate mind would not and could not think as it does, not only when engaged in writing but normally even when it is composing its thoughts in oral form. More than any other single invention, writing has transformed human consciousness.[18]

More extreme forms of this claim have also been put forward, some of which are very reminiscent of eighteenth-century views

---

[17] W.J. Ong, *Orality and Literacy*, London, Methuen, 1982, Ch. 4.
[18] Ong, op. cit., p.79.

concerning the superiority of alphabetic writing. According to Marshall McLuhan, for example, 'the Chinese are tribal, people of the ear', their writing is non-alphabetic and only the alphabet 'has the power to translate man from the tribal to the civilized sphere'.[19] R.K. Logan relates 'the lack of theoretical science in China' to the non-alphabetic nature of Chinese writing.[20]

If these or similar propositions have any foundation, then there would seem to be grounds – at least in principle – for saying that Johnson and Rousseau, together with some nineteenth-century anthropologists and their successors, may not have been altogether misguided in attributing to the advent of writing, or particular forms of writing, a diagnostic status. That would still leave room for a great deal of argument about the details. But if it is – or may be – true that there is a huge gulf separating the mentality of the preliterate individual from the mentality of one who can read and write (and habitually does so), it is not difficult to see how writing falls into place as one of the most crucial developments in human evolution. And if so, the eventual regression to a Wellsian post-literate society would be a matter of considerable and legitimate concern, not only for educationists but for everyone else. A future without writing would be, quite simply, an impoverished form of living with an impoverished form of thinking; a life from which the 'bare idea' of writing had vanished.

Perhaps this recognition of the cognitive role of writing marks the beginning of the transition from utilitarian literacy to full literacy. Perhaps it heralds at long last the advent of a mature literate society. But how are we to assess these possibilities? By what criteria are such claims and their validity or invalidity to be evaluated? The contention motivating the present book is that the only sound basis for such an evaluation depends on developing an objective and independent semiology of writing. 'Objective' and

---

[19] M. McLuhan, *The Gutenberg Galaxy*, Toronto, University of Toronto Press, 1962, p.38.
[20] R.K. Logan, *The Alphabet Effect*, New York, Morrow, 1986, Ch.3.

'independent' in that it will be free from the more or less ethnocentric assumptions discussed above, which have shaped the study of writing and of its history hitherto; free from any tendency to flatter our literate self-esteem by tacitly equating the readers and writers of the world with its civilized population. And this, for obvious reasons, is a problematic task. How can scholars distance themselves from presuppositions that are exemplified by – and enshrined in – their own publications, their own scholarly endeavours and their own institutional existence?

What is needed – the goal – is nevertheless clear enough. It must be a semiology which breaks with the old tradition of treating writing systems as indices of cultural progress or cognitive advancement, the tradition which judges writing systems by their 'accuracy' in transcribing the spoken word, the tradition which invariably treats the alphabet, either tacitly or overtly, as the ultimate human achievement in the history of forms of writing. For only then can we feel confident that we have available a semiology of writing which does not merely recycle the old prejudices.

One might have hoped that such a semiology would emerge from the work of the two great founders of modern thinking about signs, Saussure and C.S. Peirce. Peirce, however, has disappointingly little to say about writing: he is, in fact, a telling – one might even say shocking – example of the intellectual myopia that utilitarian literacy can induce about its own procedures and their semiological implications. Saussure, on the other hand, at least saw to what extent his own society's views of linguistic matters were distorted by the accumulated biasses of literacy. He therefore insisted as a prerequisite for any modern science of language and languages that a clear separation should be made between the spoken and the written.

That lesson was scrupulously learnt by his successors and became one of the maxims of twentieth-century linguistics. Unfortunately, the lesson was generally interpreted as meaning that linguists need not bother with writing, because writing was not really 'language'. Thus, as one observer put it, 'the study of writing began to suffer at the hands of linguists.' It still does.[21] Any opportunity that linguistics might have had to contribute to the self-understanding of a literate society was thus lost. For while insisting on that separation, Saussure at the same time reinstated (for reasons connected with his own academic politics) some of the most questionable traditional assumptions about writing.

Today, as a result, we are still lacking a viable semiology of writing, one which will be sufficiently robust to stand up to the critical scrutiny of a generation willing to take less for granted – both about language and about communication in general – than Saussure's did. The rethinking of writing that was already needed in Saussure's day still remains to be done.

---

[21] K.H. Basso, 'The ethnography of writing', p.425. (R. Bauman and J. Sherzer, *Explorations in the Ethnography of Speaking*, Cambridge, Cambridge University Press, 1974, pp.425–32.) The passage continues: 'Depicted by members of the emergent structural school as a pale and impoverished reflection of language, writing was consigned to a position of decidedly minor importance. Textbooks continued to include brief chapters on the subject, but this was to emphasize that writing and language were entirely distinct and that the former had no place within the domain of modern linguistics.'

CHAPTER ONE

Aristotle's Abecedary

Plato was the first authority we know of who questioned the thinking about writing that was current in his day. His conclusions, if we can rely on the *Phaedrus* and the authenticity of *Letter 7*, were deeply sceptical.[1] He thought that writing compared disadvantageously with speech, because it gave a specious permanence to words. This is a contention which does not make sense unless addressed to a society already well into the stage of utilitarian literacy, where one of the great advantages of this surrogate form is seen as being, precisely, that it gives words a permanency – or at least a durability, a verifiability – that the human voice does not afford. Plato's objection to writing, in short, is not theological or metaphysical or pragmatic but semiological. He objects that writing does not do what people commonly assume it can do, i.e. stand as an alternative to or even a definitive version of an oral discourse. This objection implies that what a written text signifies cannot be equated with what the corresponding oral discourse signifies. (It is a purely negative objection, i.e. Plato does not commit himself as to what a written text *does* signify. Aristotle later exploited this lacuna.)

Plato had parallel misgivings about painting as a way of

---

[1] Plato, *Phaedrus and Letters VII and VII*, trans. W. Hamilton, London, Penguin, 1973.

capturing what the eye can see.[2] The eye can see a person; but all the painter can produce is a lifeless image.

> The productions of painting look like living beings, but if you ask them a question they maintain a solemn silence. The same holds true of written words; you might suppose that they understand what they are saying, but if you ask them what they mean by anything they simply return the same answer over and over again.[3]

Here we glimpse the beginnings of what was to become a cross-modal semiological *topos* in the Western tradition, whereby writing is commonly assumed to be a kind of 'depiction' of speech. It is clear from the comparison, however, that what Plato is objecting to about writing is not the *accuracy* of the depiction – the question that was to preoccupy the grammarians of antiquity and their successors. He is not, in other words, complaining that the Greek alphabet is deficient in resources to capture all the nuances of spoken Greek. That would be like complaining that the portrait does not resemble the sitter. Plato's objection goes much deeper than that. What he is rejecting is the whole assumption that writing provides a viable surrogate for speech, or at least denying that writing can be treated as a reliable substitute where important (i.e. philosophical) matters are concerned. Adopting a semiological perspective on writing, as far as he is concerned, is a move in an argument about language and philosophy. Had he lived to witness the advent of the tape-recording he would have said exactly the same thing about that. The problem is not that writing does not let us hear the voice of the author. The problem is, rather, that writing (like the tape-recording) is not language *in vivo*, but merely the lifeless shell or trace that language leaves behind.[4] To suppose

---

[2] For detailed discussion of Plato's reservations about art, see Iris Murdoch, *The Fire and the Sun*, Oxford, Oxford University Press, 1977.

[3] *Phaedrus*, 275.

[4] A superficially similar but much shallower complaint reappears in the work of some twentieth-century linguists. (See Chapter 8.)

otherwise is to make the mistake of equating language with its material residuum. And this Plato implicitly compares with mistaking the portrait for the living person.

Plato's scepticism strikes at the very foundations of utilitarian literacy. It questions the validity of divorcing the speech from the speaker, the text from the writer. And insofar as writing encourages us to believe in the viability and usefulness of that divorce it is, for Plato, a deception. It masquerades as something it cannot possibly be. From this conclusion it is not a million *stadia* to St Paul's famous warning that 'the letter killeth'. Utilitarian literacy needs its detractors. They play an essential role in maintaining the perception that writing and the interpretation of writing are forms of *expertise*, not to be entrusted to fools. The lawyer, the theologian, the historian, the grammarian and the literary critic all have a vested professional interest in perpetuating that perception.

* * *

Part of the background to Plato's complaint concerns the pervasive practice in his time of discussing speech in terms of writing.[5] There were two terms *stoikheion* and *gramma* that could be used either to refer to letters of the alphabet or to the sounds of speech. As we see from Plato's *Cratylus*, Plato himself tends to use them interchangeably. To add to the problem, both letters and sounds were commonly identified by their letter-forms or letter-names (*alpha*, *beta*, etc.). The earliest surviving Greek grammatical treatise, that of Dionysius Thrax, bears witness to the fact that this potentially confusing state of affairs survived long after Plato's

---

[5] Saussure, more than two millennia later, castigates his own immediate predecessors for doing exactly the same. But they did not have the excuse that might be offered on behalf of Plato's generation; namely, that no adequate metalinguistic terminology was available. The longevity of this conflation points to the endemic scriptism of Western thinking about language.

day.[6] There we find a section devoted to the *stoikheion* which starts by announcing that there are twenty-four letters (*grammata*) in the alphabet and that they are called *grammata* because etymologically that means 'scratches' or 'traces'. But then we are told that they are also called *stoikheia* because they are arranged in a row (*stoikhon*). But the subclassification which is then given into vowels, diphthongs, consonants, etc. seems to be based on phonetic criteria. The letter-shapes themselves are never discussed, although they are used to identify the *stoikheia*.[7]

A similar state of affairs, as Françoise Desbordes points out, is found in Latin with the terms *littera* and *elementum*. As she goes on to observe, however, although authorities of this period are apparently quite capable of declaring that 'the human voice consists of letters' and so on, it would be absurd to suppose that they imagined armies of little black marks issuing forth from the speaker's mouth.[8] But what exactly did they imagine? And what did they mean? These are difficult questions. But perhaps no more difficult than the corresponding questions concerning people who nowadays claim that some words, and even some languages, are 'pronounced as they are written'. It seems unlikely that they believe the movement of the vocal organs imitates the movement of the hand holding the pen. Or perhaps they do?

These are questions that bring us face to face with the difficulty of conceptualizing and explaining, even in a quite sophisticated literate society, exactly what the relationship between speech and writing is. And especially difficult if one wishes to interpret the

---

[6] Dionysius himself seems to have lived in the 2nd century BC, but the surviving treatise that bears his name is probably a much later composition.

[7] A good modern edition is that of Jean Lallot, *La Grammaire de Denys le Thrace*, Paris, CNRS, 1989. The section on the *stoikheion* is Chapter 6 of the text.

[8] F. Desbordes, *Idées romaines sur l'écriture*, Lille, Presses Universitaires de Lille, 1990, p.113.

relationship in semiological terms, as Aristotle, for one, certainly wished to do.

* * *

Aristotle's response to Plato (if that is the right way to look at it) is to counter Plato's scepticism by conceding, in effect, that one must not confuse the functions of speech and writing and then proceeding to draw a clear semiological distinction between the two. He is the first to try to explain the semiological gap between speech and writing; i.e. exactly *why* the written forms do not capture the thought expressed by the corresponding spoken forms.

Sounds produced by the voice are symbols of affections of the soul,[9] and writing is a symbol of vocal sounds. And just as letters are not the same for all men, sounds are not the same either, although the affections directly expressed by these indications are the same for everyone, as are the things of which these impressions are images.[10]

This turns out to have been one of the most cryptic but also one of the most influential statements about writing ever made in the Western tradition. Because it is so cryptic, certain details are less than clear, but it nevertheless leaves us in no doubt that for Aristotle the essential function of writing is to provide signs for other signs, i.e. visual metasigns which 'symbolize' the sounds of speech.

How are we to intepret this? The first requirement, often neglected by commentators, is to determine the level of abstraction at

---

[9] 'Affections of the soul' is the traditional translation, which I retain here in preference to replacing it by 'concepts' or 'mental impressions', partly because either of the latter would stand as much in need of interpretation as 'affections of the soul'. Keeping this somewhat quaint term at least draws attention to the obscurity of what Aristotle meant by it. Even in the latter part of the nineteenth century there were still linguists who referred to language as an external revelation of 'acts of the soul' (e.g. W.D. Whitney, *The Life and Growth of Language*, New York, Appleton, 1875, p.303).

[10] *De Interpretatione*, 16 A.

which Aristotle's account is situated. For it is probably only the synopsis of a more elaborate discussion by Aristotle that has not survived in the extant texts.

Aristotle evidently recognizes four basic elements, including two types of sign: oral and written. The former belongs to spoken discourse and the latter to visual communication. He further distinguishes an internal element, the 'affection of the soul', which is related to an external element (the object or thing in question). So, according to Aristotle's schema, there are two channels of communication which link certain elements occupying, so to speak, two different spaces: an internal, psychological space and an external, physical space.

EXTERNAL	INTERNAL
objects	affections of the soul
vocal sounds	
letters	

Let us take, for example, talking about the city of Athens. According to Aristotle's semiology, the starting point is the object, the city itself as an existing complex. Then there is the affection of the soul, a psychological item, the idea one forms of this city. Third, there is the name of the city, the name we utter when we talk about Athens. Finally, there is the written form of this name, that we find in edicts, inscriptions, etc. So there are four elements, each perfectly distinguishable from the other three.

The passage from *De Interpretatione* is concerned with setting out the general relations obtaining between these four types of element; i.e. between what we say, what we write, what we think and the thing about which we speak, write and think. Straight away it is evident that the discussion is situated at a higher level of abstraction than that which relates to the study of particular languages, or even that of logic. And there is nothing surprising in that. For we are dealing here in *De Interpretatione* with the preface to a treatise on the proposition.

But what is remarkable in Aristotle's presentation of this very general and preliminary discussion is that the relation between the vocal sign and the written sign is assumed to be *of the same order* as the relation obtaining between the vocal sign and the affection of the soul, as indicated by the use of the term *symbolon*. This is Aristotle's contribution to rethinking writing. In both cases we are dealing with a 'symbolic' relation. Written signs are *symbola* of vocal sounds, and vocal sounds in turn are *symbola* of affections of the soul.

What does Aristotle mean by this? What is a *symbolon*? According to Liddell and Scott, it is one half of an *astragalos* or similar object that two *xenoi* or parties to a contract broke in two, each keeping half as proof of the contractual relationship.[11] Modern translations commonly render it as 'symbol' although, as Whitaker observes, this is 'not the most informative word to choose'.

The normal use of the Greek word was for a tally or token. A contract or other agreement might be marked by breaking a knucklebone or other object in two, one portion being taken by each of the parties to the agreement. Each person kept his piece, and could identify the person who presented the other piece by matching it with his own. The word hence comes to denote any token, for instance, for admission to the theatre.[12]

As a communicational metaphor, Aristotle's use of the term is both striking and profound. What is involved is both an agreement (between the two parties) and a physical relationship between the items (since the two halves were one before being sundered). Furthermore, they were broken apart deliberately (by the parties in question) in order to provide proof of that relationship.

Here we have a basic type of connexion which is of great semiological interest. For the two disjoint parts of the *symbolon* have no value at all individually. *Each is significant only as a counterpart of the other.* More importantly still, this relationship is *not*

---

[11] H.G. Liddell and R. Scott, *Greek-English Lexicon*, rev. ed., Oxford, Clarendon, 1996, p.1676.

[12] C.W.A. Whitaker, *Aristotle's De Interpretatione*, Oxford, Clarendon, 1996, p.10.

representational. Unlike the relationship between the affection of the soul and the object: that *is* representational.

Aristotle draws this distinction quite clearly, albeit succinctly. It is all the more dispiriting to read modern commentators who rabbit on about 'representation' without apparently noticing that right from the beginning of the Western tradition the more alert minds were perfectly capable of distinguishing representation from symbolism.[13] Semiology today might perhaps take the rehabilitation of that distinction as ranking among its urgent priorities. Without it any attempt to think clearly about writing – and many other practices involving signs – is on a hiding to nothing.

With the two halves of the *symbolon* there is no question of one *representing* the other or being a *substitute* for the other. They are not identical, nor equivalent. Substituting one for the other is a meaningless operation. (It would leave things exactly as they were.) Nor is there any question of one half being a copy of the other. (On the contrary, it is important that they should differ.) The whole point is that they are both *different* and *unique*. Both their difference and their uniqueness are united in their complementarity. Anyone who does not grasp that has not understood what a *symbolon* is, at least as Aristotle is using the term.

Aristotle invites us to see certain relations as 'symbolic'. (Whether we accept that invitation is another matter.) He invites us in effect to see a Greek writing down the name of the city of Athens as someone inscribing *grammata* which are *symbola* of the sounds uttered when this name is spoken. At the same time – and one might say almost in the same breath – he invites us to see the sounds uttered as *symbola* of something in the mind of the speaker (the idea of the city thus named, i.e. the city of Athens). The point to note is that according to this account the *grammata* as such have nothing to do with Athens. It would not matter if Athens were a

---

[13] Oddly, perhaps as the legacy of nineteenth-century poetry, *symbolism* is now the vaguer term. Almost anything can be a symbol of something else, provided the mind makes the requisite connexion. That was not the case in Aristotle's day.

country village or a foreign land or another planet. All that matters (in this relationship) is that the *grammata* 'symbolize' the right sounds, the right sounds being those of the name 'Athens'. However, there is an *indirect* relationship between these *grammata* and the city in question, which hinges on the name 'Athens' being – as a matter of fact – the name of that very city.

But what is it to be 'the name of' that city? The name, according to Aristotle, is the sound uttered which symbolizes that 'affection of the soul' relating to the city of Athens. (Presumably someone who has never seen or heard of Athens will not have any corresponding affection of the soul: so for such a person the name will be meaningless, i.e. the sound in question will not be a name of anything, or else a name of something unknown.) The affection of the soul, it should be noted, is not a *symbolon* of the city of Athens, but its image (*homoioma*). In other words, symbolic relations do not, for Aristotle, obtain generally between external and internal elements. Vocal sounds are symbols of affections of the soul, but letters are not. The city of Athens is not a symbol of anything.

According to Aristotle the affections of the soul (*pathemata tes psyches*) are *homoiomata* of objects or events (*pragmata*). So it is the external world which supplies the originals for those images that dwell in the soul. This world of *pragmata* outside, which is the same for all of us, thus has only an indirect connexion with speech and an even more indirect connexion with writing.[14]

---

[14] At the beginning of *De Sophisticis Elenchis* Aristotle seems to suggest that names (*onomata*) are symbols of things (*pragmata*) and we employ them because we could not use the things themselves for purposes of discourse. But this is not to be taken too seriously, as Swift saw when he turned it into a joke in *Gulliver's Travels* about the sages who save the wear and tear on their vocal cords by carrying around large sacks of things on their backs in order to obviate the need for words. Aristotle's purpose here becomes clear when the remark is put in context. He is warning against the dangers of supposing that the world of words provides a faithful image of the world of things. His point is, precisely, that words are *not* to be taken as standing in a one-to-one relationship with particular things. A single name signifies more than one thing.

In the same passage in *De Interpretatione* Aristotle distinguishes between a *symbolon* and a *semeion*. The latter is speech as a sign of what is happening in the speaker's soul (*psyche*) at a given moment. In other words, when I pronounce the name of the city of Athens, that is for my listeners a *semeion* of what I am thinking, i.e. an indication of the fact that I have that city in mind. My listeners, however, will not know that unless they know what the name in question is a *symbolon* of. So understanding the *semeion* presupposes acquaintance with the *symbolon*. Aristotle also distinguishes between what we write (*graphomena*) and the letters (*grammata*) we use for that purpose.

Aristotle, in short, is quite careful to distinguish terminologic-ally between the units of the communication system (spoken or written) and their use in given circumstances. But unfortunately these distinctions were not always preserved in the exegetical tradition. Already in the Latin translation of Aristotle by Boethius the two terms *symbolon* and *semeion* are rendered by a single Latin word, *nota*, which in any case has no technical mean-ing corresponding to that of *symbolon* in Greek. This example illustrates how easy it is to lose in translation the nuances of Aristotle's quite subtle formulation. Boethius has already blurred the schematic picture that Aristotle took some trouble to delineate quite precisely, and many subsequent commentators have done no better.

If the above interpretation of this key passage is on the right lines, Aristotle's semiological framework provides for a series of relations between quite separate theoretical items, which can be arranged by order of origin as follows:

object > affection of the soul > vocal sign > written sign.

The series begins with objects in the external world, which generate affections of the soul (*psyche*). These in turn give rise to vocal signs, through the social institution of language. Vocal signs in turn give rise to written signs, through another social institu-tion, which is writing. Thus the affection of the soul presupposes the object, the vocal sign the affection of the soul and the written sign the vocal sign. Relations between written signs and vocal signs, as between vocal signs and affections of the soul, are symbolic. Relations between affections of the soul and external objects are based on likeness.

Thus Aristotle's solution to the problem of defining the relationship between writing and speech is to incorporate both into a model of language which displays their respective roles with respect to (i) thought, (ii) the expression of thought and (iii) the external world. In this model, writing does not *directly* express thought. (To that extent, Plato would have been pleased.)

* * *

Aristotle's solution became incorporated into the body of received truths about language that were handed down in the Western tradition. Thus, for example, we find the grammarians of Port-Royal in the seventeenth century initiating their young pupils into the mysteries of grammar by explaining the relation between writing and speech as follows:

> Grammar is the Art of speaking. Speaking is explaining one's thoughts by signs, that men have invented for this purpose.
> It was found that the most convenient of these signs were vocal sounds.
> But because these sounds do not last, other signs were invented to make them durable and visible, which are the written characters that the Greeks call *grámmata*, from which came the word Grammar.[15]

This is unadulterated (albeit simplified) Aristotle, with the *topos* of 'visible speech' added for good measure.[16]

Where does Saussure stand in relation to the Aristotelian

---

[15] *Grammaire générale et raisonnée*, Paris, 1660, p.5.

[16] The Platonic parallel between painter and poet had long since been epigrammatized in Horace's famous dictum *ut pictura poesis*. The concept of writing as 'visible speech' extends this. If poetry is depiction, the written poem is a depiction of a depiction.

legacy? When Saussure says that writing exists only to represent spoken language he at first sight appears to align himself unambiguously with this tradition. Indeed it might seem that what he says on the subject adds nothing new.

> A language and its written form constitute two separate systems of signs. The sole reason for the existence of the latter is to represent the former.[17]

However, Saussure does not follow Aristotle all the way. When Saussure refers to the 'sounds' of a word, it is important to be clear what he means.

> A linguistic sign is not a link between a thing and a name, but between a concept and a sound pattern (*image acoustique*). The sound pattern is not actually a sound; for a sound is something physical. A sound pattern is the hearer's psychological impression of a sound, as given to him by the evidence of his senses. [. . .]
> We grasp the words of a language as sound patterns. That is why it is best to avoid referring to them as composed of 'speech sounds'. Such a term, implying the activity of the vocal apparatus, is appropriate to the spoken word, to the actualisation of the sound pattern in discourse. Speaking of the *sounds* and *syllables* of a word need not give rise to any misunderstanding, provided one always bears in mind that this refers to the sound pattern.[18]

No such interpretation can reasonably be put on what the Port-Royal grammarians say about writing; for they make it quite clear that its basic purpose is to make ephemeral sounds 'durable and

---

[17] F. de Saussure, *Cours de linguistique générale*, 2nd ed., Paris, Payot, 1922, p.45. All page references are to this edition. English translations are from *F. de Saussure, Course in General Linguistics*, trans. R. Harris, London, Duckworth, 1983.

[18] Saussure, op. cit., p.98.

visible'.[19] And these ephemeral sounds can only be what Saussure refers to as the actualisation in discourse (*parole*). Aristotle likewise is talking explicitly about the sounds produced by the human voice, not anything in the 'soul' of the speaker. On this point, therefore, Saussure takes very great care to distance himself from Port-Royal and Aristotle. He is insistent that if there are 'sounds' signified by alphabetic letters, these sounds must already be envisaged as psychological entities.

The result of Saussure's refusal to commit himself fully to that line of thinking raises a problem about what exactly the relation is between 'what we hear' in one sense and 'what we hear' in another. For an auditory impression, mediated by acquaintance with the language (*langue* in Saussurean terminology), may quite possibly *not* be an accurate reflection of the sounds, i.e. the external acoustic facts. So how do the latter stand in relation to the former?

In the Aristotelian tradition this is not a problem because the question of auditory impressions does not arise. So the 'accuracy' of a written transcription can only depend on correspondence between the sounds uttered and the letters inscribed. In fact, in this perspective 'words' as linguistic units do not strictly come into the picture. In theory, at least, the Aristotelian secretary does not need to *understand* what is being dictated: all that is necessary is a good ear for speech sounds and a knowledge of the grapho-phonic correspondences.

For the Saussurean secretary, however, that would not be enough. Only an adequate knowledge of the language (*langue*)

---

[19] They also concede, however, that a legitimate function of spelling is to 'help us to grasp what the sound signifies.' Thus they think that it is useful to spell *champ* ('field') with a final -*p* (even though it is not pronounced) because it reminds us of the derivation from Latin *campus* and thus avoids confusion with the homophone *chant* ('sing'). For a discussion of the view of writing in the Port-Royal grammar, see J-C. Pellat, 'La conception de l'écriture à Port-Royal', in J-G. Lapacherie (ed.), *Propriétés de l'écriture*, Pau, Publications de l'Université de Pau, 1998, pp.153–60.

would yield the information necessary to identify the internal sound patterns (*images acoustiques*) correctly. Otherwise, as far as Saussure is concerned, writing would have no connexion with language at all. It would be an external instrument quite detached from the signs involved in discourse, rather as a camera enables the spectator to take photographs of what is going on in the stadium, but does not help at all in understanding the rules of play.

Now Saussure *qua* linguist needed a theory of writing which would justify, in principle, the use of written texts as linguistic evidence (because otherwise the past history of languages would be inaccessible to 'scientific' study). And that is exactly what the Aristotelian account could not provide. For a linguist operating on strictly Aristotelian lines writing would be of dubious value. In order to establish phonetic correspondences for letters, the testimony of written texts would be worthless unless confirmed by speakers of the language. But if the direct evidence of speakers is available, the linguist does not need the texts anyway.

* * *

There is also a more profound difference between Saussure's view of language and that taken for granted by Aristotle and his successors. The Aristotelian tradition is a nomenclaturist tradition. It is natural within that tradition to view the relationship between letter and sound on the model of the relationship between name and item named. This explains how and why, within that tradition, the question of the phonetic adequacy of alphabetic writing is constantly being raised as a problem. Quintilian, for example, has this to say about it:

> It is for the grammarian (*grammaticus*) [. . .] to consider whether our alphabet lacks certain letters, not for writing Greek [. . .] but for writing Latin words. For instance, in writing the words *seruus* and *uulgus* we lack the Aeolian digamma. There is also a sound intermediate between *u* and *i*, for we do not pronounce *optimum* and *opimum* in the same way. In the word which is written *here*, neither the vowel *e* nor the vowel *i* is clearly

heard. And then there is the question of superfluous letters
[...][20]

In this connexion, Quintilian asks whether one might not discard the letter *x*.

Now Quintilian did not have either the mind or the temperament to try rethinking writing from scratch on his own account; but he did confront certain questions arising within the semiological model of his day, which is Aristotelian. The way Quintilian discusses the Latin alphabet would be incomprehensible except within a theoretical framework where two things are taken for granted:

(a) the number of sounds to be heard in speech should determine the number of letters in an alphabet, and
(b) that should result in a neat set of one-to-one correspondences between sounds and letters.

Without these twin assumptions Quintilian's examples make little sense. In the words *seruus* and *uulgus*, the two letters *u* are not identically pronounced: therefore, according to Quintilian's reasoning, they should not be written identically either. But the Latin alphabet has no letter to indicate the sound of the first *u* – i.e. no letter which corresponds to the Greek digamma. Likewise, in the two words *optimum* and *opimum*, despite what the orthography seems to indicate, the vowels of the middle syllable are not the same: therefore, they should not both be written *i*. In the word *optimum*, the vowel is half-way between *i* and *u*. (In Latin texts the spelling is sometimes *optimum* and sometimes *optumum*.) But in this case the Greek alphabet offers no letter to fill the gap. A similar case of an 'intermediate' sound is illustrated by *here*. This is a vowel which is not quite *i* and not quite *e*.

According to Quintilian, therefore, there are Latin sounds which cannot be indicated by the Latin alphabet (as it existed in the Classical period). On the other hand, this alphabet included at

---

[20] *Institutio Oratoria*, I, iv, 7–9.

least one unnecessary letter: *x*. This letter is superfluous because it is simply a means of indicating the combination of two sounds that can be separately represented as *c* followed by *s*.

Quintilian's verdict, then, is that the Latin alphabet is doubly defective. On the one hand, it does not have enough letters to register unambiguously the sounds of spoken Latin. On the other hand, it has letters that serve no useful purpose, because the sounds they indicate are already catered for.

Quintilian never asks why it should be assumed that all the minutiae of pronunciation have to be indicated alphabetically; nor whether that scrupulousness might not complicate Latin orthography unnecessarily. He proceeds as if the recognition of a phonetic difference is *eo ipso* a sufficient reason for trying to find some way of indicating it alphabetically. Given this perspective, the alphabet becomes a basic vocabulary for constructing descriptions of any speech event. Such a vocabulary will be adequate insofar as its inventory of terms matches the number of items to be distinguished in the description required; and a nomenclature is automatically inadequate if it emerges that there are nameless items to be taken account of. These assumptions about an adequate writing system conform to a more general concept of 'representation' in the Graeco-Roman world, where representation is envisaged ideally as a matter of one-to-one relations between the thing represented and that which represents it.

* * *

The whole of Aristotle's schema as outlined in *De Interpretatione* is based on bold (or naive?) pragmatic and psychological assumptions that have particularly struck modern commentators; namely, that not only the external world but the internal world (the affections of the soul) are the same for everyone. It is on precisely this issue that Saussure rejects the foundations of Aristotelian semiology lock, stock and barrel. For according to Saussure our internal mental world, or at least that part of it which includes the conceptual domain, is language-dependent; and since languages vary from one society to another there can be no question of conceptual uniformity for the whole human race. Saussure is quite categorical on this point:

> In itself, thought is like a swirling cloud, where no shape is intrinsically determinate. No ideas are established in advance, and nothing is distinct, before the introduction of *la langue*.[21]

For Saussure, this is a basic problem and he keeps coming back to it. We cannot take it for granted that the world out there is full of things waiting to be given names, as Adam named the animals in the Garden of Eden. Saussurean semiology sets itself the task of explaining what Aristotelian nomenclaturism simply takes for granted.

* * *

Saussure's need for a theory of writing that legitimizes the use of written texts as linguistic evidence is not the only relevant factor to bear in mind in assessing his account of writing. An even more serious requirement now needs to be considered. Saussure could not afford to admit that writing played a role, however small, in the articulation of thought; that is to say, in establishing a conceptual system which finds its mode of expression in language. For that would have necessitated setting up two separate branches of general linguistics, each with a different theoretical basis: one for pre-literate communities and another for literate communities. In order to avoid this embarrassing schism, it was necessary to limit the function of the written sign to the representation of speech.

Aristotle, with quite different preoccupations from Saussure's, faced no such restriction. What the modern reader finds difficult to understand in Aristotle's case is why he placed the relationship between sounds and letters on the same footing as that between sounds and affections of the soul. Treating the relationship between word and object as an indirect one, with a 'concept'

---

[21] Saussure, op. cit., p.155. The students' notes suggest that what Saussure may have said was not *la langue* but *le signe linguistique* (the linguistic sign).

playing the intermediary role, is reasonably uncontroversial, and passed unchallenged into medieval and modern philosophies of language. That is exactly how it is treated (allowing for differences of terminology[22]) by two latter-day Aristotelians, C.K. Ogden and I.A. Richards, more than two thousand years later. In their 'triangle of signification', the path between symbol and referent is indicated by a dotted line to indicate an indirect relationship.[23]

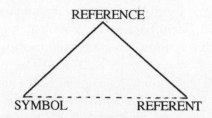

Now it would be perfectly possible to incorporate the distinction between speech and writing into this structure as follows:

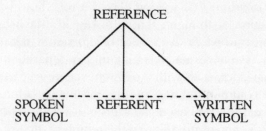

That would be both a simple and an elegant solution. But Aristotle rejected it in favour of:

---

[22] Ogden and Richards' *symbol* corresponds to Aristotle's symbol, their *reference* to his affection of the soul, and their *referent* to his object in the external world.

[23] C.K. Ogden and I.A. Richards, *The Meaning of Meaning*, London, Routledge & Kegan Paul, 1923, p.11.

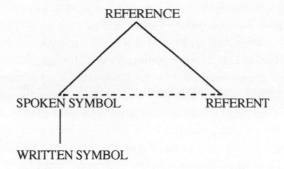

REFERENCE

SPOKEN SYMBOL   REFERENT

WRITTEN SYMBOL

Thus Aristotle's semiology makes the relation between spoken and written language quite independent of the relation between reference and referent. The questions we must ask are: Why does Aristotle treat writing as no more than the use of *grammata*? Why does he think *grammata* have nothing to do with thought? Why does he regard *grammata* as no more than phonetic symbols?

A possible clue lies in the fact that Aristotle was born about twenty years after an important orthographic reform: the official introduction of the Ionic alphabet to Athens (403 BC), replacing the previously used local Attic alphabet. Naturally, documents and inscriptions in the old Attic alphabet did not disappear overnight. Every educated Athenian of Aristotle's generation was perfectly well acquainted with the two systems, and therefore with the following facts. First, it is possible to change alphabets (deliberately) without changing the spoken language in the slightest. Second, changing alphabets is a matter of changing a few *grammata* – nothing more. Third, comparison between alphabets is not just a matter of comparing different letter-shapes but comparing the correspondences between letter-shapes and sounds. Finally, the possibility of changing alphabets shows that there are no intrinsic links between *grammata* and sounds: *grammata* can be invented, borrowed or adapted to suit any needs. (They are, in the Saussurean sense, 'arbitrary'.)

It does not take a great deal of perspicacity to realize that these four propositions between them cover the whole of Aristotle's semiology of writing. In other words, Aristotle's model is derived directly from the experience of alphabetic writing as practised in the Greece of his day, and from this experience he extrapolates to linguistic communication in general, even though his remarks on writing are presented in *De Interpretatione* as a kind of casual after-thought. One wonders whether the apparent afterthought is not in reality the source of the whole Aristotelian schema. (Otherwise, why mention writing at all? It is quite irrelevant to an analysis of propositions.) If this is so, it becomes easy to explain (i) why Aristotle recognizes the same (i.e. 'symbolic') relationship in two apparently quite different cases, and also (ii) why the two sets of symbols in question (spoken and written) are nevertheless treated separately, even though both are used in the service of linguistic communication in one and the same society. In the case of (i) what matters is that changing alphabets is seen as a paradigmatic case of the independence of form from meaning *when the semiological relationship is based on complementarity, not on likeness*. In the case of (ii) what matters is that adopting the Ionic alphabet does not mean that an Athenian has to adopt Ionic words or pronunciations.

The practical implications of this new pattern of relations between speech and writing are worth pausing to consider. For the Athenian writer all that is initially required can be based on rela-tively simple substitution formulae ('For old spelling x, substitute new spelling y'), which will be valid independently of the spoken forms. So x acquires a new value, in virtue of functioning as inter-mediary between the unchanged pronunciation and the changed spelling y. But as familiarity with x recedes (being replaced for new generations by y) the need arises for putting in place a pattern that does not rely on x at all. So a new set of written forms has to be redistributed or re-mapped on to an old set of spoken forms in the language. Since the new alphabet left many words orthographic-ally unchanged in any case, that requirement reduced to assigning a phonetic value to (a few) new letters. Thus the sounds came to be seen as holding the key to the whole system, not the letters, since the sounds remained unaltered *whichever system was adopted*. Here we have the origin of the phonoptic assumption that became incorporated into the Western view of writing.

* * *

Let us now consider what Saussure says about 'phonetic' writing against this historical background. Once it is assumed that utterances contain a determinate number of vocal units (or 'sounds'), each corresponding to a single letter in the corresponding written form, then any combination of sounds can be represented by the corresponding combination of letters. Seen from this perspective, an ideal phonetic alphabet will provide exactly the right number of letters necessary for writing the language in question (an ideal already explicitly recognized by Quintilian); and on that basis it will be possible to construct an orthography in which the appropriate written form is determined automatically by the phonetic composition of the oral message. This dispenses with any need for orthographic 'conventions', spelling being regulated in advance by the initial correlations between letters and sounds. Or, more exactly, given a perfect alphabet (see Chapter 4) the only conventions needed will be those determining the direction of writing (right-to-left, top-to-bottom, etc.).

With this set of assumptions established early in the Western tradition, Saussure's pronouncements mark a deviation to note. His position is one which concedes that spoken sounds – in what he calls *parole* – are infinite in number, and hence that it is chimerical to hope to create an ideal form of writing that will succeed in distinguishing them all.[24] Any such idealization, furthermore, is

---

[24] This was already taken for granted by other linguists in the second half of the nineteenth century. See, for example, Ch. 21 of Hermann Paul, *Principien der Sprachgeschichte*, 2nd ed., Halle, Niemeyer, 1886, where it is recognized that the series of possible speech sounds is 'infinitely numerous'. Where Saussure goes beyond Paul is in trying to explain how this infinite variety can nevertheless be 'reduced' to a small, fixed inventory of elements which is not an arbitrary selection from competing phonetic classifications.

for Saussure an irrelevance, since what counts is not the actual sound but the *image acoustique*. Unlike its (variable) realization in utterance, the *image* consists of a determinate number of elements. It is this structure that 'phonetic writing' can – if appropriately organized – render accurately. There is no harm in calling the relevant phonetic units 'sounds', provided it is clearly understood that they are not to be confused with the raw phonic products of the human vocal apparatus.

Why are these units of the *image acoustique* determinate in number and identity? Because they are elements of *la langue*. That is why, in principle, the phonetic value of a letter depends essentially on the language in question, and not – as it might first appear – on the corresponding activity of the vocal apparatus.

In order to grasp the full force of this answer, it will be necessary to situate it in the context of Saussure's proposals for semiology (Chapter 2). But already it is apparent that Saussure's intellectual strategy for dealing with the problem of writing is very like Aristotle's in at least one respect: it is a strategy which interrelates speech and writing by referring both to a more general linguistic model.

CHAPTER TWO

Structuralism in the Scriptorium

Neither Plato nor Aristotle ever suggested setting up a separate branch of inquiry devoted to the study of signs and signification. Their semiological arguments were incidental to other concerns. Locke, in the seventeenth century, was the first to identify *semeiotike*, or 'the doctrine of signs', as one of the three main branches of science, 'the business whereof is to consider the nature of signs, the mind makes use of for the understanding of things, or conveying its knowledge to others.'[1] But it was not until the very end of the nineteenth century that any general framework which would accommodate the study of all signs was proposed.

The proliferation of semiological studies has undoubtedly been one of the salient features of intellectual life in the humanities since then. On all sides we have been offered general introductions to semiology, together with semiological approaches to almost every subject under the sun. There have been semiological analyses of works of literature, of paintings, of films, of ceremonies, of musical compositions, of buildings. Most of these studies either originated or were eventually published as written texts. In other words, writing has functioned as the preferred – or even the indispensable – form for semiological studies: it has become

---

[1] *An Essay Concerning Human Understanding*, 5th ed., London, 1706, ed. A.C. Fraser, 1894, repr. New York, Dover, 1969, Bk.IV, Ch.21.

the semiological filter through which the semiologist's exposition is obliged to pass. It is all the more ironical that during all that time almost the only applications of semiological theory to writing itself have been those derived directly or indirectly from Saussure.

It seems, in short, that in the twentieth century most writing about writing has simply taken the status of the written sign for granted. In this respect the writers concerned followed faithfully in the footsteps of their predecessors. This might even be regarded as the defining feature of utilitarian literacy: one does not ask questions about those useful writing techniques one is familiar with. Even those who regard the status of the written sign as being, on the contrary, highly problematic evidently do not see this as any hindrance to writing volubly about writing themselves, or even treating the written sign as a paradigm of the linguistic sign in general. Thus, for example, Jacques Derrida's ambition to 'destabilize' traditional Western discourse about writing, while substituting a preferred discourse about an 'arche-writing' which can never be subject to scientific investigation, would be an example of the more ingeniously and absurdly self-defeating extremes to which this kind of intellectual engagement with writing can be taken.[2] So between blind confidence on the one hand and self-stultifying scepticism on the other, recognition of the need for taking the semiology of writing any further than Saussure took it goes by default. That is doubtless because admitting that there is any such need to rethink writing might be seen as tantamount to challenging an education based on textbooks, or even calling in question the profession of literate intellectual itself. And that, in a culture which prides itself on the level of literacy it has reached, would verge on the unpardonable. (Plato would have found it all unutterably depressing.)

* * *

Implicit in Saussure's semiology of writing is a critique of all previous thinking on the subject. Before either accepting or

---

[2] J. Derrida, *De la grammatologie*, Paris, Minuit, 1967, p.83.

rejecting Saussure's conclusions, it is important to understand the basis of this critique, and how, from Saussure's perspective, the enterprise of a semiology of writing is to be conceived.

The birth of Saussurean semiology was announced, somewhat prematurely, in 1901 in Adrien Naville's *Nouvelle Classification des sciences*.[3] This was a revised and expanded version of a work by the same author dating from 1888. In the new edition there was a section devoted to sociology, in which appears the following statement:

> M de Saussure insists on the importance of a very general science, which he calls *semiology*, having as its object the laws governing the creation and transformation of signs and their meanings. Semiology is an essential part of sociology. As human conventional language is the most important sign system, the most advanced semiological science is *linguistics*, the science of the laws governing the life of language.[4]

It is not clear whether this is Naville's own formulation or Saussure's. How semiology would set about its scientific task is not explained. Nor, apparently, did Saussure ever elaborate it to his students in his Geneva lectures. However, in the posthumously published *Cours de linguistique générale* we are told:

> A language is a system of signs expressing ideas, and hence comparable to writing, the deaf-and-dumb alphabet, symbolic rites, forms of politeness, military signals, and so on. It is simply the most important of such systems.
>
> It is therefore possible to conceive of a science *which studies the life of signs as part of social life*. It would form part of social psychology, and hence of general psychology. We shall call it *semiology* (from the Greek *semeion*, 'sign').[5]

---

[3] A. Naville, *Nouvelle Classification des sciences. Étude philosophique*, Paris, 1901.

[4] Naville, op. cit., p.104.

[5] Saussure, op. cit., p.33.

What is interesting for our present purposes is to note that, at the very moment when the curtain rises on modern semiology, we find a comparison between languages and writing as systems of signs. This is surprising in view of the exceptional status that Saussure proceeds to assign to writing: its sole purpose, according to the *Cours*, is to represent other systems of signs.[6] This can hardly be regarded – at least from Saussure's point of view – as typical. It is rather like introducing a science of currency by drawing attention to the existence of travellers' cheques.

The account of semiology in the *Cours* does not match that given fifteen years earlier by Naville. There, as noted above, semiology was introduced as 'an essential part of sociology'. In the *Cours* it is placed under the aegis of a different discipline – psychology. This is confirmed by the statement on the same page of the text that 'it is for the psychologist to determine the exact place of semiology'. It would seem from this that Saussure is not too concerned about exactly where semiology fits into the academic scene: what matters much more is to establish the claim of linguistics to constitute a legitimate branch of the new science.

Again, whereas in Naville's version this science would be concerned with the 'laws governing the creation and transformation of signs and their meanings', according to the *Cours* it would study 'the life of signs as part of social life'. There are two striking differences here: they relate to (i) the 'creation' of signs, and (ii) their 'transformations'. Both repay consideration.

The question of the 'creation' of linguistic signs is one which Saussure explicitly refuses to consider in the *Cours*: refuses, in fact, twice over. He rejects it when it arises in the context of the initial stages of language, both as a problem about how children learn their native language and as a problem about the early history of the human race. Why? Because, says Saussure, there is nothing to be gained by pursuing such questions:

It is quite illusory to believe that where language is concerned

---

[6] Saussure, op. cit., p.45.

the problem of origins is any different from the problem of permanent conditions.[7]

He rejects the same question again when it crops up in connexion with linguistic change:

No individual is able, even if he wished, to modify in any way a choice already established in the language. Nor can the linguistic community exercise its authority to change even a single word. The community, as much as the individual, is bound to its language.[8]

And on the following page:

In fact, no society has ever known its language to be anything other than something inherited from previous generations, which it has no choice but to accept. That is why the question of the origins of language does not have the importance generally attributed to it. It is not even a relevant question as far as linguistics is concerned. The sole object of study in linguistics is the normal, regular existence of a language already established.[9]

The idea that, however far we go back, 'the language has always been there' is one which has very important implications as far as writing is concerned. This thesis, which might be called the doctrine of 'linguistic priority', is not to be confused with the more familiar doctrine of the 'primacy of speech'.[10] The two often go together, but their theoretical status is by no means the same.

---

[7] Saussure, op. cit., p.24.

[8] Saussure, op. cit., p.104.

[9] Saussure, op. cit., p.105.

[10] This is the doctrine that 'in the natural order of language . . . speech comes first' (as it was put in the editorial preface to the first volume of the *Oxford English Dictionary*). For discussion of Saussure's position with respect to this doctrine, see R. Harris, *Reading Saussure*, London, Duckworth, 1987, pp.17ff.

What is clear enough is that whenever the question of the 'creation' of linguistic signs threatens to come to the fore, Saussure heads it off. And one wonders whether that would not be Saussure's strategy with respect to any system of signs, i.e. to insist that what counts, semiologically, is not how the system originated but its 'normal, regular existence'. Thus if Saussure shows no interest in questions concerning the origin of writing or the origin of any particular kind of writing (including alphabetic writing), this would seem to be not a lacuna in his account but an exclusion on principle.

That may have some bearing on the second striking difference between Naville's account of semiology and that given in the *Cours*. It would be reasonable to suppose that the laws governing the 'transformation of signs and their meanings' would fall under diachronic semiology. For Saussure, however, there presumably could be no question of embarking on diachronic semiology before studying the 'normal, regular existence' of signs – in other words, synchronic semiology. For unless that 'normal, regular existence' were understood, the investigator would be in no position to analyse changes in it. Any other programme would be tantamount to repeating in semiology the mistake already made in nineteenth-century historical linguistics. There is no reason, in brief, to suppose that Saussure would not have carried over from linguistics to semiology in general his insistence on an absolute separation between synchronic and diachronic studies. Nor can we suppose that he would have failed to give priority to the former in semiology, as in linguistics. The distinction between synchronic and diachronic, the *Cours* tells us, is fundamental for any science that deals with values.[11]

* * *

The next question worth pondering in the account of semiology presented in the *Cours* concerns the 'life of signs as part of social life'. The exact wording here is probably the editors'; but the

---

[11] Saussure, op, cit., p.115.

double use of the biological metaphor is a deliberate repetition, not a stylistic blemish. This reference to a life within a life is a way of insisting on the symbiotic relation between signs and society. For Saussure, semiology is not a science of signs *in abstracto*. It proposes neither a general philosophy of signs nor a logic of their relations but, quite specifically, a study of their mode of existence in society. It excludes, in other words, signs *which have no publicly recognized signification*. The point comes out even more forcefully in Albert Riedlinger's notes for the Second Course than it did subsequently in the published text of the *Cours*. According to Riedlinger's version:

> We <therefore> recognize as semiological only that part of the phenomena which characteristically appears as a social product, <and we refuse to consider as semiological what is properly individual.>[12]

Thus it is the community which validates and guarantees the operation of the sign system.

On this important point Saussurean semiology differs markedly from the semiotics of Peirce.[13] According to Umberto Eco, the

---

[12] E. Komatsu and G. Wolf (eds), *F. de Saussure, Deuxième Cours de linguistique générale (1908–1909)*, Oxford, Pergamon, 1997, p.14.

[13] Some commentators appear to treat the terms *semiology* and *semiotics* as more or less synonymous. According to S.E. Larsen, the difference merely marks a 'superficial distinction' (P.V. Lamarque (ed.), *Concise Encyclopedia of Philosophy of Language*, Oxford, Pergamon, 1997, p.177.) The superficiality, however, lies not in the distinction but in dismissing it as unimportant. It is difficult to understand how anyone more than superficially acquainted with the work of Saussure and Peirce could reach the conclusion that Saussure's semiology and Peirce's semiotics had much in common. Retaining the Saussurean term, in preference to Peirce's, is a reminder of the difference between two quite diverse approaches to signs. Saussure can be seen as continuing the European tradition, where Peirce marks a notable divergence from it. That is why it is far less misleading to call the European tradition 'semiological' than to rebaptize it (and presumably Saussure as well) with Peirce's term.

main difference between Saussure and Peirce is that semiology is based on the concept of communication, which in turn implies intentional activity.

[For Saussure] the sign is implicitly regarded as a communicational device taking place between two human beings intentionally aiming to communicate or to express something. It is not by chance that all the examples of semiological systems given by Saussure are without any shade of doubt strictly conventionalized systems of artificial signs, such as military signals, rules of etiquette and visual alphabets. Those who share Saussure's notion of *sémiologie* distinguish sharply between intentional, artificial devices (which they call 'signs') and other natural or unintentional manifestations which do not, strictly speaking, deserve such a name.[14]

Eco is wrong about the intentionality, at least as far as Saussure is concerned. It is true, however, that the idea he draws our attention to is expressed quite explicitly by certain theorists working in the Saussurean tradition. Buyssens, for example, proposes the following definition:

Semiology may be defined as the study of processes of communication; that is to say, of means used to influence another person *and recognized as such by the person one wishes to influence.*[15]

Buyssens's insistence on communication and the intentions of the participants is very clear. That insistence, in effect, redefines semiology as the study of *speech acts* in the sense of modern analytic philosophy.[16] What is highly questionable, however, is

---

[14] U. Eco, *A Theory of Semiotics*, Bloomington, Indiana University Press, 1976, p.15.

[15] E. Buyssens, *La Communication et l'articulation linguistique*, Paris/Brussels, Presses Universitaires de France, 1967, p.11. Italicization in the original.

[16] See e.g. J. Searle, *Speech Acts*, Cambridge, Cambridge University Press, 1969. NB A speech act, in this sense, is not necessarily verbal, much less oral.

whether that was Saussure's conception of semiology. Nowhere does Saussure mention the speaker's intentions. Nor do these intentions play any part in the Saussurean 'speech circuit': there we find only 'concepts' – that is 'significations' (*signifiés*). And that is something quite different. We are dealing with communication indeed; but not with the intentions of the communicators. Saussure's *signifiés* do not belong to the speakers: they belong to the language. Intentions, on the contrary, belong not to the language but to individual speakers. Speakers use the concepts provided by the language in order to express, as best they can, their own intentions.

It is important to be clear what is at issue here, because the question of intentions makes a vital difference to theories of the written sign. (Is it the writer who is ultimately in control of 'what is written'?) Speech-act theory is indeed a semiological theory in Saussure's sense; but to conflate it with Saussurean semiology would be to distort beyond recognition Saussure's thinking about writing.

The following discussion will proceed on the assumption that Saussure neither claims nor presupposes that the semiological function of the written sign has anything to do with the intentions of the writer. An interesting piece of evidence on this point is provided by a passage in Constantin's notes. In the lecture he gave on 4 November 1910, it appears that Saussure spoke of a psychology of sign systems. Constantin summarizes as follows:

Any psychology of sign systems will be part of social psychology – that is to say, will be exclusively social; it will involve the same psychology as is applicable in the case of languages. The laws governing changes in these systems of signs will often be significantly similar to laws of linguistic change. This can easily be seen in the case of writing – although the signs are visual signs – which undergoes alterations comparable to phonetic phenomena.[17]

---

[17] E. Komatsu and R. Harris (eds), *Ferdinand de Saussure, Troisième Cours de linguistique générale (1910–1911)*, Oxford, Pergamon, 1993, p.9.

The first point to note is the proviso 'exclusively social'. In other words, this is *not* a matter of individual psychology; so there is no question of bringing in the intentions of those involved. Thus what Saussure proposes regarding linguistic signs applies equally to any system of signs. That is not made very clear in the published text of the *Cours*. (But Bally and Sechehaye did not have Constantin's notes available when they produced their edition.)

In the second place, one is struck by the explicit comparison between changes a writing system may undergo and phonetic changes. That does not appear in the *Cours* either. The comparison is very significant, because Saussure repeatedly makes it quite clear that phonetic changes have nothing to do with speakers' intentions. These are changes brought about by members of the linguistic community through their speech, but they have no awareness of what they are doing. (Whether Saussure's comparison between sound change and changes in writing conventions is valid is another question: the point here is that in Saussure's eyes it evidently is.)

What does all this amount to? If Constantin is a reliable witness, it means that Saussurean semiology envisages studying signs only insofar as they comprise systems with an independent social life – independent, that is, of their users' intentions. This conclusion has important consequences, to which we must return in due course. Straight away, however, it is worth noting that this limitation of the domain of semiology fits perfectly within the framework of Saussure's ideas. For if the limitation were not in place, it is difficult to see how linguistics could serve as a 'model for the whole of semiology', as we are told it does in the *Cours*.[18] Such a claim would make little sense if semiology were envisaged as needing also to deal with signs subject to the will of the individual.

* * *

Another valuable piece of evidence is the passage in the chapter on 'linguistic value' in the *Cours*, where a detailed comparison

---

[18] Saussure, op. cit., p.101.

between languages and writing is presented. This passage deserves detailed examination, because it attempts to demonstrate that the 'material' element in linguistic value is solely a function of relations and differences between linguistic signs. Having commented on the latitude which speakers are allowed in the way they pronounce sounds, the discussion continues as follows:

An identical state of affairs is to be found in that other system of signs, writing. Writing offers a useful comparison, which throws light upon the whole question. We find that:

1. The signs used in writing are arbitrary. The letter *t*, for instance, has no connexion with the sound it denotes.

2. The values of the letters are purely negative and differential. So the same individual may write *t* in such variant forms as:

The one essential thing is that his *t* should be distinct from his *l*, his *d*, etc.

3. Values in writing are solely based on contrasts within a fixed system, having a determinate number of letters. This feature, although not the same as 2 above, is closely connected with it; for both 2 and 3 follow from 1. Since the written sign is arbitrary, its form is of little importance; or rather, is of importance only within certain limits imposed by the system.

4. The actual mode of inscription is irrelevant, because it does not affect the system. (This also follows from 1.) Whether I write in black or white, in incised characters or in relief, with a pen or a chisel – none of that is of any importance for the meaning.[19]

With this key passage, structuralism makes its entrance into the

---

[19] Saussure, op. cit., pp.165–6.

Western scriptorium, at a carefully chosen moment and with a very specific objective in view.

It must be noted, first of all, that these observations occur under the heading 'Linguistic value: material aspects'. In the immediately preceding section we have already had comments on the conceptual aspects of linguistic value. There, clearly, the thesis that values are purely negative is more plausible, or at least less difficult to maintain, since in the conceptual domain we are automatically dealing with abstractions; whereas in the material domain we appear to be dealing with concrete, positive facts. And precisely at that moment – a pivotal one for the argument in question – Saussure appeals to writing.

Why? Doubtless because in the case of writing the 'concrete' facts are more evident than in the case of speech. As a medium, sound is invisible and ephemeral. The identification and re-identification of particular sounds already requires some kind of abstract analysis. Writing, on the other hand, presents us with stable, visible marks that can be examined at leisure and repeatedly, without indulging in any analytic jiggery-pokery. (It may be worth reminding ourselves that in the classroom of Saussure's day there were no sound spectrograms or video screens to make speech 'visible'.) So if, in spite of the 'material' nature of writing, it can be shown that the *formal* value of the written sign is purely negative, extending that conclusion to the linguistic sign would be a natural corollary.

This argument patently relies on the written sign and the linguistic sign being semiologically comparable in the relevant respects. Hence the first point to establish is the arbitrary character of the written sign. Here we encounter an initial difficulty. Is it beyond doubt that the written sign is in fact arbitrary? Saussure offers no proof, but merely cites the example of the letter *t*. Are we to assume that it is only the alphabet he has in mind as an arbitrary system of writing? No such restriction is apparent in the terms in which the case is presented.

For Saussure the differentiation between what is arbitrary and what is not is sufficiently important to be worth marking by a terminological distinction. He proposes reserving the term *symbole* for devices that are not entirely arbitrary. (For example, the scales as a symbol of justice.) Now it is noticeable that Saussure never applies the term *symbole* to elements of writing. It is presumably also significant, given that he must have been familiar with the widespread belief in his day that writing originated with pictography. So the question of what Saussure understands by 'arbitrary' assumes a particular importance for his semiology of writing.

* * *

Enough has been said above to indicate how intimately Saussure's thinking about writing is intertwined with his thinking about signs in general. That is doubtless what one would expect of a theorist whose knowledge of languages was so indebted to the study of ancient texts (as was that of most nineteenth-century European linguists). Saussure, however, is also regarded as a theorist who reinstated the notion of the essential orality of language and emphasized the importance of not equating languages with their written texts. He accuses the comparative philologists of his day of working with a mistaken perception of the relationship between speech and writing. He clearly holds no high opinion of the way they had treated the written evidence on which they based their reconstructions of linguistic history. His comments on their failure to grasp that an oral tradition is not always faithfully reflected in surviving documents are revealing.

The first linguists were misled in this way, as the humanists had been before them. Even Bopp does not distinguish clearly between letters and sounds. Reading Bopp, we might think that a language is inseparable from its alphabet. His immediate successors fell into the same trap.[20]

---

[20] Saussure, op. cit., p.46. Franz Bopp (1791–1867) published a comparative study of the conjugation systems of Sanskrit, Greek, Latin, Persian and Germanic in 1816. This is often regarded as the beginning of comparative Indo-European linguistics.

The implications of these remarks should not be under-estimated. Not distinguishing clearly between letters and sounds is an accusation that could be levelled at many of Bopp's predecessors, going all the way back to Plato. It is the traditional 'literate' perspective of Western thinking about language that is being questioned here. What Saussure is saying is that failure to understand the relation between speech and writing is responsible for failure to understand what language is. In other words, it is not just a question of correcting a misguided view of writing but of setting our whole thinking about language straight. The semiology of writing is about much more than writing.

* * *

For Saussure, the blind spot in traditional Western thinking about writing (and other forms of communication) is a failure to grasp the systematicity involved. Writing, for Saussure, is not just an *ad hoc* appendage to speech. Writing systems are *systems* in their own right, even though they subserve or supplement forms of oral communication. For Saussure, the beginning of wisdom here is to grasp the (semiological) fact that writing and speech depend on *different* systems of signs. The writing system is not just a copy or mirror image of the speech system, *and cannot be.*

There is nothing in the Aristotelian semiology of writing that recognizes this. On the contrary, if we take Quintilian or the grammarians of Port-Royal as representative practitioners of the Aristotelian theory of writing it seems that one could add to or simplify one's inventory of written signs almost at will, depending on the decisions about whether or not it was worth 'recognizing' a particular sound (i.e. providing it with a 'letter' or mark of its own). Quintilian's view, as noted in the previous chapter, was that the Latin alphabet should provide separate letters for *all* the distinguishable sounds of speech in Latin, but no more.

For Saussure, the assumption that one might simply 'add' or 'remove' letters as required would be not only a failure to realize the systematicity of writing, but in addition a manifestation of closet 'nomenclaturism'. Nomenclaturism, for Saussure – as later for Wittgenstein – was the original sin of Western thinking about signs. It is no accident that the foundational mythology of language in the Western tradition is the Biblical story of Adam naming the animals. This is a profoundly nomenclaturist account. The creatures exist before they are named: Adam merely supplies a separate vocal label for each. The 'vocabulary' thus created can extend indefinitely, for as long as Adam can think of new names for new creatures. The only constraint on the Adamic nomenclaturist (presumably) is that one should avoid giving different creatures the same name, since that would defeat the purpose of the exercise. Adam did not say to God 'Why not just call them all the same?' (That would have been the first semiological heresy.)

Although Saussure does not single out individual linguists by name, it is not difficult to find examples of naive nomenclaturism in the work of his contemporaries. A blatant case is one of the most eminent American linguists of the day, W.D. Whitney of Yale. According to Whitney the basis of all language is 'the name-making process'. This, says Whitney, is very easy to understand.

When a human being is born into the world, custom, founded in convenience, requires that he have a name; and those who are responsible for his existence furnish the required adjunct, according to their individual tastes, which are virtually a reflection of those of the community in which they live.[21]

According to Whitney, this is merely a conspicuous example ('only with variety in the degree of consciousness involved') of the process of name-making in all its varieties. We give names not only to people, places and things but to the many and various conceptions our mind entertains.

First, there is always and everywhere an antecedency of the conception to the expression. In common phrase, we first have our idea, and then get a name for it. This is so palpably true of all the more reflective processes that no one would think of denying it; to do so would be to maintain that the planet, or

---

[21] Whitney, op. cit. p.135.

plant, or animal, could not be found and recognized as something yet unnamed until a title had been selected and made ready for clapping upon it; that the child could not be born until the christening bowl was ready. But it is equally true, only not so palpable, in all the less conscious acts, all the way down the scale to the most instinctive.[22]

Quintilian's approach to the alphabet might be described as naive nomenclaturism of this order. (Another sound? No problem. Invent another letter.) It would be comforting to think that naive nomenclaturism was dead; but it has continued to flourish in various guises in all kinds of scholarly thinking about writing during the late twentieth century.

* * *

In what respects did Saussure think that naive nomenclaturism failed to recognize the systematicity of writing? A diversion, which will be less of a diversion than it may seem, is necessary at this point in order to put Saussure's concept of a writing system in its proper theoretical perspective.

Systems, for Saussure, create their own semiological values. That may be as concise a way as any of summing up the approach to culture that was subsequently called 'structuralism'. For Saussure, as a pioneer of structuralism, society would be impossible without systems of signs, of which the most important are linguistic signs. In the *Cours* Saussure explains his concept of systematicity – i.e. of 'structure' – by constantly invoking comparisons between language and chess. There are three passages from the *Cours* that are worth examining in detail in this connexion.

(1) The language itself is a system which admits no other order than its own. This can be brought out by comparison with the game of chess. In the case of chess, it is relatively easy to distinguish between what is external and what is internal. The facts that chess came from Persia to Europe is an external fact,

---

[22] Whitney, op. cit., p.137.

whereas everything which concerns the system and its rules is internal. If pieces made of ivory are substituted for pieces made of wood, the change makes no difference to the system. But if the number of pieces is diminished or increased, that is a change which profoundly affects the 'grammar' of the game.[23]

(2) But of all the comparisons one might think of, the most revealing is the likeness between what happens in a language and what happens in a game of chess. In both cases we are dealing with a system of values and with modifications of the system. A game of chess is like an artificial form of what languages present in a natural form.

Let us examine the case more closely.

In the first place, a state of the board corresponds exactly to a state of the language. The value of the chess pieces depends on their position upon the chess board, just as in the language each term has its value through its contrast with all the other terms.

Secondly, the system is only ever a temporary one. It varies from one position to the next. It is true that the values also depend upon one invariable set of conventions, the rules of the game, which exist before the beginning of the game and remain in force after each move. These rules, fixed once and for all, also exist in the linguistic case: they are the unchanging principles of semiology.

Finally, in order to pass from one stable position to another or, in our terminology, from one synchronic state to another, moving one piece is all that is needed. There is no general upheaval. That is the counterpart of the diachronic fact and all its characteristic features. For in the case of chess:

(*a*) One piece only is moved at a time. Similarly, linguistic changes affect isolated elements only.

(*b*) In spite of that, the move has a repercussion upon the whole system. It is impossible for the player to foresee exactly

---

[23] Saussure, op. cit., p.43.

where its consequences will end. The changes in values which result may be, in any particular circumstance, negligible, or very serious, or of moderate importance. One move may be a turning point in the whole game, and have consequences even for the pieces which are not for the moment involved. As we have just seen, it is exactly the same where a language is concerned.

(*c*) Moving a piece is something entirely different from the preceding state of the board and also from the state of the board which results. The change which has taken place belongs to neither. The states alone are important.

In a game of chess, any given state of the board is totally independent of any previous state of the board. It does not matter at all whether the state in question has been reached by one sequence of moves or another sequence. Anyone who has followed the whole game has not the least advantage over a passer-by who happens to look at the game at that particular moment. In order to describe the position on the board, it is quite useless to refer to what happened ten seconds ago. All this applies equally to a language, and confirms the radical distinction between diachronic and synchronic. Speech operates only upon a given linguistic state, and the changes which supervene between one state and another have no place in either.

There is only one respect in which the comparison is defective. In chess, the player *intends* to make his moves and to have some effect upon the system. In a language, on the contrary, there is no premeditation. Its pieces are moved, or rather modified, spontaneously and fortuitously. [. . .] If the game of chess were to be like the operations of a language in every respect, we would have to imagine a player who was either unaware of what he was doing or unintelligent.[24]

(3) Consider a knight in chess. Is the piece by itself an

---

[24] Saussure, op. cit., pp. 125–7.

element of the game? Certainly not. For as a material object, separated from its square on the board and the other conditions of play, it is of no significance for the player. It becomes a real, concrete element only when it takes on or becomes identified with its value in the game. Suppose that during a game this piece gets destroyed or lost. Can it be replaced? Of course it can. Not only by some other knight, but even by an object of quite a different shape, which can be counted as a knight, provided it is assigned the same value as the missing piece. Thus it can be seen that in semiological systems, such as languages, where the elements keep one another in a state of equilibrium in accordance with fixed rules, the notions of identity and value merge.[25]

If writing depends on writing systems, all this applies *pari passu* to writing. Thus the implications of (Saussurean) systematicity might be spelt out as follows.

1 Writing is not merely making marks, even if the marks happen to conform to what readers would recognize as a written form. Playing chess is not just making random moves on the board, even if they correspond to those recognized by the rules of chess. Chess is a system. So is writing.

2 Writing does not depend on the shapes of the marks. Any other shapes could be substituted, provided they were accorded the same semiological values in the writing system. Just as we could substitute a button for a chess piece, so we could replace a letter-form by an asterisk (provided in both cases we did so 'systematically').

3 The identity (and value) of any written character depends on its differentiation from other characters in the same system. (Hence Saussure's example of various ways of writing the letter *t* as a paradigm case of semiological identity.) It does not matter whether one knight is exactly the same size and shape as

---

[25] Saussure, op. cit., pp.153–4.

another knight, provided it is recognizably distinct from a king, a queen, a bishop, etc.

4 If we introduce extra characters into our alphabet, or eliminate others, that automatically restructures the entire writing system. For there are now new combinations that have to be recognized, new combinatorial possibilities, new spellings.

5 In analysing a writing system, its past history is irrelevant (the 'previous states of the board'). All that matters is the set of characters currently in use ('in play') and their respective values.

This structuralist semiology of writing challenges the traditional Western notion at a very basic level, since questions about formal contrasts within the visual system now take priority over questions about what 'sounds', if any, the units of the system are paired with. That is, in any case, left open; for, unlike Aristotle, Saussure was also concerned to account for writing systems that cannot plausibly be regarded as operating on the basis of pairing letters with sounds at all.

* * *

The trouble with Saussure's semiology of writing is that, as applied by Saussure himself, it does not deliver on its promises. His handwriting example is a case in point. For Saussure, a sign pairs a form (*signifiant*) with a meaning (*signifié*) in the mind of whoever is using the system of signs in question. Now Saussure's handwriting example takes it for granted that the letter *t* designates a specific linguistic unit; that the former functions as the *signifiant* of the latter. But nowhere does he explain the process of semiological analysis which led to this conclusion. The question is rather crucial; for this linguistic unit supposedly corresponding to the letter *t* is itself a theoretical abstraction. (In actual practice, the letter *t* appears to answer to a variety of possible pronunciations.) Furthermore, there are different possible ways of identifying this linguistic unit. How in practice do we identify it? And what of the numerous cases where the letter *t* appears in the orthographic form of a word, but no 'sound [t]' is heard in the corresponding pronunciation? From a semiological point of view these are serious questions.

The difficulty does not stop there, however. For exactly parallel questions arise with regard to 'the letter *t*' itself. Are we quite sure that this letter in fact *is* a Saussurean *signifiant*? Saussure evidently assumes so, but again gives no semiological justification for the assumption. This emerges as a problematic lacuna when we consider his examples of the different handwritten variants which the letter may have. By citing these examples Saussure evidently wishes to demonstrate that the semiological status of a sign does not depend on the intentions of its users. In other words, what links the three variants – indeed *makes* them semiological variants – of a single letter is not the fact that the writer *intended* them to be, nor the fact that they resemble one another, but the (negative) fact that in each case the form is distinct from that of an *l*, a *d*, etc. ('In the language itself, there are only differences.'[26]) So that is 'what makes it' a *t*. The identity of the written *signifiant* and the link between its variants are – for Saussure – aspects of one and the same semiological fact.

This much is clear. But it is nevertheless open to question, and on more grounds than one. First, within a Saussurean theoretical framework the identification of signs requires a simultaneous co-determination of both *signifiant* and *signifié*. Neither is given in advance. It is not a question of starting out with a list of *signifiants* and looking around to find their *signifiés*; nor vice versa. We are not matching up pairs from separate inventories already known.

Once this is realized, the example of the three variants of the letter *t* becomes particularly awkward for the Saussurean semiologist. It is an example which appears to suggest that all that needs to be taken into account is the visual configuration of the marks. The comparison in question is a visual comparison between these marks and the only relevant question is whether or not any given configuration is visibly distinct from the possible variants of *l*, of *d*,

[26] Saussure, op. cit., p.166.

etc. What remains unexplained is *how to make sense of this task* (i.e. of identifying the variants of *t*) without the assumption that there is indeed a finite list of letters (including *t*) determined in advance. Otherwise we are sifting through the visual haystack for a needle that may not be there.

How might Saussure have responded to this objection? Presumably he would *not* have wished to say that any identification of the variants of *t* proceeds on the assumption that we know there are only a certain number of basic sounds ([t], [d], [l], etc.) to be represented by any alphabet. That would be a disastrous answer from a Saussurean point of view. It would immediately introduce a concrete and 'positive' factor into the situation, undermining straight away the claim that the *only* thing that counts is avoiding possible confusion between letterforms. Thus the last thing Saussure would concede is that we identify variants of the same letter simply on the basis of whether or not they all have the *same* pronunciation. For that destroys any need to appeal to his somewhat more mysterious notion of semiological identity defined negatively in terms of differences.

On the other hand, if the *signifié* is ignored and all that matters are similarities and differences between visible marks, it is difficult to see why anyone should be driven to the conclusion that the three examples we are offered in the *Cours* are all versions of a single letter. Working on the Saussurean principle that a single sign cannot have more than one *signifiant*, four other conclusions are possible: (i) that the first two marks are variants, while the third represents a separate letter, (ii) that the first and third marks are variants, while the second represents a separate letter, (iii) that the second and third marks are variants, while the first represents a separate letter, and (iv) that all three forms represent different letters. What we are *not* told is how to choose between these possibilities. In short, visual similarities and differences alone fail to yield adequate criteria for the semiological concept 'graphic variant'. And this is precisely the concept on which the plausibility of Saussure's example rests.

The concept becomes even more problematic when we reflect that Saussure's example gives us no information about the language (English? French? Spanish?) in which the hypothetical text in question is written. Given that not all languages using alphabetic scripts employ the same inventory of letters, one might have expected Saussure, in accordance with his own structuralist principles, to claim that the semiologist needs to distinguish between a different 'letter *t*' in each such case (on the ground that the sum total of contrasts within each system of writing will be different). But no such proviso is mentioned in the text of the *Cours*. The reason why is not difficult to fathom. That would have ruined the immediate plausibility of the example, which depends entirely on our lay acquaintance with the fact that handwriting, unlike printed text, does not reproduce uniform shapes of each letter. We grasp the point about variants of *t* without even bothering to inquire whether it is an English *t*, a French *t*, a Spanish *t*, or any other *t*.

From a strictly Saussurean perspective, however, that *ought* to matter. It is all very well to claim that 'values in writing are solely based on contrasts within a fixed system, having a determinate number of letters'; but that does not explain *how* the number of letters is determined. To put the point another way, there is no guarantee that the number of distinct letters in the (semiological) system corresponds to the number of letter-names currently in use. (If *that* could be safely assumed, being a semiologist of writing would be a sinecure.) The fact that a lay observer might call three distinct graphic shapes all '*t*' does not necessarily reflect anything other than a certain nomenclature derived from the observer's education: in itself it proves nothing about the semiological structure of the writing system or about the number of signs it comprises. Indeed, the lay nomenclature of 'letters' traditionally permits each letter-name to be applied right across the range of such distinct shapes as 'the capital letter', 'the small (or lower-case) letter', 'italics', etc. But it is open to question whether all these function semiologically as 'the same sign'. That might perhaps depend on the text in question and the purpose of the analysis.[27]

The critical point here is that as soon as the possibility of discovering alternative semiological analyses of alphabetic writing is taken seriously, that automatically undermines any assumption that the alphabet is 'a fixed system, having a determinate number of letters'.

It seems difficult to reconcile the notion that 'the alphabet' is itself a system of signs, determinate in number and having determinate phonetic values, with the notion that alphabetic units are to be identified semiologically only on the basis of contrastive relations. To take an obvious example, in written English the graphic shape we call 'capital T' occurs initially in names like *Tom* which begin with the dental stop [t], but also in names like *Thelma* which have no initial [t]. Nevertheless, no literate English person would claim on the basis of pronunciation that the names *Tom* and *Thelma* are not spelt with the same initial letter. That same letter is recognized as occurring as the initial letter of the first word in this sentence. The same word ends with a 'small' *t*. What is the semiological relation between the 'small' and the 'capital' letter? Clearly they are not interchangeable, since in English orthography we do not encounter spellings like *thaT*. Nor, in general, are 'capital letters' found in word-final position in English unless the whole word is written 'in capitals': e.g. *THAT*. These and similar facts about the dissimilar distributions of T and t in written English, quite apart from their coincidence and non-coincidence with the occurrence of the consonant [t] in corresponding spoken forms, make it clear that the question of determining how many alphabetic units we are dealing with, and the question of giving an exact semiological definition of each, is far more complicated than at first sight might appear. It might even turn out that neither our

---

[27] The Port-Royal grammarians had already pointed out the usefulness of the distinction between capital letters and 'small' letters, even though that difference corresponds to nothing in pronunciation (*Grammaire générale et raisonnée*, I,v).

traditional 'capital *T*' nor our traditional 'small *t*' unambiguously represents such a unit.

Evidently, analysing the spelling of English – as even this one example shows – involves considering similarities and differences which simply do not arise in the analysis of spoken English. What, then, are we to make of Saussure's contention that writing exists solely in order to represent speech? What semiological status can be assigned to written distinctions that have no counterpart in oral communication?

Finally, what of Saussure's contention that 'the actual mode of inscription is irrelevant'? A letter *t* in black or in white, in ink or in chalk, is still a letter *t*. Quite so. But that is a mere tautology, not a principle of semiological analysis. From the semiologist's point of view, a black letter or a white letter, an ink mark or a chalk mark, may well be different signs with quite different significations.

The further we pursue Saussure's claims about writing, the more inextricably we find him enmeshed in a semiological snare of his own making. By insisting *both* that writing systems are semiologically separate systems of signs from those of speech and, at the same time, that written signs are merely metasigns which serve to signify the signs of speech, he creates a dilemma for himself. A theorist can opt for one or the other: what is disastrous is trying to have it both ways at once.

CHAPTER THREE
Writing off the Page

Anyone satisfied neither with Aristotle's semiology nor with Saussure's is inevitably led to look for another theoretical framework within which to rethink writing. There are not many options to choose from.

One possibility would be a framework based on C.S. Peirce's theory of the sign. This would have to be constructed 'on Peirce's behalf', so to speak; for in Peirce's voluminous *œuvre* there is remarkably little on the subject of writing. For Peirce, written signs are 'symbols', but not symbols in the Aristotelian sense.

A Symbol is a Representamen whose Representative character consists precisely in its being a rule that will determine its Interpretant. All words, sentences, books, and other conventional signs are Symbols. We speak of writing or pronouncing the word "man"; but it is only a *replica*, or embodiment of the word, that is pronounced or written. The word itself has no existence although it has a real being, *consisting in* the fact that existents *will* conform to it.[1]

There are already enough metaphysical problems in this passage alone to make it clear that constructing a Peircean 'semiotics

---

[1] J. Buchler (ed.), *Philosophical Writings of Peirce*, New York, Dover, 1955, p.112.

of writing' would be a considerable task in itself. It will not be attempted here. Peirce defines a sign as 'an object which stands for another one to some mind', or, even more vaguely, as 'something that stands to somebody for something in some respect or capacity'. The visible letters in ink on a page (which Peirce calls 'tokens') are in his view signs of, i.e. stand for, invisible graphic abstractions (which he calls 'types'). But the formula 'x stands for y' does not seem to take us any further than Aristotle's 'x symbolizes y'. It merely defers the problem. What now has to be explained is the 'standing for' relation, just as in Aristotle's case what remains to be explained is the symbolic relation. Peirce's sign is in any case pre-Saussurean, and reverting to a pre-Saussurean model of the sign is not an attractive move if we are looking for a framework which will provide a critical perspective on both nomenclaturist and structuralist accounts of writing.

The only current framework that has no prior nomenclaturist or structuralist commitments at all is that of integrational semiology.[2] Integrational semiology matches the scope and generality of both Saussurean semiology and Peircean semiotics, inasmuch as it covers the whole range of human communication. At the same time, it leaves open exactly the questions about writing that Peirce deferred and Saussure foreclosed. On both counts it provides a viable independent basis for rethinking writing.

For an integrationist, however, the problem of glottic writing has to be seen in a quite different way from the way Saussure, Peirce and their predecessors saw it. For integrational semiology takes a radically different view of what a sign is.

* * *

Aristotelian and Saussurean thinking about signs share a serious flaw in common: both start at a level of abstraction where signs are already decontextualized theoretical items. The question of the 'working conditions' under which signs actually function *as*

---

[2] R. Harris, *Signs, Language and Communication*, London, Routledge, 1996; R. Harris, *Introduction to Integrational Linguistics*, Oxford, Pergamon, 1998.

signs is already bypassed. Essential to this level of abstraction is a dualist conception of the sign, whereby it is taken for granted that what identifies any given sign is the pairing of a 'form' with a 'meaning'. The meaning of the sign is what it signifies: the form is the signal or indicator of that meaning. This binary relationship itself – and this alone – identifies the sign. A sign, on this view, may – or may not (in some versions) – have more than one form or more than one meaning. Nevertheless, differences of form or of meaning or of both are what distinguish one sign from another. On the dualist view, signs are distinct from one another only on condition that they differ in at least one of these respects.

As Michel Foucault observes, dualism (or the 'binary theory of the sign', as he calls it) is one of the essential foundations of Western theories of 'representation'. Its ramifications extend far beyond the domain of language. Saussure was in this respect a very conservative revolutionary. Thus although Saussure's definition of the sign

> may have appeared to be 'psychologistic' [. . .] in fact that was a way of reinstating the classic condition for conceptualizing the binary nature of the sign.[3]

Dualism leaves room for many different interpretations of what counts as form and what counts as meaning; but they all have in common the notion that in order to recognize the sign we have to know which forms go with which meanings. The relationship between form and meaning is usually assumed to be established by social convention, at least for 'arbitrary' signs, including those of language. (Aristotle says explicitly that names are established by convention, no sound being by nature a name.[4] Saussure describes *la langue* as 'a body of necessary conventions adopted by society'.[5]) Thus the flag at half mast, the red traffic light, the 'EXIT' notice,

---

[3] M. Foucault, *Les Mots et les choses*, Paris, Gallimard, 1966, p.81.

[4] *De Interpretatione*, 16A 20–30. Whitaker (op. cit. p.19) points out that this is confirmed by what Aristotle says in *De Sensu*.

[5] Saussure, op. cit., p.10.

etc. are all assumed to be forms to which a public meaning has been assigned by social convention. The traditional assumption is that anyone who does not grasp the relationship between the form and the meaning does not understand the sign (and is to that extent not a communicationally competent member of that society). What this dualist way of conceptualizing signs does not explain is how a sign ever came to signify what it (supposedly) does. (Aristotle never addresses this question: Saussure, as noted in the previous chapter, explicitly refuses to address it.)

The integrationist theory of signs begins one stage further back and invites consideration of precisely that question. In other words, it does not assume that one can take 'form' and 'meaning' for granted as established. Why not? Because, for one reason, it leaves the theorist with no satisfactory way of dealing with cases where two people disagree about what the sign signifies. The dualist cannot afford to concede that *whatever* people think a form signifies *is* what it signifies; for if everybody is right automatically, that amounts to abandoning the social-conventionist view altogether. The alternative is to claim that some people are (sometimes) just wrong about (some) signs. But that involves spelling out how we establish the 'right' meaning for any given sign. It is no use saying at this point that the right meaning is the meaning established by the social convention, because that is just what is at issue. It is possible for two people to disagree about what the social convention is. So do we hold a referendum? Do we defer to some higher authority? Do we take it that whoever produced the sign in question is the person who knows what it means? Or hand over the decision to whichever of the people in the dispute has a gun? Or how, exactly? These are unattractive options for the dualist, and whichever one is chosen leads to further conundrums of its own.

The integrationist proposal is that dualist assumptions about form and meaning do not provide a very good basis for approaching these questions in the first place. In order to understand signs and signification, we have to begin at a much more elementary level of human behaviour. We certainly do not have to start with the notion of a social convention already *in situ*. For our own experience tells us that we *attribute* significations to things and events, irrespective of whether there is any social convention about the matter or not. Signs do not necessarily have a social dimension at all. Here, straight away, there is a fundamental difference between integrational semiology and Saussurean semiology; i.e. the integrationist does not accept that one must recognize as semiological 'only that part of the phenomena which characteristically appears as a social product'. On the contrary, the integrationist would argue that unless semiology starts below the social level it will never be able to explain publicly recognized signs at all.

Take, for example, the case of the familiar landmark. There are doubtless landmarks that almost everybody in a community recognizes. But there may also be landmarks recognized by certain individuals only. I may look out for a particular tree, knowing that I have to take the first turning on the left after that tree on my usual way home. (On reaching the tree, I change down into a lower gear, move into the left-hand lane, etc.) Thus for me the tree signifies something, has a certain semiological value. Perhaps it does for others too; but that is strictly irrelevant. It is a landmark *as far as I am concerned*, and that is already sufficient. Its value as a sign arises simply – and solely – from the fact that I rely on it to integrate certain programmes of activity in my daily comings and goings. In terms of integrational theory, the tree thereby acquires an integrational function, i.e. becomes a sign, in virtue of the role it plays in those activities. Outside that framework, it has no semiological status (unless it plays a comparable role in some other programme of activities). But as far as I am concerned it requires no co-operation from anyone else; that is, the 'tree' sign does not depend on my interaction or agreement with another person, any more than tying a knot in my own handkerchief does.

It is important to note that none of this means (a) that somehow the physical tree has now become a 'form' with its own 'meaning' (e.g. 'Take the next left'), or (b) that one object, the tree, now 'stands for' another object, the first turning on the left, or (c) that a mental image of the tree, tagged with the conceptual 'take-the-next-left' label, has now been added to my brain's stock of equipment. To refer to the tree as a *sign* – at least in the sense that integrational semiology construes that term – implies simply that I recognize and contextualize it in a certain way in relation to certain activities. (How I manage to do that is another question, but it is a question for neuropsychologists, not for semiologists.) The tree is a sign only insofar as I *make* it a sign.

Signs, for the integrationist, provide an interface between different human activities, sometimes between a variety of activities simultaneously. They play a constant and essential role in integrating human behaviour of all kinds, both publicly and privately, and are products of that integration. Signs are not given in advance, but are made. The capacity for *making* signs, as and when required, is a natural human ability. Some signs (e.g. the landmark) are recurrently useful and are constantly being remade as often as required; but others may serve the purpose just for one particular occasion (as when the reader turns down the corner of the page before putting the book aside, in order to mark the point at which to resume reading next time). Signs do not have any superhuman capacity for outliving their makers. When languages die, it is because no one is any longer engaged in remaking them. But this is the case for all signs.

Signs, therefore, in an integrationist perspective are not *invariants*: their semiological value depends on the circumstances and activities in which, in any particular instance, they fulfil an integrational function. Thus even *for me* the semiological value does not somehow remain permanently attached to my landmark tree. If I change my usual route home in order to avoid the traffic, looking out for the tree may cease to play any orientational role at all in my daily journeys. Its semiological value will then lapse as far as I am concerned: it will no longer be a sign.

If the basic process by which signs are created and function is as the integrationist construes it, then the notion of a sign which integrates the activities of two or more individuals is not difficult to establish. And from there the notion of a sign with a common (i.e. public) value is not too difficult either. What it requires minimally is that A assign a semiological value to x, and B assign a semiological value to x, and that A and B both carry out mutually integrated programmes of activity on that basis. The tree, for example, can become a landmark for you too. Suppose I give you directions to my house: 'Take the first left after the tree . . . etc.'. The fact that I told you about the tree does not affect the point at issue. What matters is how you integrate spotting the tree into your journey. What makes the tree a landmark *for you* is the use you make of it in finding your way to where I live. The difference between us is simply that I worked it out for myself but you did not. But that does not somehow rob the tree of its landmark function in your case. That function is put to the test, i.e. established, for both of us by exactly comparable procedures. There is no philosophical puzzle about 'sameness' here: we *demonstrate* the integration of our activities by both ending up in the right place on the basis of planning our route by reference to the tree in question. (There could be various reasons why this does not work out – roadworks, a puncture, a heart attack – and also possible scenarios in which either you or I end up at the right place in spite of having missed the tree, but these are irrelevant to the semiological point.)

As this example illustrates, from an integrational point of view the difference between a private sign and a public sign is not particularly puzzling. Public signs are public because more people are involved: i.e. more people assign a semiological value to certain things or to certain practices and integrate their activities accordingly. And the more people do this the more they take it for granted that other people are familiar with these signs too. But what the signs signify is established in exactly the same way, irrespective of how many or how few people are involved. Thus the appeal to social conventions which underlies both nomenclaturist and structuralist theories of the sign is in the end a red herring. We do not have to start by presupposing that the relevant social conventions are already in place.

The integrationist approach to writing is based on the assumption that this applies just as much to the written sign as to any other kind of sign. The implications of this are far-reaching. Whereas Saussure assumes, in common with his predecessors in the Western tradition, that in order to explain the written sign we have to start from the spoken sign, as already established in some public code (i.e. the relevant oral language), the integrational semiologist makes no such assumption. Integrational semiology offers no warrant for believing that written signs bear some kind of constant relation to spoken signs anyway. On the contrary, the integrationist will assume that in any semiology of writing we need to begin with the written sign itself.

Thus, to illustrate the difference in terms of Saussure's own example, the identity of a 'letter *t*' in a particular instance is not established by reference to the internal contrasts in the writer's habitual handwriting. For an integrationist, the fact that the writer has fulfilled all the conditions Saussure mentions (forming his *t* differently from his *l*, his *d*, etc.) does not prevent someone else, particularly someone unfamiliar with the writer's hand, from taking this particular mark for an *l* and thus, say, reading *seat* as *seal*. Exactly how important this might be will depend on the circumstances of the case. But however important or unimportant, the fact remains that there is only one mark on the paper, but there are two written signs: one which the writer identifies as '*t*' and another which the reader identifies as '*l*'. The mark itself has no semiological value other than that attributed to it by writer or reader; and that value depends on how the written message integrates communication between them. In sum, integrational function, and that alone, is the criterion for establishing what a sign is.

At first sight this might not seem to yield a very different analysis of the handwriting example from Saussure's. However, it does differ on three important counts.

1 According to the integrationist analysis, the conflicting interpretations of the mark remain unresolved, unless settled by negotiation between reader and writer. ('I can't read your writing. Is it a *t* or an *l* at the end of this word?') But (a) it may not occur to the reader that there is any doubt about the identity of

the letter, so the question may never be asked, and (b) any such negotiation with the writer is itself a further attempt to integrate the mark in question into some communicational programme. The mark is now, in effect, recontextualized (by the questions the reader asks and the writer's response).

2 In the integrationist account, there is no appeal to the semiological systematicity supposedly manifested in the writer's formation of the letter, i.e. no recourse to structural criteria for resolving the problem. (Asking the writer is a pragmatic not a structural solution. The writer may just insist that it is a *t* even if it is patently indistiguishable from an *l* in the very next word.)

3 For the integrationist, there is no question of whether it 'really' is a *t* or not. In other words, the form of the sign is itself indeterminate.

It is this third point which brings out the most radical difference between the Saussurean and integrationist positions. In Saussurean structuralism, a sign is always a doubly determinate unit (determinate in *both* form *and* meaning); for that is a condition of its existence within the system to which it belongs. Integrational theory, by contrast, treats the intrinsic *indeterminacy* of the sign as the foundation of all semiological analysis.[6]

* * *

The integrationist thus takes a quite different view of human communication from that which underlies traditional Western thinking on the subject. The basis of traditional thinking is what integrationists refer to as the 'fixed-code' fallacy. This is the notion that communication (in particular, linguistic communication) depends on the establishment of publicly recognized systems of

---

[6] For further discussion of the indeterminacy of the sign, see R. Harris, 'The integrationist critique of orthodox linguistics', *Integrational Linguistics: a First Reader*, ed. R. Harris and G. Wolf, Oxford, Pergamon, 1998, pp.15–26.

correlation between forms and meanings. Thus 'a language' (English, French, Swahili, etc.) is assumed *ab initio* to be

a fixed code which, by relating entities in a dimension called 'form' to entities in a dimension called 'meaning', provides language-users with a means of transmitting and receiving thoughts.[7]

This in turn relies on the traditional assumption that communication is telementational, i.e. a process of thought-transference from A's mind to B's mind.[8] The essential role of the (linguistic) sign is seen as being to facilitate that mental transfer. Thus the fixed-code fallacy and the doctrine of telementation feed off each other. For if communication is to be successful, the internal logic of the process requires that B's mind shall eventually 'receive' the thought that set out from A's mind. If B's mind receives some *different* thought, or no thought at all, then communication has broken down somewhere along the line. As Locke put it in his classic formulation of the telementational thesis,

[men] suppose their words to be marks of the ideas in the minds also of other men, with whom they communicate: for else they should talk in vain, and could not be understood, if the sounds they applied to one idea were such as by the hearer were applied to another, which is to speak two languages.[9]

Locke's statement provides a brilliantly concise synopsis of the communicational implications of Aristotle's semiology. The 'affections of the soul' have to be the same in both speaker and hearer for verbal communication to be successful. The difference is that for Locke this is a problem, whereas Aristotle circumvents the

---

[7] N. Love, 'The fixed-code theory', in R. Harris and G. Wolf (eds.), *Integrational Linguistics: a First Reader*, Oxford, Pergamon, 1998, p.55.

[8] For an integrationist view of telementation, see M. Toolan, 'A few words on telementation', in R. Harris and G. Wolf (eds), *Integrational Linguistics: a First Reader*, Oxford, Pergamon, 1998, pp.68–82.

[9] Locke, op. cit., III, ii.

problem by simply assuming that the 'affections of the soul' are the same for all.

As Talbot Taylor notes,
the telementational picture of communication, passed down to us from Locke, takes the understanding of an utterance to be an unobservable, private, mental event.[10]

If we take this privacy condition seriously, Taylor argues, we are led inevitably to the paradoxical conclusion that 'we can never know if our hearers understand what we say to them'. Here, in effect, Aristotelian semiology (at least as far as language is concerned) has its bluff called. Either the communicational question is being dodged, or else we are missing an explanation which Aristotle takes to be so obvious as not to require elaboration.

How does all this affect our understanding of written communication? Rather profoundly. To see why we need only follow through Nigel Love's simple example of the word *postman*. In spoken English, unstressed vowels are commonly 'reduced' (as phoneticians describe it) to such an extent that the singular *postman* becomes indistinguishable from the plural *postmen*. In written English the two are always distinct, unless (for reasons such as those pertinent to Saussure's example of the letter *t*) a writer's hand blurs the visual difference between *a* and *e*. So how does that leave the grammatical distinction between singular and plural? Do we have one grammar for spoken English but another for written English? To paraphrase Locke, is this a case of 'two languages'? Love lists six possible pronunciations of the plural *postmen*, some of which overlap with possible pronunciations of the singular *postman*. Some of these might only be articulated when a speaker wished to avoid a possible ambiguity. In other words, the speaker

---

[10] T.J. Taylor, 'Do you understand? Criteria of understanding in verbal interaction', in R.Harris and G. Wolf (eds), *Integrational Linguistics: a First Reader*, Oxford, Pergamon, 1998, p.207. The whole question of Lockean 'scepticism' about communication is discussed at much greater length in T.J. Taylor, *Mutual Misunderstanding*, Durham, Duke University Press, 1992.

can always 'make' the distinction between *postman* and *postmen* phonetically obvious when – but only when – required. Thus a secretary taking dictation can use forms with 'unreduced' final vowels to ask 'Was that [pous'man] or [pous'men]?'. But this is not a question about what was said, because what the speaker said was neither. It is a question about how the secretary is to integrate the current scribal operation with the (speaker's) previous utterance (and, consequentially, with any later optical scanning by readers of the letter). And that is already a problem for any theorist who supposes that writing is merely a 'visible' reflection of speech. For in effect this avoidance of ambiguity reverses the canonical priority normally assumed, i.e. the assumption about the 'primacy of speech', as well as undermining the thesis that a language is a fixed code.

This is why the structuralist language-describer is reluctant to include within the scope of his description deviations from canonical forms brought about by awareness of communicational difficulties that might arise from use of the canonical forms in particular circumstances. For if he were obliged to take account of such variants, the task of exhaustively enumerating or in some sense 'defining' a language's stock of form-meaning pairs would be impossible.[11]

Anyone who realizes the implications of Love's point will see that it casts doubt upon a whole set of traditional assumptions about relations between speech and writing. What it means is that in a literate society both speakers and writers are free to opt between alternative ways of trading off speech against writing and vice versa, not by special dispensation but as *a matter of course*. These are, indeed, *integrated* forms of communication and not just parallel but separate forms of communication which happen to be available. Furthermore, the disparity between the grammar of singularity and plurality reopens the whole question of how these *could be* just parallel forms of communication. From this point on,

---

[11] Love, op. cit., p.55.

thinking about writing becomes a different enterprise. Or, at least, it should do.

But traditional beliefs die hard, and in Saussure's case we have a remarkable example of the lengths to which theorists will sometimes go to defend them. Saussure was just as well aware as Quintilian that there are cases in which written alphabetic forms do not 'match' the corresponding spoken forms. But instead of concluding from this that what needs rethinking is the relationship between the two, Saussure puts the entire blame on inadequate spelling systems. He complains about their 'inconsistencies' (*inconséquences*), 'aberrations' (*aberrations*) and 'irrational spellings' (*graphies irrationnelles*). For him it is 'irrational' to spell *Zettel* in German with a double consonant, because it is spelt that way 'simply in order to indicate that the preceding vowel is short and open'. Similarly, *made* in English creates the misleading appearance of having a second syllable, whereas in fact the final -*e* is simply an indication of the pronunciation of the preceding vowel. Even worse are cases like *bourru*, *sottise* and *souffrir* in French, where the spelling shows 'illegitimate double consonants' (the doubling having no phonetic justification at all). In short, Saussure concludes, 'writing obscures our view of the language'. It is 'not a garment, but a disguise'.[12]

Saussure's arguments on this score will be considered in more detail in the following chapter. They are well worth examining not only because they show how Saussure allowed the traditional view of alphabetic writing to override his structuralist principles, but also because these are in any case arguments of the kind that have often been deployed by linguists since Saussure's day, whether or not they would count themselves as 'structuralists'. For integrationists, this is a paradigm case of how semiological analysis can be led astray when written forms are treated as decontextualized items and simply compared, one by one, to their equally decontextualized 'pronunciations'.

* * *

[12] 'pas un vêtement, mais un travestissement'. Saussure, op. cit., pp.51–2.

An important piece of historical evidence in support of the integrationist approach to writing is that writing tends to develop over time a symbiotic relationship with speech. The evolution of alphabetic writing in Europe provides some prime examples of this symbiosis in the form of reciprocal influences. What one might expect in any society where speech and writing come to be closely integrated practices is that eventually the interrelationship would be reflected in changes in both. That is to say, not only would the way words are pronounced come to affect the way they are written, but also the way they are written would come to affect the way they are pronounced. This topic will come up again for discussion in a later chapter, but it is worth commenting at this point on Saussure's reluctance to face up to the semiological implications of the phenomenon.

Although Saussure was well aware of these reciprocal influences, he regarded the influence of the spoken form on the written form as natural and desirable, but the influence of the latter on the former as pernicious. He is quick to castigate such manifestations as exceptional, or even 'monstrous'. He fulminates against instances where the written form gives rise to 'erroneous pronunciations'. This phenomenon, according to Saussure, is 'strictly pathological'.[13] He laments the probability that these deformations will become increasingly frequent, and that 'more and more dead letters will be resuscitated in pronunciation'.[14] He waxes indignant that in Paris 'one already hears *sept femmes* ('seven women') with the *t* pronounced. Darmesteter foresees the day when even the two final letters of *vingt* ('twenty') are pronounced: a genuine orthographic monstrosity.'[15] This remarkable tirade against the baneful influence of writing concludes:

> These phonetic distortions do indeed belong to the language but they are not the result of its natural evolution. They are due

---

[13] Saussure, op. cit., p.53.
[14] Saussure, op. cit., p.54.
[15] Saussure, op. cit., p.54.

to an external factor. Linguistics should keep them under observation in a special compartment: they are cases of abnormal development (*cas tératologiques*).[16]

But Saussure's conception of 'teratology' touches on one limited aspect of an area of study which includes a whole network of complex relations. These are relations which inevitably arise, as an integrationist would point out, from the coexistence of two forms of communication – speech and writing – which both compete and complement each other in the life of a society. We are dealing in such cases with exactly that 'life of signs as part of social life' that Saussure elsewhere posits as the authentic domain of semiology. How ironic that he should relegate these examples to a special laboratory for linguistic monstrosities!

It would be a mistake, however, to suppose that this is just a personal idiosyncrasy of Saussure's. We find the same notion of 'monstrosity' invoked in the following passages from Max Müller's Rede lecture of 1868:

In the natural history of speech, writing [...] is something merely accidental. It represents a foreign influence which, in natural history, can only be compared to the influence exercised by domestication on plants and animals.[17]

This 'artificial domestication of language' by 'literary cultivation', according to Müller, produces 'unnatural' results, just as in the biological world, so that

however perfect, however powerful, however glorious in the history of the world, – in the eyes of the student of language, Sanskrit, Greek, and Latin, Hebrew, Arabic, and Syriac, are what a student of natural history would not hesistate to call '*monstra*', unnatural, exceptional formations which can never

---

[16] Saussure, op. cit., p.54.
[17] F.M. Müller, *Chips from a German Workshop*, Vol.IV, London, Longmans, Green, 1875, p.74.

disclose to us the real character of language left to itself to follow out its own laws without let or hindrance.[18]

Here it is not just spelling pronunciations but the whole literary language which is 'monstrous'. The conception is a direct result of a certain way of thinking about writing and written texts as 'unnatural' products.

* * *

Like Saussure, the integrational theorist proceeds on the assumption that the question of graphic differences lies at the heart of any semiological analysis of writing; but unlike Saussure, the integrational theorist proceeds on the assumption that the question of 'phonetic values' of letters is pertinent only to those communicational practices involving the integration of writing with speech. Even there the first requirement is graphic differentiation – i.e. the establishment of features which distinguish one letter or character from another. Without an unambiguous identification of its units, writing cannot fulfil its integrational function. This is a practical as well as a theoretical requirement, as we are reminded every time we try to read an illegible hand. To solve practical problems of this order it is (in most cases) quite irrelevant to concern ourselves about how the writer might have pronounced the word(s) in question. That has nothing to do with the *reader's* difficulty, which consists in the first instance in identifying the written forms, however incompetently or negligently they may have been inscribed. In other words, even in glottic writing there are structural features of the written form which are quite independent of any 'phonetic value'.

A similar conclusion emerges if we consider the case of the so-called 'braille alphabet' for the blind, which is not an alphabet in the historical sense of the term, but a transcription system used to transpose certain visual shapes into patterns of dots in relief, thus allowing them to be 'scanned' by touch (Fig.1). These

---

[18] Müller, op. cit., p.74.

equivalences are established at the 'letter' level. Any phonetic or other values that the letters may have are an irrelevance, and it is possible to translate quite precisely into braille a text of which one understands nothing except its alphabetic composition. Which does not mean that braille lacks any semiological structure of its own.[19] On the contrary, the alphabetic equivalences are 'arbitrary' inasmuch as the utilization of the six dots available in the braille system does not correspond in any way to the shape of the letter translated.

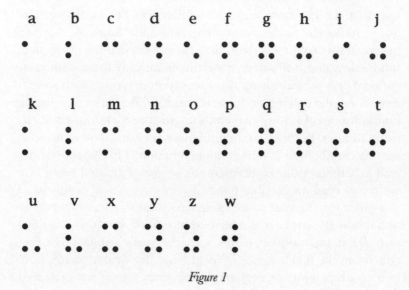

Figure 1

What is missing from Saussure's account of alphabetic writing is any theoretical recognition that there are two levels of structure involved. From an integrational point of view, this is a major lacuna, the full implications of which will be considered in the following chapter.

* * *

---

[19] The system also allows for a large number of contractions and abbreviations.

Saussurean semiology, then, is a semiology of fixed codes. The *langue* recognized in Saussurean linguistics is always a language that enjoys the privilege of being 'already there', waiting to be used, given in advance. The code itself comprises a set of decontextualized forms and meanings, together with 'rules' for their combination into equally decontextualized 'messages'. The first step towards freeing semiology from this theoretical straitjacket is to reject the conception of context as something *extra*, belonging outside the signs themselves. The basis of integrational semiology is recognition that all communication is intrinsically context-dependent. The sign itself is the product of contextualization.

To put it another way, what sets integrational semiology apart from Saussurean and neo-Saussurean semiology is the premiss that *there are no contextless signs*. Given this premiss, it becomes possible to envisage a semiology of writing which is not tied umbilically to the traditional belief that writing has to be understood – and analysed – as a mode of 'representing' a spoken language. The relations between speech and writing, from an integrational perspective, are construed in a quite different way. First, because an integrational semiology recognizes that there are forms and features of writing which have nothing to do with speech at all. Second, because in those cases where speech is *one* of the activities that is integrationally relevant, its connexions with writing can take a variety of different forms, depending on the circumstances of the case and on the other activities involved. So there is no simple, universal relationship between the written sign and the spoken sign of the kind that Saussurean semiology postulates.

Signs, seen from this perspective, are not pairings of form and meaning, already set up in some pre-established code. They arise from actual events and circumstances in which the participants are involved. Thus, in a particular situation, *any* object, action, etc. can acquire a semiological value. Furthermore, it is not essential that all the participants should agree on what that value is, or even agree on which particular features of a given communication situation have such a value. On the contrary, everyday life is full of situations which are of such semiological complexity as to defy any definitive interpretation, whether by the participants or by an observer-analyst. Writing is not magically exempt from these problems.

So the sign of integrational semiology will be not the *signifiant-signifié* of Saussure (a postulated psychological pairing), nor Peirce's *token* (an existing physical entity), nor Peirce's *type* (a purely abstract invariant) but the working sign; in other words, the sign with all the practical limitations, doubts and problems that its function in an actual communication situation may bring with it. The constant creation of such signs in human interaction *is* what Saussure called their 'social life' – the social life that his semiology proposed to study. But whereas the Saussurean sign is put away back in its system after each occasion of use in *parole*, rather like a chess piece being returned to its box after the game, ready to come out again when next needed, the integrational sign is not a discrete autonomous entity. It has no continuous identity outside the contextualization that brought it into existence. Anyone who supposes that writing is not subject to the same ephemerality as speech is mistaking the document or the inscription for the written sign. And that mistake has been the other major obstacle (i.e. apart from the traditional misconstrual of the relationship with speech) standing in the way of setting up a serious semiology of writing.

* * *

An integrational perspective thus reverses the priority taken for granted in traditional accounts of writing. Attention is focussed not on some system of supposed correlations between written and spoken signs, but upon the particulars of written communication in specific circumstances. But this reversal of priorities entails others.

Rethinking writing from an integrational point of view involves recognizing how powerfully modern thinking on the subject has been moulded by one of the outstanding post-Renaissance products of utilitarian literacy: the printed book. Written communication, from an integrational point of view, is a form of communication in which contextualized integration relies in the great majority of cases on a visual framework and visual analogies. The full implications of this are in part obscured because we find it nowadays difficult to escape from the intellectual legacy of a literacy in which the mechanically produced printed book is presented as the paradigm case of a written text. Typically, we are dealing with a work comprising scores or hundreds of pages, reproduced in hundreds or thousands of more-or-less identical copies. Typically, it is portable. It is a work designed so that its reading shall be entirely controlled by the individual reader, who can pick it up or put it down at will, turn the pages at leisure, go back and forth within its confines in whatever idiosyncratic patterns personal interest dictates. It will be the reader who decides whether to read aloud or silently, when, where and – in the case of reading aloud – to whom. In short, this paradigm case offers a product which, of all forms of writing, is the least context-bound and has the highest degree of autonomy (at least, if these properties are measured in terms of the distance – physical, temporal, cultural – separating writer from potential reader). But the book is also a somewhat unusual example of writing in that it presupposes no particular visual framework, except – in certain cases – one that is provided by accompanying 'illustrations'. So the visual analogies that predominate are the internal analogies emerging from the written text itself: these are the analogies that link one ink mark to another, one configuration of such marks to another, that enable the reader to recognize 'the same letter' or 'the same word' twice on one page, etc. These are the analogies that underlie Peirce's distinction between 'types' and 'tokens'. With such a text, there is no need for the reader to look for any *other* visual framework: the book is self-sufficient. It can be read anywhere (provided there is light to read by). One could sum up all these salient features of the printed book by saying that it represents the limiting case in which, insofar as it is humanly possible, *the written text is made to supply its own context.*

However, that is not the case for the written sign in general; and that is why it would be a mistake for any semiologist of writing to treat the printed book and its familiar features as a tacitly accepted model, to which all other forms are imperfect approximations. If we wish to rethink writing, perhaps the first thing we need to think about is the full extent of this atypicality.

* * *

The image of the printed book hovers over the term *context* itself, and has done since the sixteenth century. It is no accident that *context* is commonly used, and not only by linguists, to designate the immediate verbal environment, the words preceding and/or following some other word or words: thus, for example, in *a big man* and *a big mistake* the word *big* is said to appear in two different 'contexts'. A quotation taken 'out of context' is one removed from the rest of the text in which it originally appeared. These and similar usages tacitly appeal to – and bolster – the notion that the written text is self-sufficient: it is the whole which contextualizes its own parts.

From an integrational point of view, this is a quite inadequate notion of what context is. A written text does not appear, nor is it read, in a communicational vacuum but in a specific communication situation. It is this situation, with all its constituent circumstances, verbal and non-verbal, which provides the basis for contextualization. A written text must be written *by* someone: its production is necessarily integrated into some wider pattern of events in the life of the writer. Similarly, reading a text is necessarily integrated into some wider pattern of events in the life of the reader. These are not just banal truisms but statements of the conditions of existence for every written text; and it is these conditions which, in any given instance, supply the basis for contextualizing what is written. When a readable form is produced under these conditions – and only then – a written sign appears. That is why the notion of a contextless sign is, for integrational semiology, a contradiction in terms.

* * *

The term *context* calls for another preliminary observation. It is often used in the singular. But in practice we are never dealing with *a* context or *the* context, but always with multiple contexts. There is not only a spatio-temporal or physical context but a psychological context. The psychological context of the writer is not that of the reader. This plurality of contexts must always be borne in mind. From an integrational point of view, the sign is invariably at the centre of a whole series of actual and possible contexts, i.e. surrounded by other potentialties for contextualization.

The most important factor in the contextual integration of the written sign, if we leave aside for the moment the case of writing by and for the blind, is visual location. A written message has to be written *somewhere*. But since writing is not always a question of marking a surface already available, it is preferable to adopt a less specific term and refer to the *installation* of the written sign. Anyone who wishes to communicate by means of writing is obliged to find or prepare an installation for the written message. From this there will follow automatically a whole range of integrational constraints, since not *anything* can be written *anywhere* or *anyhow*.

But the constraints which apply to writing are not those which apply to speech, because different biomechanical activities are involved. All signs have a biomechanical basis, provided by the human body and its sensory equipment. (Unless I could *see* the tree, there would be no question of its becoming a landmark in my journey home.) No semiologist can afford to ignore these biomechanical factors, since in the end they determine limits beyond which communication is not possible. The point being made here is simply that, at the biomechanical level, writing requires a form of contextualization which is quite different from that of speech, and that difference has far-reaching semiological consequences. In the case of speech, we have what might be regarded as a default installation already supplied by Nature. Silence is the background against which the sounds of the human voice are best heard. Now in the case of writing it might perhaps be urged that the surface of the blank page offers a default installation equivalent to silence. But the comparison will not do, for the page has been artificially prepared as a setting for the text. (The psychological and socio-political implications of this are by no means negligible.) In short, unlike the spoken sign, the written sign *requires installation*. The presentation of writing most commonly depends on an artifact deliberately prepared for that purpose. The exceptions one can think of confirm rather than disconfirm the foregoing generalization. Shakespeare could doubtless have written a sonnet on the sea shore by tracing words with his finger in the damp sand; but the text would have vanished with the next tide. The whole development of writing presupposes right from the beginning a society that has reached a level of technological advancement which allows the preparation of durable surfaces, ready to receive more or less permanent marks, made by means of instruments designed specifically for such a purpose. In the development of oral language, by contrast, technology played no comparable role. But that difference is the source of much confusion about the relationship between the two. It is what underlies the thesis that writing is 'unnatural' – a thesis which already conflates the sign with its installation.

* * *

Writing and speech, then, have quite different biomechanical bases. (Leroi-Gourhan made this the foundation of his theory of primitive 'mythological' writing, insisting on the difference between the role of the hand in tool-making and the role of the face in the elaboration of oral language.[20]) What is of interest from an integrational point of view is how the biomechanical difference underpins various semiological differences. In particular, the notion of 'context' is not identical in the two cases, since the contextualization of a written message typically assumes a set of preparatory conditions involving the availability of writing materials, writing instruments, etc.

These 'material' requirements play a role which has long been

---

[20] A. Leroi-Gourhan, *Le Geste et la Parole*, I. *Technique et Langage*, Paris, Albin Michel, 1964, Ch.6.

recognized, insofar as historians of writing have acknowledged that the visual form of the written sign often depends on what is available for the writer to work with: paper, stone, reed, wax tablet, baked clay, pattra, bronze, bamboo, silk, tortoise shells, etc. According to Béatrice André-Salvini:

> There are two necessary conditions for the invention of writing in any civilization: the existence of an established society – which presupposes awareness of collective unity – with symbols recognized by all which can be materialized, 'transcribed', and the discovery of a durable basis which can be easily obtained and used.[21]

Where the integrationist takes issue with claims of this kind is over the suggestion that the starting point in the development of writing is a social convention ready and waiting to be implemented, i.e. an embryonic inventory of signs already agreed in advance, but waiting for the appearance of a suitable technology which will allow them to be 'materialized'. The precise form of this 'materialization' will then depend on the technology that becomes available. But is this a viable hypothesis?

It seems rather obvious that people do not write on paper as they write on soft clay or on wax. But it would be a mistake to conclude that the material is no more than an adventitious or 'external' factor (to adopt Saussurean terminology) in the birth of a writing system. In other words, it is implausible to suppose that the written sign exists from the beginning at a level of abstraction which is independent of its biomechanical realization, i.e. as a pure geometric configuration.

For the integrationist, the importance of the material elements involved in writing is of quite a different order. Their semiological function is complex. The entire syntagmatics of the written text may be determined by limitations imposed by these elements. But, more important still, it is the interplay of these material elements

---

[21] B. André-Salvini, *L'Écriture cunéiforme*, Paris, Éditions de la Réunion des musées nationaux, 1991, pp.2–3.

and the biomechanical factors involved that acts, semiologically, to transform marks into written messages.

It is at this level that we encounter important semiological differences between the tree that functions as a private 'signpost' for me on my journey home and the public signpost that has been put up by the municipal authority. A commonplace but instructive example is provided by the old-fashioned finger-post, nowadays confined to rural roads (Fig.2). Here the material support, the post

Figure 2

itself, acts as a semiological vehicle indicating how the text it bears is to be understood. The form of the post is usually distinctive (traditionally in Great Britain a white post of wood or metal, with alternating black and white bands on the upright, and black lettering on a white ground along the horizontal arm). The occurrence of the text in this position and on this kind of object already determines to a large extent the range of possible intepretations. In other words, the written marks are only part of a larger semiological complex.

The function of this complex whole is, manifestly, of an integrational character: it serves to integrate certain programmes of anticipated activities. Travellers coming from a certain direction are assumed to be in need of certain information in order to get their bearings and continue their journey. In a world where no one travelled by road, this form of integration would be unnecessary and the finger-post would not exist.

The crucial semiological point to grasp is that *this* integrational function depends on the traveller's understanding of the written forms. In the case of the 'tree' sign, there is nothing to understand other than the topographical relationship between the location of the tree and my destination. But in the case of the finger-post, that understanding (of one's present location in relation to one's destination) is mediated by writing. It would be simplistic, however, to treat the writing as a semiological device which transforms what would otherwise be just a metal upright and an arm into a source of topographical information. That would be to ignore the other side of the relationship. For it is also true that the traveller's understanding of what a signpost is contributes to the semiological value of the written forms. The metal upright and the horizontal arm provide the installation for the text, thus turning what would otherwise be just sequences of letters into a message. This is not a simple conjunction of elements but a functional complementarity.

The written sign must not be confused either with the signpost or with the visible configuration of letters (e.g. 'GODSTOW') that it bears. The sign, for an integrationist, is not a physical item of either kind, nor the mental correlate of either. Discarded signposts, complete with their lettering, still survive as material objects long after having ceased to play a role in any system of communication (Fig.3). But they do not carry their semiological status around with them. For the sign *qua* sign is neither the support nor the marks that appear thereon.

There is no theoretical contradiction between recognizing the radical *impermanence* of the written sign and the (relative) *permanence* of the visible marks. Traditional wisdom of the kind that utilitarian literacy promotes tends to confuse the two, thus giving rise to the mistaken belief that what distinguishes written sign from spoken sign is that the former is not subject to the intrinsic ephemerality of the latter. And this in turn, as Plato saw, gives rise to the illusion that writing 'fixes' words, whereas speech cannot.

Figure 3

But once we see semiological value as depending on integrational function the role of writing appears in a quite different light. In the case of glottic writing there are typically at least three bio-mechanically different operations to be integrated: (i) graphic (manual), (ii) vocal, and (iii) optical. No dualist theory of the written sign can possibly accommodate all three. Freeing writing from this traditional Procrustean bed is the first requirement if we wish to understand it as a mode of communication.

CHAPTER FOUR

Notes on Notation

The first step in any rethinking of writing within an integrational framework must be to recognize the validity of a distinction that Saussure failed to draw. His failure to draw it is entirely attributable to following the traditional wisdom about the phonoptic function of letters. Although the distinction in question is commonly recognized by virtually every European child who learns at school to read and write a 'foreign language', there are no traditional pedagogical terms for referring to it (another lacuna which points to the blind spot in traditional thinking). In integrational terms it is the distinction between a *notation* and a *script*.

This distinction corresponds to typically different patterns of integration between the activities associated with reading and writing, and also to different questions that may be asked about them. 'Is it a *t* or an *l*?' is a question about a notation. 'How do you spell [kat]?' is a question about a script. The relationship between script and notation can be stated generally and informally as follows: the same notation may serve as a basis for more than one script (in fact, theoretically, for any number of scripts). That is why it is important not to confuse the elements of a notation with the (homographic) elements of a script.

It is through its incorporation into a script that an element of notation acquires its value as a written sign *in the texts of that system*. This is the conclusion Saussure ought to have reached if he had been faithful to his own structuralist principles.[1] That conclusion would have allowed him to recognize and account for such facts as the existence of interlingual homography: e.g. that the letter-sequence *c-h-a-i-r* spells one word in English but a quite different word in French. The members of this homographic pair are differently pronounced and have different meanings, but are nevertheless orthographically indistinguishable.

The integrationist's rationale for drawing this distinction again rests on the premiss that semiological values are determined by the structure of the activities integrated. In order to copy accurately a text containing the letter-sequence *c-h-a-i-r* a medieval scribe familiar with the alphabet does not need to know whether this is a French text or an English text; nor what the texts 'says'. Modern printers can and do set type in languages with which they are quite unacquainted. The viability of such activities as these already shows that there is something missing from Saussure's semiological analysis of the written sign. What is missing turns out to be a basic level that we can identify if we consider more elementary forms of semiological structure than writing. Examples of such structures are provided by children's games that are based on simple matching of shapes and/or colours from a given inventory of pieces. (Children are sometimes, as Quintilian recommended, introduced in this way to the letters of the alphabet; but the point being made here is of far wider application.) It would be quite mistaken to dismiss such games as 'meaningless'; on the contrary, they exemplify particularly clearly how meaning emerges from the integration of activities. Nowadays games of this kind are quite carefully devised to develop the child's skills of recognition and

---

[1] A remark from the Second Course, recorded by Patois, but omitted from the published text of the *Cours*, bears on this question. On the subject of letter-forms, Saussure notes that 'P' does not denote the same consonant in the Latin alphabet as in the Greek. But this is because he takes it as signifying [p] in one case and [r] in the other. He draws no general distinction between notation and writing system on this basis. (Komatsu and Wolf, op. cit., p.113.)

manipulation. But to determine the value of each piece in the set of pieces we do not need to look further than the way it functions in the game. Thus, for instance, a circle will mean something different from a square because it does not fit into the same slot on the child's board. However, if the relevant matching criterion were colour, not shape, the circle and the square might be equivalent. Some games, such as the card game commonly called 'Snap', depend entirely on matching two samples of the same configuration. Others, such as jigsaw puzzles, depend entirely on fitting together parts of a pre-determined configuration. Saussure's myopia about the alphabet, seen from an integrational perspective, is like that of someone who insists that a jigsaw does not make sense unless it fits together to form a picture. (Landscapes by Constable and interiors by Dutch masters seem to be traditional jigsaw favourites.) But the fact is that Constable's landscape provides an extra layer of meaning, superimposed on the more basic geometry of the jigsaw. In the Constable jigsaw there are two semiological structures involved, not just one.

In retrospect it may seem astonishing that Saussure failed to see the implications of interlingual homography and draw the appropriate semiological lessons. But it is worth pointing out that he also failed to see a very similar distinction in the domain of spoken language; namely, the distinction between phonetic units and phonological units. This latter distinction turned out to be indispensable for the development of modern structural phonology. Consequently retrospective attempts were made to trace it back to Saussure. In this connexion a great deal was made of his early *Mémoire sur le système primitif des voyelles dans les langues indo-européennes*, which Saussure had published in 1878 at the age of 21. Some Saussurean scholars detected in this essay a concept of the phoneme which anticipated that of the Prague school half a century later. The suggestion is certainly an attractive one and, if it were right, would fit admirably into the general framework of Saussure's ideas about language. What throws doubt upon it, unfortunately, is that nowhere in Saussure's Geneva lectures, or in the text of the *Cours*, do we find anything approaching an unambiguous statement of the distinction in question. If Saussure had already grasped the phoneme principle as early as 1878, it is difficult to explain why he left it undeveloped for the next thirty years of his academic career. One would have expected its applications, on the contrary, to have become one of the major themes of his teaching. It would also have supplied what is conspicuously missing in the *Cours*. As has been pointed out in Chapter 2, it is in the section on the 'material aspects' of linguistic value that the exposition of Saussure's ideas runs into all kinds of difficulties through its question-begging appeal to the analogy of writing. This could have been avoided if a clear formulation of the phoneme principle had been available. So there seems to be a significant connexion between Saussure's failure to draw the semiological distinction between a notation and a writing system on the one hand and his failure to distinguish phonetic from phonological units on the other.

* * *

The general idea that a notation must not be confused with any superimposed system of values it is used to express is perhaps more important in mathematics than it is in linguistics. In lay mathematical terms, the basic point is easily made: figures must not be confused with numbers. There is no such simple and perspicuous statement available in the case of language. ('Letters must not be confused with sounds' makes a quite different point. Perhaps where Saussure went astray was in assuming that this *was* the appropriate linguistic parallel.) In the first mathematical treatise to be printed in Europe, the *Practica* of Treviso (1478), the author begins with this distinction as the foundation for all mathematical reasoning: 'numeration', as he puts it, is the 'first operation':

> Numeration is the representation of numbers by figures. This is done by means of the following ten letters or figures: *i* [sic], *2, 3, 4, 5, 6, 7, 8, 9, 0*.[2]

---

[2] D.E. Smith (ed.), *A Source Book in Mathematics*, New York, McGraw-Hill, 1929, pp.2–3.

This 'first operation' is, in effect, the choice of a notation, and the notation here presented has become one of the most familiar in modern Western culture: the so-called 'Arabic numerals'. From this 'first operation' there will follow a whole range of decisions that need to be taken concerning the system(s) of mathematical writing to be based upon it. For example, if it is desired to express more than ten numbers, some convention will have to be determined for combining the individual notational marks (*i, 2, 3,* etc.) into complex mathematical signs. Any such convention, however, will belong to that particular system of mathematical writing, not to the notation as such. Many such conventions might be devised, all based on the same original notation, and irrespective of the numerical values assigned to the basic notational marks.

For non-mathematicians, however, it is very easy to fall into confusion about what belongs to the notation and what does not. For example, there may be a temptation to suppose that *5* always designates the number five, this value being somehow built in to the definition of that notational unit. That temptation arises, if it does, simply because of the arithmetic value most commonly assigned to the figure *5* in the calculations of daily life. Worse still, it is not uncommon to speak of 'the number five' to refer *either* to the number *or* to the figure, as if the two were indissolubly associated. Thus National Lottery results are announced as winning 'numbers'. This and similar usages may encourage people to suppose that the figure *5* always has a numerical value, even when it occurs in post-codes or telephone 'numbers'. (This is exactly parallel to the assumption that the letter *t* always designates the sound [t] or the phoneme /t/.)

Such confusions have to be set aside if we are ever to grasp the (semiological) fact that *5* retains its identity as a notational unit regardless of what numerical value it may be assigned in any given instance, and regardless of whether it has any numerical value at all. This fact is reflected (although somewhat indirectly) in our acquaintance with the possibility of two ways of reading certain arithmetic expressions aloud. To read *555* as 'five five five' is to read it as a figure, whereas to read it as 'five hundred and fifty five' is to read it as a number.

Most of the above observations about 'Arabic numerals' have their counterparts with respect to those other familiar notational forms in Western culture which we call 'letters of the alphabet'. (Thus, for example, like the figure *5*, the letter *E* retains its notational identity irrespective of how it is pronounced or whether it is pronounced at all; we read letter-sequences aloud differently depending on whether we treat them as words or not, cf. reading *CAT* as [si ei ti] or as [kat].)

A notation is not just a haphazard collection of autonomous marks. It has an internal systematization. *5* has its own place in the numeral series (. . . *3, 4, 5, 6* . . .) Similarly *E* has its own place in the alphabetic series (. . . *C, D, E, F* . . .) There is no notational series which combines the two. The 'places' that individual notational marks occupy in their respective series are features of notational structure, and are not to be confused with the variable 'places' that may be occupied in written signs; e.g. the place of *5* in the numeral *5000*, or the place of *E* in the word *Edinburgh*. These latter places are features of the structure of particular scripts, not of notational structure. In the case of letters, notational place-sequence is commonly referred to in English as 'alphabetical order'. It has nothing whatsoever to do with place-sequence in the signs of written English. Similarly, we recognize for figures what might be called a 'counting order', although that term is not in common usage. Thus the instruction 'Count up to five' requires one to recite the names of the relevant figures in a certain order: the place of each in that traditional order is independent of the place(s) it may occupy in the expressions of any particular system of mathematical writing. (European children commonly start to learn 'counting order' before they can actually count or write.) Considerations of this kind point again to the necessity for a semiological distinction between notations and scripts. Just as a supply of metal discs of various shapes and sizes does not in itself constitute a currency system, even though it may provide the necessary materials, so a notation does not in itself constitute a script, but may provide the basis for one.

The distinction between notation and script is also relevant to understanding an ambiguity in the everyday use of the term *letter*. When we talk, for example, about a word beginning with a certain letter or about how many letters there are in a certain word (as, for instance, in connexion with crossword puzzles or other word games) we are referring to letters as notational units and we refer to them either by their letter-names (in speech) or by instantiating them (in writing). We can also, although perhaps less frequently, refer to them by their place in alphabetical order, as e.g. 'the first, second, third, etc. letter of the alphabet'. This notational sense of the term *letter*, however, does not capture the sense in which there are important differences between capitals and 'small' letters, between roman and italic letters, etc. These contrasts between corresponding shapes also have to be taught and learnt in an apprenticeship to alphabetic literacy. So there is a sense in which a capital *A* and a small *a* are indeed different letters (as typographers and printers insist), even though in the notational sense both are 'the same letter'. Differences of the kind that distinguish capitals from small letters, roman from italic letters, etc. are features of scripts, not notational features. Capital *A* and small *a* do not occupy different places in alphabetical order: both have the same place and share the same letter-name.[3]

* * *

By insisting on a semiological parallel between the way writing works and the way speech works, Saussure overlooked a profound

---

[3] It is perhaps worth pointing out that the distinction between letters as notational units and letters as units of scripts is not to be confused with the Peircean distinction between 'types' and 'tokens'. In Peirce's sense, every letter-shape, whether capital, lower-case, roman, italic, etc. will have its own type and innumerable tokens. The number of letter-tokens on this page remains the same, regardless of how many letter-types are distinguished.

structural difference between the two, a difference which tends to develop in all civilizations where writing becomes a widespread form of communication. This difference hinges on the fact that writing may be based on units which have a certain degree of independent organization; or, in other words, on structures which to some extent live a social life of their own, not geared to the immediate demands of communication. This is because a tradition of writing requires mechanisms of apprenticeship, conservation and transmission to be put in place, mechanisms which are far more complicated and specialized than those of speech, and hence become a focus of social attention in themselves.

In this way, notational units acquire a social existence that is denied to individual speech sounds. The consonant [t] on its own has no existence at all except one conjured up by linguists and phoneticians. It has no history either, any more than the sound of coughing has a history. But the history of the letter *t* is quite a different matter: we can trace it back over the centuries to the original emergence of alphabetic writing. To ask for the history of the sound [t], on the other hand, is to ask a nonsense question. One can describe the mechanism of articulation of the sound and its acoustic properties; but that is all.

The history of alphabetic letters is often illustrated in textbooks by tables showing the variations of form at different chronological stages. Thus the modern *A*, for example, turns out to be an inverted form of an original pictograph representing the head of an ox. There is nothing wrong with tabular histories of this kind, provided the information they contain is accurate and provided we do not treat them as anything more authoritative than schematic guides to the evolution of certain visual configurations. Similar tables, after all, can be drawn up to illustrate the evolution of patterns which have nothing to do with writing; for instance, in textiles or ceramics.[4] What would be a mistake, however, would be to ascribe a similar validity to the tables of sound changes that

---

[4] See R. Harris, *The Origin of Writing*, London, Duckworth, 1986, p.125 for a table illustrating the evolution of corner decorations on Delft tiles.

authors of textbooks on historical linguistics are fond of compiling. These have a quite different status. The 'sounds' represented in such tables are abstractions reconstructed by linguists on the basis of certain hypotheses and the application of certain analytic methods. The supposed 'evolution' of these 'sounds' is equally hypothetical, and metaphorical to boot. Yet the misleading impression is given – and accepted by many students – that the table of letter-form changes and the table of sound changes are somehow on an equal footing, and merely exhibit different facets of the same linguistic story. This only serves to obscure a fact which the semiologist of writing must bring out into the open and place in the forefront of any investigation: *letters and figures are cultural artifacts.* Sounds are not (except insofar as their identification is a second-order activity which itself depends on familiarity with writing).

The history of metalanguage is very revealing in this connexion. In most European languages, letters have names but speech sounds do not; with the result that a letter-name is frequently pressed into service in order to identify a particular vowel or consonant. ('He slurred his esses.' 'French people can't say tee aitch properly.') Throughout the European tradition there is a tendency to conceptualize sounds in terms of letters. Greek and Roman authors so frequently refer to sounds as 'letters' that one might be forgiven for supposing that they failed to distinguish between the phonetic phenomena and the marks on the page. It was this pervasive tendency to think of the sound by reference to a written form that Saussure had in mind when he warned his students against looking at language through the grid imposed upon it by conventional orthography. He speaks of the 'tyranny' of the letter.[5] More explicitly:

> the written word is so intimately connected with the spoken word it represents that it manages to usurp the principal role. As much or even more importance is given to this representation of the vocal sign as to the sign itself. It is rather as if people

---

[5] Saussure, op. cit., p.53.

believed that in order to find out what a person looks like it is better to study his photograph than his face.[6]

In spite of these warnings, Saussure himself does not seem to see that, as cultural artifacts, letters lead a life of their own 'within the life of society', whereas speech sounds do not. Nor does he see that for this very reason the semiologist of writing cannot take it as a basic premiss that the sole function of letters is – or should be – to designate sounds. This would be like starting from the assumption that the alphabet was the creation of the International Phonetic Association.

Even odder, however, is Saussure's failure to recognize in writing what he recognizes very promptly in speech: the existence of dual articulation. Although consonants and vowels are units in the chain of speech, they are not *ipso facto* signs. But when it comes to writing, Saussure treats individual letters not only as units in the graphic chain but as signs, each signifying a given sound. The bizarre result of this theoretical move is that he is then obliged to devote a long discussion to explaining away the 'discrepancies' between orthography and pronunciation.

The causes of these discrepancies, according to Saussure, are many and various. He mentions only the most important. The first and most general is that 'a language is in a constant process of evolution, whereas writing tends to remain fixed'.[7] Thus, he points out, the French word for 'king' is still spelt *roi*, which corresponds to its thirteenth-century pronunciation.

This example is worth pausing over, since it epitomizes some of the basic problems with the utilitarian view of writing. On the one hand, writing is praised for its capacity to 'fix' the spoken word: on the other hand, it is blamed for 'fixing' it too permanently. Thus the chimerical ideal of a spelling system which would somehow automatically adapt to changes in pronunciation is conjured up. Saussure seems to have regarded current proposals for French

---

[6] Saussure, op. cit., p.45.
[7] Saussure, op. cit., p.48.

spelling reform with caution, if not with contempt (presumably because he thought they were advocated by people linguistically incompetent to judge the 'real' relationship between the writing system and *la langue*). But the explanation he himself offers for the 'discrepancy' between the spelling of the word *roi* and its modern pronunciation does not inspire confidence in the ability of linguists to deal with the problem either, since it raises as many questions as it answers. He cites it as an example of the 'immobility' of writing. But this alleged immobility is clearly extrapolated from a comparison between modern texts and medieval texts, from which it emerges that the modern spelling *roi* and the medieval spelling *roi* coincide. Now to conclude from such a comparison that here we have a typical example of inertia or conservatism in the writing system involves assuming that the same orthographic principles are operative in both periods. In other words, we are tacitly invited to judge the twentieth-century spelling by the practice of the medieval scribe. Does this make sense? Where do these panchronic criteria come from?

What is no less puzzling is how to reconcile Saussure's 'immobility' claim with the obvious counterevidence that this example itself provides. *If* letters represent sounds, as Saussure (bearing in mind his interpretation of sounds as elements of the *image acoustique*) maintains, then the expected conclusion would be that what has changed over the centuries, to judge by the case of *roi*, are the rules of representation. On the other hand if, as Saussure seems to be insisting here, the modern spelling *fails* to reflect the modern pronunciation, what this calls in question *prima facie* is the thesis that letters represent sounds. The case of *roi* could be argued either way; but what Saussure again seems to be trying to do is to have it both ways at once. In other words, he wants it *both* to illustrate *and* to be an exception to his main semiological thesis about the alphabet. Saussure evidently thinks that a better (i.e. more accurate, more rational) spelling for the twentieth-century word would be *rwa*, but he offers no explanation of why French people do not adopt that spelling, as presumably they could if they too thought that. What is one to conclude? One possibility is that, contrary to Saussure's claim, the modern spelling *roi* is not recognized by most people as an orthographic 'discrepancy' at all.

To sum up, Saussure seems to be guilty here of an inconsistency which he criticizes severely in other linguists; namely, mixing synchronic and diachronic perspectives. A 'discrepancy' between spelling and pronunciation – if there is any such linguistic phenomenon – must be a synchronic phenomenon and therefore requires a strictly synchronic analysis. How the word *roi* was written – or pronounced – in the thirteenth century is simply an irrelevance as far as the semiological status of the twentieth-century spelling is concerned.

The second cause of 'discrepancies' that Saussure lists is borrowing.

Another cause of discrepancy between spelling and pronunciation is the borrowing of an alphabet by one people from another. It often happens that the resources of the graphic system are poorly adapted to its new function, and it is necessary to have recourse to various expedients. Two letters, for example, will be used to designate a single sound.[8]

The example he cites is the voiceless dental fricative of the Germanic languages being spelt *th* because the Roman alphabet had no corresponding letter.

This is another puzzling case of an illustration undermining the main thesis it is invoked to support. In the first place, the very possibility of adapting and augmenting an alphabet shows that we are dealing with nothing more than a notation. Otherwise, it would be impossible to borrow an alphabet without borrowing its pronunciation at the same time. In the second place, the spelling *th* would be inexplicable if it were true that letters represent sounds, since the Germanic dental fricative was not a [t] followed by [h]. Saussure adds, for good measure, that King Chilperic tried to introduce a special letter for this fricative sound, but without

---

[8] Saussure, op. cit., p.49.

success. So what we end up with is borrowing as a variation on the theme of the 'immobility' of writing.

The third cause of 'discrepancies' that Saussure cites is 'etymological preoccupation':

It is not infrequently the case that a spelling is introduced through mistaken etymologising; *d* was thus introduced in the French word *poids* ('weight') as if it came from Latin *pondus*, when in fact it comes from *pensum*. But it makes little difference whether the etymology is correct or not. It is the principle of etymological spelling itself which is mistaken.[9]

It is difficult to know what to make of this authoritarian pronouncement. For an integrationist it would be self-evident that there is no point in trying to establish a semiology of writing (or of anything else) on the basis of prescriptive claims of this kind. Etymological spellings are obviously to be condemned if one believes that letters 'ought' to stand for sounds and nothing else. But for anyone not committed to this belief, the very existence of etymological spellings is an important piece of evidence *against* the thesis that letters are just phonetic signs.

There is little to be rescued from this disastrous chapter of the *Cours*. Even the idea of grapho-phonic 'discrepancy' does not survive. In order to make any sense at all, it would have to be construed as a synchronic concept. But now suppose we are dealing with a writing system where certain spellings or certain pronunciations cannot be explained by general orthoepic rules. The analyst then faces a simple choice. Either (i) the principle that letters designate sounds is to be upheld – in which case the orthoepic rules have to be altered in order to accommodate the previously recalcitrant examples – or else (ii) the principle is abandoned and one concedes that there must be other factors at work. In the first case there is, by definition, no 'discrepancy', since the rules are reformulated in such a way as to take care of the former exceptions. In the second case there is no 'discrepancy' either,

---

[9] Saussure, op. cit., p.50.

since the original principle is now abandoned. Either way, the notion of 'discrepancy' itself vanishes – a mirage projected by an inadequate theory of writing.

* * *

Saussure's failure to distinguish between script and notation in his analysis of alphabetic writing is not just an 'accidental' blind spot, but a consequence of his own structuralist approach to semiological questions. This becomes apparent if we go back to his own favourite example of chess. He points out – quite rightly – that the relations between successive states of the board are such that any passer-by (who understands the rules) can take in the current situation at a glance, without knowing anything about antecedent states that led to it. Such a person can even take over from one of the players and carry on the game from there. What Saussure omits to mention, however, is that in order to step in in this way the newcomer must not only know how to move the pieces but, before that, be able to *recognize* them as they stand on the board. Now chess pieces are recognized by their form. That is why Saussure's remarks about replacing a knight cannot be accepted without serious reservations.[10] According to Saussure, even 'an object of quite a different shape' will do 'provided it is assigned the same value'. That is indeed possible. But it would be a mistake to conclude on that account that the 'normal' shape of a knight counts for nothing. Replacing the knight by a spare bishop, for example, would certainly run the risk of confusing the players in the long run. And if the knight were replaced by an object having nothing to do with the game – a coin, for example – a passer-by would no longer be able to judge the state of the board simply on inspection: it would be necessary to explain the substitution.

Here again the importance of the integrational concept of notation makes itself felt. In order to play chess at all, we have first to learn certain 'notational' distinctions. That is to say, before there is any question of how the knight moves, we have to grasp

---

[10] Saussure, op. cit., pp.153–4.

which pieces are knights, which are bishops, and so on. Saussure makes no mention of the fact that in chess there is a long tradition of forms and names. These cannot be dismissed as merely 'external' elements of the game, since they articulate an essential part of the rules. The distinction between the two colours ('white' and 'black') is basic to the way chess is played, i.e. as a competition between two opposing players, each in command of a certain team. Furthermore, in the traditional chess set equivalent pieces have the same shape. The beginner grasps straight away, for instance, that all pawns move in the same way. There is no need to ask what the moves are for each pawn individually, and no need to explain that white pawns behave according to exactly the same pattern as black pawns. (Nevertheless, as chess signs, a white pawn and a black pawn mean something different.) In short, the iconography of chess is not merely 'decorative' even if it is 'arbitrary', but reflects certain crucial features of the game.

There is an interesting parallel between the way Saussure plays down the significance of these allegedly 'material' aspects of the game of chess (the colours, the characteristic shapes of the pieces) and his failure to recognize notation as a basis for alphabetic writing. In both cases what has been missed – or dismissed – is the existence of a dual structure within the semiological organization of the system.

What is the explanation? Any search for one brings us back to Saussure's notion of semiological 'differences'. The importance Saussure attached to this is a reflection of his dislike of the spirit of positivism which, he believed, had dominated nineteenth-century linguistics. The fundamental error engendered by this positivism, in Saussure's view, was the assumption that systems of signs arose from the conjunction of series of objects and thoughts given in advance. Against this Saussure argues that a word such as *arbre* ('tree') is not a mere vocal label attached to an object supplied ready-made for us by Nature. On the contrary, both the *signifiant* and the *signifié* of this word are products of a vast network of phonic and conceptual differences which constitutes the French language.

This emphasis on the importance of differences and differentiation, at the expense of positive relations, is one of the originalities and strengths of Saussure's thinking about signs. But it is at the same time the Achilles' heel of Saussurean semiology. For there are systems of signs based on something *other than* a network of differences; and scripts are among them. This is not to say that in such systems differences do not count: they do indeed. But nevertheless such systems cannot simply be reduced semiologically to series of internal oppositions, in the way Saussure believed was both possible and necessary in the case of languages.

*   *   *

The integrationist distinction between script and notation is only the application to glottic writing of a more general semiological distinction. Notations exemplify a type of structure which, far from being confined to writing, is one of the most basic structures in the domain of signs. It is the structure characteristic of any set of items fulfilling the following conditions.

1 Each member of the set has a specific form which sets it apart from all others in the set.
2 Between any two members there is either a relation of equivalence or a relation of priority. Thus every member has a determinate position with respect to all other members in the set.
3 Membership of the set is closed.

Such a structure constitutes what in integrationist terms is an *emblematic frame*. The very simplest emblematic frames comprise just two members: examples are an on-off switch with only two possible positions and a red-green traffic light where the two colours alternate but never show simultaneously. Slightly more complicated examples are the following.

A The Japanese game of *shenken* is based on a three-member emblematic frame. The three members of the set are: Knife, Paper, Stone. The priorities are: Knife beats Paper, Paper beats Stone, and Stone beats Knife. The two players simultaneously choose an emblem. The winner is the player choosing the emblem with the higher priority. It would be possible, obviously, to play with a different set of priorities; e.g. Knife beats the other two, Stone and Paper are equal. But then the game would presumably lose its interest, since the players would always choose Knife.

B In the traditional pack of playing cards, each suit has the structure of an emblematic frame. There are thirteen members: ace, king, queen, jack, etc. In certain games, the deuce takes priority over the ace and the joker takes priority over all other cards. There is no priority between suits except in certain games, including games where 'trumps' are declared. The notion 'trump' is an interesting example of a semiological concept: a priority is assigned where 'normally' there is no priority.

C The traditional Chinese calendar is based on an emblematic frame. The emblems are: Rat, Ox, Tiger, Rabbit, Dragon, Snake, Horse, Sheep, Monkey, Cock, Dog and Boar. Here the priorities are chronological. The cycle repeats every twelve years, always in the same order. Thus Horse is always preceded by Snake and followed by Sheep

D A more complex calendrical example is the *pelelintangan* of Bali (Fig. 4). This is an astrological calendar comprising thirty-five emblems, of which there are a number of variants.[11] One of these goes: *kala sungsang*, demon upside-down; *gajah*, elephant; *patrem*, dagger; *uluku*, plough; *laweyan*, headless body; *kelapa*, coconut tree; *kukus*, smoke; *kiriman*, gift; *lembu*, bull; *pedati*, cart; *kuda*, horse; *yuyu*, crab; *asu*, dog; *jong sarat*, full boat; *sidamalung*, sow; *tangis*, tears; *gajah mina*, mythological beast with the body of a fish and the head of an elephant; *lumbung*, rice store; *kartika*, the Pleiades; *tiwa tiwa*, death rites; *sangkatikel*, broken hoe; *salah ukur*, faulty measurement; *bade*, cremation pyre;

---

[11] F.B. Eiseman, Jr., *Bali: Sekala and Nisakala. Vol.1. Essays on Religion, Ritual and Art*, Berkeley/Singapore, Periplus, 1989, Ch.18.

Figure 4

kumba, urn; *naga*, snake; *banyak angrem*, brooding goose; *bubu bolong*, fish trap; *prahu pegat*, shipwreck; *magelut*, embrace; *udang*, prawn; *begoong*, headless ghost; *ru*, arrow; *sungenge*, sunflower; *puwuh atarung*, fighting quails; *pagelangan*, stare.

The order in this case is not a simple chronological succession. The place of each member of the *pelelintangan* depends on the fact that the Balinese calendar consists of several weeks that run concurrently. The two most important weeks are the *pancawara* of five days and the *saptawara* of seven days. Coincidences between days in these two weeks, of which the above emblems are allegorical representations, are considered particularly significant. The *pelelintangan*, in other words, summarizes the total set of possibilities of coincidence between days of the *pancawara* and days of the *saptawara*. Each of these is a *bintang*. So there are thirty-five possible *bintang*. The character of a child is believed to be determined by the *bintang* of the day on which it was born.

It should be noted that although the *pelelintangan* is traditionally displayed as a five-by-seven grid, the arrangement of the thirty-five emblems is not determined by the chronological succession of *bintang*, but by the sequence of days in the two basic weeks. At the same time, however, the succession of *bintang* results in rearranging the days of the weeks in a new order: 1, 6, 4, 2, 7, 5, 3 for the *sapatawara*, and 1, 3, 5, 2, 4 for the *pancawara*. (The semiological importance of this point – which will not be pursued here – is that, unlike some calendars, the *pelelintangan* is not a kind of spatial diagram of time. There is in this sense no answer to the question of 'what' the *pelelintangan* grid 'shows': any more than there is an answer to the question of what the game of *shenken* 'means'.)

* * *

In the four examples cited above, the emblematic frame is a structure determined by tradition. Its images may originally have had some rationale of a practical, religious or magical nature which has since been obscured. But, once established, the emblematic frame becomes a cultural artifact in its own right, irrespective of what purpose it may originally have served. It can be described quite precisely without reference to its beginnings or to the social practices that maintain it. A description of a Balinese *pelelintangan* could just as easily be the description of a gaming board, or a description of a pack of playing cards, or that of a cosmic symbolism. It is no coincidence that emblematic frames are often the subject of mystical or superstitious interpretations which have nothing to do with their social history.

Emblematic frames of some kind turn up in every culture that has been studied by anthropologists. They may serve very diverse functions: they feature in calendars, military uniforms, architecture, rituals and games of all kinds. The point here is that it should come as no surprise – anthropologically speaking – to find them at the basis of writing systems. For they offer just what a script needs: a notation. A notation simply *is* an emblematic frame adapted to or devised for the purpose of writing. But it is not in itself a script, any more than a set of emblems constitutes in itself a calendar.

It is sometimes possible to utilize or devise emblematic frames in such a way that the emblems correspond on a one-to-one basis with units of some other structure. In such cases the result is an isomorphism between the two structures. That possibility is certainly available, in principle, in the case of notations. But, as far as the semiologist is concerned, it cannot be taken for granted that such isomorphisms regularly occur, or are even common.

* * *

It is ironic that Saussure, of all theorists, should have overlooked the distinction between a notation and a script, for this is bound to make a great difference to any semiology organized on structuralist principles. Once that difference is given its due, there will be two levels of structure to be taken into account in every case, and the most basic mistake the analyst can make would be to conflate them. The notational structure and the structure of the script need to be kept separate because some features of a written text are to be explained by reference to the former and some by reference to the latter. In order to distinguish them for purposes of discussion let us call them *notation features* and *script features* respectively.

Usually we find that the script superimposes a more complex layer of organization on that of the notation it deploys. But that does not mean that notation contributes nothing to the final structure of the written message, or so little that it can be safely ignored. On the contrary, notation features are typically among the most prominent features distinguishing one form of writing from another.

A clear illustration of this is provided by forms of arithmetical writing that uses Arabic numerals. Consider what can be done with the classic notation *1, 2, 3, 4, 5, 6, 7, 8, 9, 0*. Given this notation, we next have to choose a set of arithmetic values. In order to express the number 'thirteen' we have a variety of scripts available. Depending on which one we choose, the appropriate numerical expression will be, for example, *13, 1101, 111, 31, 23, 21* or *11*. The binary system uses only two units of the notation whereas the denary system uses all ten. But in all cases the structure of the expression is grafted on to a more basic structure provided by the notation.

Take, for example, the sign for 'thirteen' as expressed in the binary system: i.e. *1101*. The syntagmatic organization of this expression and the numerical values are supplied by the binary system; but the two figures, the contrast between them and their relative priority come from the notation itself and have nothing to do with the binary principle. Similarly, when we compare the two signs *13* and *31*, both meaning 'thirteen', we see that the figures are the same but their position in the syntagmatic chain is different. This has nothing to do with the notation, which is the same in both cases, but is entirely due to the different value systems.

The number 'thirteen' can also be expressed in Roman numerals. Roman arithmetic notation uses the seven letters *I, V, X, L, C, D* and *M*. As regards their shape, these are recognizable as letters of the alphabet. But their order of priority is not that of alphabetical order. In this case the numerical system imposes an order of its own, on the basis of the values 'one', 'five', 'ten', 'fifty', 'hundred', 'five hundred', 'thousand'. 'Thirteen' is written *XIII*. Again, the syntagmatic structure is not determined by the notation.

It is clear from these cases, which could be multiplied *ad infinitum*, that semiological analysis requires recognition of a distinction between *notation structure* and *script structure*. How would this apply in the case of alphabetic writing? What difference would it make to the way written forms are analysed and classified? It is instructive to consider one of Saussure's examples: the French word for 'bird'.

The modern orthographic form is *oiseau*. Saussure takes this as a flagrant example of how it is possible for a writing system to obscure entirely the structure of the linguistic sign. 'Not one of the sounds of the spoken word (*wazo*),' he complains, 'is represented by its appropriate sign'.[12] But that complaint presupposes

---

[12] Saussure, op. cit., p.52.

that *oiseau* should indeed be spelt *wazo*; which is an entirely gratuitous assumption from a semiological point of view. Indeed, doubly gratuitous; for it is difficult to see what authority Saussure has for invoking a hypothetically 'correct' spelling which has no antecedents in the history of French orthography, and no less difficult to see what justification he has in any case for assuming that the written form should reveal the phonetic composition of the corresponding spoken *signifiant*. The idea that a written sign might signify simply in virtue of expressing a particular concept (in this case 'bird') is one Saussure is evidently not prepared to consider, even though that is exactly what he assumes in the case of the corresponding oral sign.[13] The result is that his semiological analysis has nothing to say about *oiseau* as a written sign at all except that it is bizarrely – even perversely – 'incorrect': i.e. it has no synchronic explanation and totally violates what Saussure takes to be the current structure of the French orthographic system.

A quite different picture emerges if instead we consider the form in the light of the distinction between notation features and script features. It is difficult to see in the case of *oiseau* that the notation contributes anything apart from the letter-shapes, and therefore it must be in the structure of the script that any explanation of its graphic form is to be sought. A synchronic rationale at this level – where Saussure never looked for it – is not difficult to find, and can be found without employing any analytic methods other than those Saussure himself recommends. It begins to emerge as soon as we consider the following two series of forms:

1. *oiseau, oisif, oiseux, Oise, toise, ardoise,* etc.[14]
2. *oiseau, beau, eau, peau, sceau,* etc.[15]

The spelling *oiseau* clearly conforms to certain orthoepic patterns quite abundantly exemplified in matching sets of modern

---

[13] Discussion of a neo-Saussurean theory (glossematics) which allows for the possibility Saussure rejected will be reserved for a later chapter.

[14] Phonetically: [wazo], [wazif], [wazø], [waz], [twaz], [ardwaz].

[15] Phonetically: [wazo], [bo], [o], [po], [so].

French words. These patterns, to be sure, are not without competitors; but such patterns rarely are (except in the case of artificially constructed languages). The existence of competing paradigms is one of the conspicuous features of linguistic structure at all levels of analysis.

When we look for patterns that reflect the meaning of the word, we find:

3. *oiseau, oiselle, oisellerie, oisillon, oiselet, oiseleur, oiselier,*[16]
4. *oiseau, corbeau, moineau, bécasseau, étourneau, vanneau.*[17]

Thus, quite independently of its pronunciation, *oiseau* also fits certain lexical and semantic patterns which find their expression in the written language. It is ironic that what prevents Saussure from reaching these eminently Saussurean conclusions is his misguided insistence on treating individual units of notation as signs of sounds.

* * *

That the concept of notation is not a mere artifact of integrational theory is shown by a great variety of literate practices. An interesting example is that of the lipogram: the literary form which is based on the systematic avoidance of certain letters. It is quite easy for the unforewarned reader to read a page or a whole chapter of Georges Perec's novel *La Disparition* without realizing that the text contains no examples of the letter *e*.[18] What is of interest here is not the ingenuity of the enterprise, nor the question of its literary value, but the simple fact that the rules would be incomprehensible if a written text could not be analysed at the level of notation. It has nothing to do with pronunciation. It has nothing to do with spelling either, except insofar as the exclusion of a particular letter automatically entails the exclusion of certain

---

[16] 'bird', 'hen-bird', 'aviary', 'fledgling', 'small bird', 'fowler', 'bird-fancier'.

[17] 'bird', 'crow', 'sparrow', 'sandpiper', 'starling', 'lapwing'.

[18] G. Perec, *La Disparition*, Paris, Denoël, 1969.

words. In short, the lipogram would be inconceivable unless there were writing systems based on fixed inventories of graphic units, and unless it were possible to classify written texts on the basis of the presence or absence of one of those units *irrespective of any phonetic value it might have or any function in the script.*

The same notion is the cornerstone of the modern dictionary, which arranges words in 'alphabetical order'. But lipograms are much older than dictionaries. Trephiodorus in the fifth century wrote an *Odyssey* in 24 books, of which each one omitted a letter: alpha from the first book, beta from the second, and so on. Before him Nestor of Laranda had composed a lipogrammatic *Iliad*. In Latin, Fulgentius is the author of an *Absque litteris de aetatibus mundi et hominis*, of which only fourteen books have survived. The oldest known lipograms are those of the poet Lasos from the sixth century BC. So there can hardly be any doubt that from a very early period in the European tradition people understood, even if they did not have a technical term for it, what a notation was: a set of graphic units with its own structure. And the proof is that they amused themselves by inventing a literate game which consists, essentially, in superimposing the structure of a notation on the structure of texts.

*   *   *

The distinction between notation and script also underlies the familiar use of letter-forms and letter-names for metalinguistic purposes. Thus 'Church begins with c' is false or nonsensical unless the first six letters of the written form are taken as identifying metalinguistically the subject of the proposition in question and the last letter as identifying the same notational unit as the first letter. All the rest of the sentence is to be interpreted non-metalinguistically. The general phenomenon whereby, depending on the circumstances of the case, letters stand to be interpreted in one way or the other may be called 'notational ambiguity'. In order to avoid notational ambiguity, writing commonly employ devices such as inverted commas, underlining and italicization. (E.g. ' "Church" begins with "c" ', or '*Church* begins with *c*'.)

Philosophers distinguish here between the 'formal mode' and the 'material mode' of expression, or between 'mention' and 'use'.[19]

Of particular interest for our present purposes is the asymmetry between speech and writing that is thrown into relief by cases of notational ambiguity. In order to avoid corresponding ambiguities in speech, it is frequently necessary to make the point more explicitly. (Thus, read aloud, 'There are twelve letters in *this sentence*' can still be misinterpreted, whereas 'There are twelve letters in the words *this sentence*' deals with that potential problem.) In short, a purely graphic device (italicization, inverted commas, etc.) can function as the equivalent of a metalinguistic term. The fact that this strategy is available – and commonly resorted to in literate cultures – means that we can if we wish, in written communication, choose to ignore or bypass the structure of the script and have direct recourse to the notational structure that underlies it. Nothing like this is possible in speech, for the simple reason that spoken discourse has no notational structure. (An impression to the contrary may sometimes be fostered by pedagogical techniques such as 'sounding out' a word, but such techniques are in fact examples of orthography projected into the domain of phonetic education. '[k] [a] [t] says [kat]' is a pseudo-sentence that has no existence outside the classroom, and it is manifestly calqued on 'C-A-T spells cat'. The proof of this is that when asked how to pronounce the word written *cat*, one answers by pronouncing it, not by attempting the curious vocal feat of articulating three phonetic isolates – unless, of course, one has been brainwashed at school by a teacher of so-called 'phonics'. In a literate culture based on alphabetic writing, 'How many letters are there in your name?' is a genuine question. 'How many sounds are there in your name?' is not.)

---

[19] For a critical discussion of the way in which philosophers have used such distinctions and the corresponding graphic devices, see R. Harris, *The Language Connection*, Bristol, Thoemmes, 1996. The case could be made that were it not for writing conventions Western philosophy would never have attributed such importance to these matters.

The semiological explanation of this asymmetry, once again, is that writing incorporates two structural levels, which it is possible to distinguish whenever that becomes necessary for purposes of communication. There is, strictly speaking, no oral counterpart to the written sentence 'C-A-T spells *cat*'. If I say '[si ei ti] is pronounced [kat]' that is self-evidently false, since I have just proposed a three-syllable pronunciation of a monosyllabic form; and even if I try to utter the elements of this form as three separate articulations separated by pauses I fare no better, since that is clearly *not* how I pronounce the word in question. I can, to be sure, utter the phonetic tautology '[kat] is pronounced [kat]'. But this still fails to match 'C-A-T spells *cat* ', since 'C-A-T spells *cat*' is no tautology at all, but states a non-trivial fact of English orthography. (There is no orthographic principle that requires C-A-T to spell anything at all, any more than Z-X-T does.)

* * *

Centuries ago Quintilian came closer than Saussure ever did to acknowledging the distinction between script and notation. He offers the following observations on the methods used in his day to acquaint Roman children with the alphabet:

I do not approve the practice which is followed in many cases: teaching infants the names and the order of the letters before their shapes. This makes it difficult for them to recognize the letters, since the children do not pay attention to the form but rely on their memory. Thus, when the teacher thinks the child has mastered the letters in their customary order, they are written out in reverse sequence, and then in all kinds of permutations, in order to get the child to recognize them by their form (= *facie*) rather than their place (= *ordine*). The best way is, as with persons, to introduce them by their appearance (= *habitus*) and by name (= *nomina*) at the same time. But what is an awkward method where letters are concerned is not to be rejected when it comes to syllables. I do not disapprove the practice of giving children ivory letters to play with, or any such method that will encourage children's interest at that age, when they love to handle things, look at them and name them.[20]

What Quintilian's recommendation comes down to is this: first teach the notation, and only when that has been mastered proceed to teach the child how to use it. What is interesting from a semiological point of view is that Quintilian has no difficulty in recognizing that notational structure as such is quite separate from the structure of the writing system and can be taught independently.

A general question about notation might appropriately be raised at this point. Why does not physical configuration alone suffice to identify the units of a notation? The answer might be that a shape, as such, lends itself to various interpretations. Given a prototypical example to copy, this can always be analysed visually in more ways than one, copied in more ways than one, and hence give rise to variants. The possibility of confusion is reduced if some alternative means of identification is added. In practice, the expedients commonly employed are to give the shape its own name or its own place in a series. What Quintilian is complaining about in the passage cited above is that Roman schoolmasters in practice commonly gave these ancillary forms of identification priority over the actual letter-shapes when it came to teaching their pupils. What he recommends instead is identifying each letter *ab initio* by a combination of physical appearance and name. For it is thus, he says, that we learn to recognize human beings.

The validity of the comparison, however, is open to question. In the case of human beings, there is no particular limit on the number we may need to be able to recognize, and there is no guarantee that two will not share the same name. Accustoming children to recite the letter-names by rote in alphabetical order serves a purpose that Quintilian does not mention. What this practice captures for the learner is the important semiological fact that the letters constitute a small closed inventory, the members of

---

[20] Quintilian, *Institutio Oratoria*, I, i, 24–26.

which stand in strict one-one correlation with their names. Quintilian's recommendation would make more sense if the written language to be learnt were Chinese.

* * *

Is the distinction between script and notation in any way parallel to that which linguists draw for spoken languages between morphology and phonology? Do not letters as notational units correspond, in effect, to phonemes as phonological units?

Yes and no. The whole history of modern phonology shows that the phoneme, as a theoretical concept, is based on the letter. However sophisticated the phonological system, its basic segmental units are invariably represented in transcription by alphabetic letters of some kind. Furthermore, the development of phonemic transcription is inextricably bound up with efforts by missionaries and others to devise writing systems for hitherto unwritten languages. In this sense, the parallel between letter and phoneme is just another manifestation of the scriptism that pervades traditional Western thinking about language.

Semiologically, on the other hand, the parallel may easily give rise to an illusion. The illusion consists of thinking that the phonemes are already there, like the pile of bricks waiting for the house to be built. Whereas it is the other way round. The phonological bricks depend on the construction of the building, not vice versa. The building in question is oral discourse. And when that building is up, it takes a great deal of sophisticated analysis to distinguish the bricks. How many went into the construction and exactly what shapes they had even the builders do not know, and these are questions that may be answered differently by different analysts. In the case of writing, on the other hand, we find nothing parallel to this. Writing starts with bricks – alphabetic bricks in the case of the languages of Europe – and no constructional progress is made without first mastering that inventory. Learning to speak is not like that: there is no list of phonemes to learn off by heart.

Perhaps someone will object that phonological analysis, even if it tells us little directly about the processes of language learning, must nevertheless reflect a speaker's cognitive organization 'at some level or other'. For, in the end, do we not have to be able to produce and recognize the acoustic differences between words like *pin, bin, tin, din, sin*, etc.? Are not these phonemic differences? And are not these minimal differential units, which 'mean' nothing in isolation, exactly parallel in that case to the corresponding letters in the written forms? So do not the phonemes of a language in effect constitute its oral alphabet?

The equation is deceptive on all counts, precisely because spoken discourse has no structural basis that corresponds to a notation. It has no list of units, determinate in number, drawn up in advance and handed down by tradition, constituting in itself an independent cultural artifact. The phonological systems recognized by modern phonologists are abstract systems of synchronic oppositions derived from – and hence valid only in respect of – the contrasts manifested in the morphology, syntax and vocabulary of a particular language. Thus the notion that the same phoneme might occur in two different languages is theoretically incoherent. Whereas the notion that the same alphabet with the same letters and letter-forms might be used in two different scripts is not incoherent at all. And this is because a notation is independent of a script and has its own existence.

But there is also a more basic reason for rejecting the equation between letters and phonemes. Phonological analysis is based on series of comparisons such as that cited above (*pin* vs. *bin* vs *tin* vs *din* vs *sin* . . .) in which isolated words are compared in order to determine minimal differences. The reasoning the phonologist then deploys, on the basis of this decontextualized 'evidence', involves assuming that such minimal pairs of words must differ by just one phoneme. But this logic is clearly debatable. That is to say, from the fact that *pin* is consistently distinguishable from *bin, tin, din, sin*, etc. it does not follow that the English language must contain a phoneme /p/ which 'accounts for' that phenomenon. No one would accept similar reasoning in chemistry, geography or botany. Minimal differences do not prove the existence of corresponding minimal units. If they did, it would not be difficult to show that a ten-pence coin consists of two five-pence coins, or large potatoes of smaller potatoes. That would be an atomistic sophistry worthy of the scientists of the Grand Academy of Lagado.

We are certainly not obliged to accept this kind of sophistry in linguistics, unless we are anxious to make phonological analysis conform to an *a priori* atomic model. And that seems, in fact, to be just what modern phonologists have been anxious to do. Now the lineage of their atomic model can hardly be in doubt. It becomes obvious as soon as we consider that nowhere in the world except in certain literate communities do we find an analysis of speech that ends up by postulating an inventory of some twenty or thirty separate atoms of sound. And those are communities whose traditional form of writing is alphabetic.

Perhaps, nevertheless, there is a temptation to justify all this by saying that the alphabet itself is an intellectual triumph of analysis, capturing a truth about speech that pre-literate communities have not yet recognized; namely that spoken discourse consists in constant repetition and recombination of the same very limited set of sounds. Here one recognizes another variant of the ancient *topos* about savages and their primitive mentality. But today it can hardly be taken seriously. No pre-literate community has so far been discovered in which speakers had no grasp of oral repetition and could not mimic or make mock of certain forms of speech and idiosyncrasies of pronunciation. The notion of pre-literates as phonetic simpletons does not stand up to a moment's investigation: in communities without writing the ear for niceties of speech and accent is as well developed as in any literate elocution class. What is beyond pre-literate comprehension, on the other hand, is why anyone should suppose that the human speaking voice is restricted to producing sounds from a mysteriously fixed inventory of phonemes. For that reduction of their natural oral capacity is comprehensible only when people have been conditioned, as Europeans are, to thinking about speech in terms of writing.

CHAPTER FIVE

Alphabetical Disorder

Perhaps the most heretical implication of an integrational semiology of writing is that it requires us to rethink the alphabet. Since
establishing the history of the alphabet is generally counted as one
of the crowning achievements of language studies in modern
times, it might seem outrageous to suggest that this great monument to learning is built on semiological foundations of sand. But
this is the conclusion to which one is led. It is not merely that
certain details of historical evolution and transmission are obscure
in the canonical history, but something much more serious. The
concepts 'alphabet' and 'alphabetical' are themselves not well-
defined. Worse still, different authorities interpret them differently
to suit their own arguments.

Saussure, as already noted in Chapter 2, held no very high
opinion of the way in which his predecessors had treated the
written evidence on which they based their reconstructions of
linguistic history. In order to avoid what he called the 'trap' into
which Bopp and his successors had fallen, Saussure made a point
of insisting from the outset that a language and its written form
constitute two quite different systems of signs.

But this decision brought immediately in its wake a problem of
academic strategy. Bopp's error was not fortuitous but in certain
respects necessary; without it the early development of Indo-
European linguistics would never have taken place. So Saussure,

intent on setting up an intellectual charter for modern linguistics, faced an awkward choice. Either reject the study of 'dead' languages as falling outside the scope of the new science (which would have been the more honest course); or else find a theoretical justification that would allow the linguist to use ancient texts as linguistic evidence, but at the same time steer clear of the 'trap'.

The solution was to postulate that the two systems of signs, spoken and written, are bound together by relations which lend themselves to semiological analysis.

It has often been noted that Saussure needed semiology (even if the discipline did not yet exist) in order to provide a guarantee of the autonomy and specificity of linguistics among the sciences. Which is true enough. But that is only, so to speak, an external reason. There was also an internal reason. Saussure also needed semiology in order to explain how the linguist can be in a position to examine a system of vocal signs which no longer exists and therefore is not amenable to observation. The answer was to proceed via the intermediary of another system of signs, of which evidence that is subject to direct scrutiny still survives. The need for that strategy was pressing if the new structural linguistics was not to deprive itself of being able to utilize whatever it needed from the labours of previous generations of linguists.

Saussure thus found himself from the start in the position of having to solve his own problem of the relationship between two systems of signs, one spoken and the other written, which could not be treated as completely unrelated. Given his theory of the sign as a bi-partite entity, established by structural oppositions internal to the system, the obvious solution was to make one of the two systems a system of metasigns. This seemed to be the only semiological connexion that could be invoked.

The range of possibilities for a Saussurean typology of metasigns is quite restricted. Given that each metasign must have its own *signifiant* and *signifié*, this yields just three hypothetical types:

1 The *signifié* of the metasign is the *signifiant* of the first-order sign.
2 The *signifié* of the metasign is the *signifié* of the first-order sign.

3 The *signifié* of the metasign is both *signifiant* and *signifié* of the first-order sign, i.e. the first-order sign as a whole.

For all practical purposes, the third possibility inevitably merges with the first two. Thus it should be no surprise to find that when Saussure proposes a typology of writing systems it has just two branches. Most commentators seem to regard this typology as reflecting either a deliberate oversimplification on Saussure's part or else his ignorance of the variety of existing writing systems, whereas in fact it is the logical outcome of his theory of signs. His typology of writing is part of his semiological theorizing, not a synoptic description of the world's writing practices.

There are only two systems of writing:

1. The ideographic system, in which a word is represented by some uniquely distinctive sign which has nothing to do with the signs involved. This sign represents the entire word as a whole, and hence represents indirectly the idea expressed. The classic example of this system is Chinese.

2. The system often called 'phonetic', intended to represent the sequence of sounds as they occur in the word. Some phonetic writing systems are syllabic. Others are alphabetic, that is to say based upon the irreducible elements of speech.

Ideographic writing systems easily develop into mixed systems. Certain ideograms lose their original significance, and eventually come to represent isolated sounds.[1]

The problem of 'ideographic' writing will be dealt with in due course. For the moment, let us focus on matters more directly relevant to the alphabet; namely, the semiological features of what Saussure classifies as writing 'commonly called "phonetic"'.

Saussure's typology makes no mention of 'phonetic' writing based on the analysis of distinctive features. Apart from modern systems of stenography, the example usually cited is Han'gul, the Korean writing system dating from the fifteenth century. It is a

---

[1] Saussure, op. cit., p.47.

remarkable system on several counts, originally introduced by King Sejong and called *Hun Min Jong Um* ('Correct Sounds for the Instruction of the People'). The royal decree promulgating Han'gul claims that the writing system previously used, based on Chinese characters, was not suitable for most people's purposes. The new system was not a simplification of the old one, but a radically different type of writing. It purported to have a meta-physical foundation, the five basic vowels corresponding to five universal elements: water, fire, wood, metal and clay. Thus, given that the material world consists of various combinations of these elements, it would follow that any vocalic sound could be repre-sented by some combination of the corresponding symbols. The logic of this explanation may not be altogether convincing, but it is of interest from a semiological point of view as an attempt to elaborate principles of phonetic representation within a cosmological framework.

The feature of Han'gul that has attracted the interest of lin-guists, however, is the formation of the letters, where certain marks appear to be used systematically to indicate phonetic rela-tions. For example, aspirated consonants are marked by a stroke added to the character for the corresponding non-aspirate. Palat-alization is likewise marked by another added stroke. It is evident that the inventors of Han'gul had made a careful study of articulatory phonetics, since they adopted letter-shapes represent-ing schematic diagrams of the positions of the vocal apparatus – another semiological complication, since this makes the charac-ters simultaneously phonetic and pictographic. More interestingly still, the royal decree claims that the system could faithfully repre-sent even the howling of the wind, the cries of birds and the barking of dogs. In short, this was an ambitious attempt to create not just a system for recording speech but a map of the whole universe of sound.[2]

---

[2] For further details, see S. Lee, *A History of Korean Alphabet and Movable Types*, Seoul, Ministry of Culture and Information, Republic of Korea, 1970 and G. Sampson, *Writing Systems*, London, Hutchinson, 1985, Ch.7.

A number of writing systems utilize diacritic marks to indicate tonal differences in a systematic way. Thai writing employs four such marks to distinguish the five tones of the spoken language. The Pahawh Hmong of Laos has no less than seven diacritics, each corresponding to a tone when superposed to a vocalic letter, but in other cases having a purely differential function with no constant phonetic correlate. For instance, the letter *H* without a diacritic stands for the diphthong [ai] with high level tone, whereas the same letter with a superscript dot indicates the same vowel with low tone. This tonal distinction is marked in the same way for all vowels. The same diacritic dot is also found with consonants, but in these cases has no fixed value. Thus *R* with no dot indicates the consonant [m], but with a dot the aspirated affricate [tsh].[3]

These examples suffice to indicate why it is difficult to accept Saussure's characterization of alphabetic writing as based on 'the irreducible elements of speech'. Even for languages like French and English, vowels and consonants can hardly be regarded as 'irreducible elements': they are phonetic segments of the 'speech chain' or, more exactly, phonetic contours which characterize certain segments. When we look further afield we find writing systems that recognize 'smaller' component elements into which consonant and vowel sounds can be analysed. It should be noted, however, that neither in the East nor the West do we ever find a set of characters entirely based on phonetic distinctive features: at most there are traces of the recognition of distinctive features in certain systems.

There are problems too with Saussure's statement that phonetic writing 'aims to reproduce the sequence of consecutive sounds in the word'. One is that syllabic systems of writing usually give no indication of the sequence of sounds within the syllable. (Saussure can hardly be defended here on the ground that in syllabic writing the syllable itself is treated as a single indivisible sound. For if that

---

[3] W.A. Smalley, C.K. Vang and G.Y. Yang, *Mother of Writing: the Origin and Development of a Hmong Messianic Script*, Chicago, University of Chicago Press, 1990, Ch.4.

argument were accepted, a system in which each character stood for a whole word – or even a sentence – could likewise be classed as 'phonetic', provided the order of characters in the written text followed the sequence of corresponding units in the spoken utterance.) Another problem is that if phonetic writing did always aim to reproduce the sequence of consecutive sounds in the spoken word there should be no systems in which the order of graphic units fails to correspond to the order of phonetic units. However, this non-correspondence is by no means a rare phenomenon. In Thai writing, for example, the position of vowel marks in relation to non-vocalic characters varies a great deal. The vowel mark may be placed above, below, behind, in front of, half in front of and half behind – or even half above and half behind – the nearest consonant character. The 'actual' sequence of sounds can always be worked out if one knows certain orthographic conventions: nevertheless, it can hardly be claimed that the order of graphic units 'reproduces' this sequence.

Saussure's typology of writing also leaves in doubt the status of so-called 'consonantal' systems, such as early Phoenician. This has attracted the attention of scholars because of its relevance to the question of the history of the alphabet. On this, opinions are much divided. It is the semiological rather than the historical aspect of the controversy which is of interest here. However, it should be said straight away that it is by no means easy to give a summary of the accepted historical 'facts' without entering into semiological interpretations. Even the term *consonantal* is suspect, inasmuch as it might be taken to imply an alphabet without vowels. It seems preferable, therefore, to approach the whole problem by considering how it has been formulated by the experts.

I.J. Gelb claims that Semitic writing of the so-called 'consonantal' type is in fact syllabic writing.[4] However, unlike more typical syllabic systems, it omits any indication of the syllabic vowel, because to mark it would have been superfluous for the

---

[4] Gelb, op. cit. pp.76ff., pp.147ff.

languages in question. Thus interpreted, each character in the system has a syllabic value, albeit a more abstract value than is usually found in syllabic writing, since it includes a whole range of possible pronunciations. Thus *k*, for instance, may represent [k] + [a], [k] + [o], [k] + [e], etc., as well as just [k].

According to James Barr, on the other hand, this is a paradoxical way of looking at it:

> From a certain point of view, indeed, one might conceivably grant that in a Semitic consonant writing, with no vowels marked, each sign represents 'a consonant plus any vowel or no vowel' and is in that sense theoretically 'syllabic'. It is, however, difficult to see any sense in *insisting* on the term 'syllabic' when the script does absolutely nothing to tell you what vowel. A Semitic writing like *dbr* or *mlk* determines graphically only the consonants and in no way registers which vowels are in the spoken form. I would say therefore that it is better to follow the traditional terminology and call a script 'syllabic' only when it does something to *specify* the vowel of the syllable. It is more economical and sensible to regard a Semitic consonant writing as an alphabetical writing in which the vowels are not marked.[5]

At first sight it might appear that Barr is merely expressing a terminological preference. The reasons he advances are not particularly compelling, and one wonders why the issue is being taken that seriously. It is difficult to see exactly what the difference is between the two propositions (a) 'Semitic writing is syllabic writing in which the vowels are not marked', and (b) 'Semitic writing is consonantal writing'. But the question lurking in the background emerges when Barr goes on to comment:

> Professor Abercrombie writes: 'The invention of a system of writing based on *segments* of the syllable has taken place once, but only once: it was the brilliant discovery of the Greeks, and it

---

[5] J. Barr, 'Reading a script without vowels'. In *Writing Without Letters*, ed. W. Haas, Manchester, Manchester University Press, 1976, Ch.4, pp.74–5.

gave us *alphabetic*, as distinct from syllabic, writing.' On page 168, note 6, he adds that 'Although the word "alphabet" is semitic in origin, semitic writing systems are not alphabetic; they are syllabic systems of a somewhat unusual kind.' I would prefer to say that the alphabetic principle, in the sense of a principle of marking in writing segments and not entire syllables, was basically Semitic in origin; but the earliest Semitic writing of this kind marked only certain segments, i.e. basically the consonants, and left others unmarked. The Greek innovation in this respect was to extend the principle and to mark all segments alike. Reasons which may have influenced them in this direction include the facts that their language structure had (*a*) many words beginning with vowels and (*b*) sequences of vowels with no consonant coming between.[6]

The mist lifts and one sees that this is not a trivial question of terminology after all, because what is at issue is who shall get the credit for having discovered the 'alphabetic principle'. This is implicitly regarded as a great triumph in the history of the human sciences, on a par with the discovery of the law of gravitation in the history of the physical sciences. In short, from a Western academic perspective, which is that adopted by most modern historians of writing, the alphabet represents what Joseph Vendryes once called 'the final perfection of writing'.[7]

In Barr's view, there is no doubt that the credit should go to the Semites. He proposes to redefine the term *consonantal* as follows.

It can be *very roughly* said that the scripts of languages like Arabic and Hebrew are 'consonantal' scripts and that the indication of vowels (*a*) historically was added at a relatively *late* stage; (*b*) graphically is clearly *additional* to the consonantal

---

[6] Barr, op. cit., pp.75–6. The reference to Abercrombie is to D. Abercrombie, *Elements of General Phonetics*, Edinburgh, Edinburgh University Press, 1967, p.38.

[7] 'le dernier perfectionnement de l'écriture'. J. Vendryes, *Le Langage*, Paris, Renaissance du Livre, 1923, p.356.

writing of a text, consisting in a series of points or marks above and below; and (*c*) is *optional*, in that these points or marks may be inserted or left out. Actually, however, even the so-called 'consonantal text' of such a Semitic writing commonly includes the marking of *some* vowels. This was done, from quite ancient times, in the following way: that certain of the consonant markers were also used to mark certain vowels. The consonant signs mainly used for this purpose were four: *h, w, y* and *aleph* (or *alif*; a glottal stop). Consonant characters used in this way are commonly called 'vowel letters' or (in Hebrew grammar) *matres lectionis*. In the major Semitic texts of historic times, as opposed to the early origins of Semitic alphabetic writing, this is an important phenomenon. In central languages like Hebrew or Arabic it is in fact omnipresent, and this is so alike in the text of the Bible or the Quran and in the modern newspaper. In fact, in the average Hebrew or Arabic text, quite apart from the marking of vowels by points and additional marks, one in four or one in five of the 'consonants' is in fact a vowel indicator. To be strict, therefore, the usual statement that a Semitic script is consonantal in nature should be amended somewhat as follows: such a script is composed of signs of which all *may* stand for consonants; of which the majority can stand only for consonants but a minority may stand for either a vowel or a consonant; and of which none can stand only for a vowel and never for a consonant.[8]

The Greeks, it seems, are up against an adversary who does not hesitate to exploit all the terminological tricks of the trade. Having started off by rejecting the term *syllabic*, and insisted that *consonantal* is the only apt designation for forms of writing that do not mark vowels, he then claims that Semitic writing marks them after all, at least sometimes. Clearly, writing in which vowels appear or disappear according to which side of the argument you are on must be alphabetic.

---

[8] Barr, op. cit., pp.76–7.

The Greek cause is not championed either by David Diringer, author of the best-known scholarly book on the history of the alphabet.

Some scholars believe that, as the North Semitic script did not possess vowels, it cannot be considered a true alphabet; according to them, only the Greeks created an alphabetic writing. This opinion is erroneous. The North Semitic was from the first moment of its existence a true alphabet; at least, from the Semitic point of view. It was not perfect. But perfection has not yet been reached by any alphabet [. . .].[9]

This claim raises the question: what would a perfect alphabetic system be? Diringer's answer runs as follows:

Perfection in an alphabet implies the accurate rendering of speech-sounds; each sound must be represented by a single constant symbol, and not more than one sound by the same symbol.[10]

Here we recognize virtually the same conception of alphabetic writing as Saussure's, except that Diringer expresses it even more bluntly. So this is an appropriate point at which to say why it is semiologically unacceptable. The problem lies in the presupposition that the pronunciation of a word or phrase combines a finite number of discrete elements which are its constituent 'sounds'. This is a misconception, whether considered from an articulatory or an acoustic point of view. To the extent that the notion has any psychological plausibility at all, that is probably a *post facto* product of acquaintance with alphabetic writing itself. The phonetic events that occur in the course of any given utterance are highly complex: they can be described and analysed quite exactly in various ways, depending on the criteria adopted. Experimental phonetics leaves no room for doubt on this score. But the impression we may have of repeating exactly the same sounds when we

---

[9] Diringer, op. cit., p.217.
[10] Diringer, op. cit., pp.217–218.

repeat a word is an illusion. To ask 'How many sounds are there in this word?' is to ask a nonsense question (for the same kind of reason as it is nonsense to ask how many movements it takes to stand up): a continuum can be described and analysed, but it does not consist of a finitely denumerable concatenation of single elements. It follows that the idea of an optimally 'correct' written record as one that indicates the exact number of sounds occurring in spoken discourse is nonsense too.

Diringer's naive belief in a complete set of one-to-one correlations between letters and sounds should not be confused with a more subtle misconception that is popular among linguists. Although rejecting as absurd the idea that a perfect alphabet would allow for the separate representation of every single sound, or even of all the phonetic similarities and differences the human ear can recognize, many linguists suppose that systems of alphabetic writing can be judged according to whether or not they give an accurate representation of all the phonologically pertinent *oppositions* in a language. This too is an absurdity if coupled – as it usually is – with the theoretical assumption that there is a finite number of such oppositions. The fact, for instance, that the words *pin* and *bin* are phonologically distinct in English certainly provides a good reason for distinguishing them orthographically in the written language (i.e. in order to avoid confusion for the reader). But from this it does not follow – and it would be an illusion to suppose – that it must be possible to count exactly how many such distinctions there are in English and provide a distinctive way of marking each one alphabetically. The method of counting depends on the principles of phonological analysis adopted. Here too a perfect alphabet (one – and only one – letter for each member of a phonological opposition) is a nonsensical ideal.

Diringer's notion of alphabetic perfection runs into another problem. Any study of the human voice will detect certain resemblances between the many and various sounds it produces. Although the initial sounds of *pin* and *bin* are different, they are nevertheless similar. These similarities are problematic in the sense that one is tempted to say that a common phonetic element is shared. Yet Diringer's principle lays down that the same sound must always be indicated by the same symbol and that two different symbols must never be used to indicate one sound. Now within the resources of an inventory of letters of the kind that is traditionally called 'alphabetic' it is difficult to see how to deal with cases of the *pin / bin* type, where difference and similarity are equally recognizable. Diringer's perfect alphabet, it seems, would work only with a language where the sounds were as different from one another as, say, [p] from [r] or [b] from [s]. In many languages, however, this is far from being the case: contrasting sounds tend to fall into pairs or sets sharing common features. So the paradoxical side of the perfect alphabet turns out to be that if Diringer's requirements were strictly applied the expected conclusion would be the rejection of the alphabet altogether and the adoption of a graphic matrix of phonetic features instead.

Thus, far from throwing any light on the status of writing systems like early Phoenician, discussions of the so-called 'alphabetic principle' reveal a total failure by the historians of writing to think through the logic of their own criteria.

This is already bad enough; but there is worse to come. Not everyone agrees that 'consonantal' writing systems are phonetic anyway. J.G. Février in his book *Histoire de l'écriture* expresses serious doubts. Having pointed out that archaic Phoenician, with its alphabet of 22 letters, does not use *matres lectionis* and retains no vestiges of ideograms, determinatives or syllabic writing – and is thus a perfect example of a 'pure' consonantal system – Février adds:

> This is writing that has rejected the ideogram but remains ideographic to some extent, since it notes only the root, irrespective of the vowels.
>
> In order to understand the birth of a conception of writing which seems so strange to us Europeans, it is necessary to compare the structure of an Indo-European word with the structure of a Semitic word. In both we have a root, which gives the sense, and modifications of this root which indicate the function of the word in the proposition. But in Indo-European this root, developed into a radical, forms a compact and relatively stable

block, to which prefixes and suffixes are added as functional indicators. In French, starting from the radical *parl* ('speak'), we have *parl-er* ('to speak'), *parl-ant* ('speaking'), *parl-é* ('spoken'), *parl-ons* ('let us speak'), etc. In Hebrew, by contrast, starting from the root *QTL* ('kill'), we have *QeTôl* ('to kill'), *QôTéL* ('killing'), *QâTúL* ('killed'), *QâTaLnu* ('we have killed'). Thus what remains stable in the word and corresponds to the idea, not the function, is not a kind of solid block of consonants and vowels but an abstract group of consonants. Every Semite who hears a word decomposes it, by instantaneous mental gymnastics, into consonantal root and vocalic flexion. In writing, he is careful to avoid anything which might occasion confusion between root and flexion.

Considered from this point of view, Phoenician writing does not seem to be so defective. Completely consonantal, it highlights with admirable clarity the consonant skeleton of the word. Punctuation marks also help to isolate each root [. . .]

Forms of Semitic writing derived from Phoenician have inherited this desire to indicate clearly, above all, the consonant skeleton, the root of the word. This is what explains their reluctance, so strange in our eyes, to create for vowels signs like those the consonants have. The example set by the Greek and Latin alphabets was tempting; but they obstinately refused to follow it because it would have drowned the consonants amid the vowels. They preferred to have recourse to the system of vocalic dots (Hebrew, Syriac, Arabic), or to the rather special kind of syllabic writing found in Ethiopia, because in that way the root retains its graphic autonomy.

One wonders whether such a conception of writing, even though it was to lead to the comprehensively phonetic writing of the Greeks, is not basically much nearer to primitive ideography than the syllabic writing into which the various cuneiform systems tended to develop.[11]

---

[11] J.G. Février, *Histoire de l'écriture*, 2nd ed., Paris, Payot, 1984, pp.210–212.

Thus according to Février the idea of consonantal writing as a half-way stage between syllabic writing and alphabetic writing is a *trompe-l'œil* effect created by adopting a Eurocentric perspective. In other words, we are dealing with a classification of written signs and writing systems based on the assumption that the history of writing consisted in a long, laborious progress towards a final peak of achievement. The culminating point was the invention of the alphabet in roughly the form we become acquainted with from our childhood onwards; that is to say, as applied to the languages of Europe. This prejudice is widespread among historians of linguistics and of writing. (A typical example is the typology of writing proposed by Pedersen.[12] It is also the typology adopted more recently by Higounet.[13])

The same prejudice is to be found, although it may be less obvious, among scholars who dispute the importance of the Greek contribution and give the accolade for the invention of the alphabet to the Semites. Their view is that consonantal writing already *is* alphabetic, whereas according to their opponents that was merely a tentative groping towards the alphabet. But on both sides there is, in effect, agreement that alphabetic writing surpasses all previous systems. Where they differ is over the point at which the alphabet emerges.

What is a semiologist to make of this sterile debate? From an integrational point of view, the so-called 'alphabetic principle', in spite of all that has been written about it, lacks a valid semiological definition. And this lacuna is not fortuitous. It is no coincidence that the alphabetic principle floats in this curious theoretical vacuum: *an alphabet is only a notation.* On the basis of a single notation it is possible in principle to construct an infinite number of sign systems which have nothing in common as regards

---

[12] H. Pedersen, *Linguistic Science in the Nineteenth Century. Methods and Results*, trans. J.W. Spargo, Cambridge, Mass., Harvard University Press, 1931, p.142.

[13] Ch. Higounet, *L'Écriture*, 7th ed., Paris, Presses Universitaires de France, 1986.

their semiological structure *other than* using that particular notation. In itself a notation does not determine the structure of
a script.

That is why in the end the only sense that can be made of the
term *alphabetic writing* is: 'a form of writing that uses notational
units derived historically from the series traditionally known as
"alphabetic" and employed in various cultures from the second
millennium BC onwards'. This is not as circular as it may sound.
For the only way to check whether a script is or is not alphabetic is
to trace its historical affiliations: the variations of form are now so
great that it is no longer possible to recognize 'the alphabet' on
inspection. To say 'Alphabetic writing is writing that uses the
alphabetic principle' is vacuous in the absence of any coherent
definition of the principle in question.

To test this out, let us go back to Saussure's famous example of
the word *oiseau*. Is this written form an example of alphabetic
writing? How do we determine whether it is or not? It would be
folly to try to resolve the question on the basis of pronunciation
(i.e. to determine whether the spelling conforms to any 'alphabetic
principle'). Everyone agrees that however *oiseau* may nowadays be
pronounced that pronunciation is the result of a whole series of
historical accidents in the history of French that could not possibly
have been predicted. So whatever the original justification for the
spelling might have been, it no longer holds. The form survives
today as a graphological fossil. And yet, it will be said, *oiseau*
remains an 'alphabetical' spelling. But what does that amount to
other than saying that it perpetuates the historical employment of
letters belonging to a certain written tradition?

One could propose on the basis of exactly the same considerations the opposite conclusion: *oiseau* is no longer (if it ever was)
an alphabetical form, because it fails to meet the conditions of
correspondence between letters and sounds that the 'alphabetical
principle' requires. This line of argument would have to be
backed up by providing a list of the correspondences claimed as
being in accord with the principle. That could doubtless be done
(although Saussure fails to do it in defence of his condemnation of

the spelling *oiseau*): the trouble is that it could be done only too easily, and differently by different arbiters. What is less clear is how the listing could be anything other than an attempt to impose normative standards on the orthography of French. But a more serious objection is the risk of finding as many different – and conflicting – 'alphabetic principles' as there are demonstrable correlations between letters of the alphabet and the pronunciation of French words. (Thus, for instance, the letter *s* correlates with a voiceless sibilant in *sire* and a voiced sibilant in *bise*. But we cannot have both. How does the arbiter decide which of the two correlations is in accordance with the alphabetic principle and which is not? And likewise for countless other cases?)

*   *   *

None of this means that it is impossible to take an alphabetic notation and construct a script based on one-to-one correlations between letters and phonetic units. On the contrary, that is often done and the results utilized in modern dictionaries to give a rough indication of how words are pronounced. It can indeed be done for any language and at almost any pedagogic level. What does not follow, however, is that this rather specialized use of alphabetic notation is more 'correct' than its use in everyday, traditional spelling. Even less does it prove retrospectively that this was what the original inventors of the alphabet (whoever they were) had in mind.

From a strictly phonetic point of view, every syllable is a continuum with a certain duration, which can be divided for purposes of analysis into as many consecutive segments as may be wished. By means of modern electronic equipment it is possible to obtain detailed acoustic information about any one of these segments. But the question 'How many such segments need to be represented in a faithful transcription of the syllable?' is self-defeating. For the only kind of representation which is 'faithful' to the phonetic facts would be one which did not divide the continuum into segments at all – as we see in a sound spectrogram. Alphabetic transcription inevitably misrepresents speech to the extent that it is obliged by its own conventions to mark a series of subdivisions that do not exist. For the semiologist, any belief that an optimally accurate alphabetic transcription mirrors the structure of the utterance is rather like supposing that the best kind of drawing of a jet of water must be one in which each droplet is separately shown.

The problem cannot be resolved by making a few minor emendations to currently held theories of the alphabet, or correcting overambitious claims that historians have made for it. Once the integrational distinction between script and notation is recognized, the whole question of the alphabet appears in a different light. We are led inevitably to the conclusion that, from a semiological point of view, *there is no such thing as alphabetic writing*.

In other words, in spite of the importance that is – justifiably – ascribed in cultural history to what are described as systems of 'alphabetic' writing, the heterogeneous scripts thus classified do not in fact have any special status at all in the semiology of writing. It is not even clear that they belong unequivocally in the domain to which Saussure (along with others) unhesitatingly assigned them – that of 'phonetic' writing. The alphabet is the keystone to Western thinking about writing. Without that keystone securely in place, everything else about writing needs rethinking too.

CHAPTER SIX

Ideographic Hallucinations

Reasons for rethinking the notion of 'phonetic writing' inevitably go hand in hand with reasons for rethinking other forms of writing. Saussure's other main category is ideographic writing. In ideographic writing, according to the *Cours*:

a word is represented by some uniquely distinctive sign which has nothing to do with the sounds involved. This sign represents the entire word as a whole, and hence represents indirectly the idea expressed.[1]

This definition calls for examination, being in certain respects remarkably un-Saussurean. Here the term *sign* (*signe*) seems to do duty for what Saussure elsewhere calls the *signifiant*. So what are we to make of this *signe unique*?

Are ideographic systems those in which each word has only one written form? That is, are there no graphic variants in ideographic writing? Or are ideographic systems those in which each word has a written form which belongs to it alone? More exactly, are there no homographs in ideographic writing? These questions are not made any easier to answer in the light of the fact that Saussure chooses Chinese as his 'classic example' of ideographic writing. For it would be hard to maintain that Chinese

---

[1] Saussure, op. cit., p.47.

characters have no variants or that Chinese writing has no homographs.

Another possibility would be that Saussure subscribed to the common (Western) view that Chinese is a 'monosyllabic' language. And since each syllable has its own written character, it would then be easy to assume that in Chinese the number of words equals the number of syllables. Is this what he means? Whatever the answer, it is difficult to see why ideographic writing as such should be forced to comply with any principle of one-to-one correspondence between word and ideogram.

A certain amount of light is thrown on the enigma by comparing the text of the *Cours* with the corresponding passage in Constantin's notebooks. There we read, in the notes on Saussure's lecture of 6 December 1910:

Two main systems of writing are known.

(1) the ideographic system which attempts to represent the word without bothering about the constituent sounds <(but the aim is indeed to represent the word, not the idea)>, using therefore a single sign, which can only relate to the idea contained.[2]

This at least allows us to follow Saussure's train of thought a little more clearly. He is trying, apparently, to distinguish between (a) systems of writing in which each word is represented by a *signifiant* which comprises a single monolithic block, and (b) systems of writing in which each word is represented by a sequence of *signifiants*. In other words, *signe unique* is to be interpreted as implying a simple, autonomous graphic unit. This is the exact opposite of alphabetic writing, where each word is normally composed of a sequence of individual letters which are themselves (in Saussure's view) signs. Hence the otherwise puzzling 'therefore' (*donc*) in the latter part of Constantin's sentence. In short, the idea is that in ideographic writing the whole word is represented by a single sign, because this kind of writing pays no attention to the vocal *signifiant* as such.

---

[2] Komatsu and Harris, op. cit., pp.41–2.

What also emerges clearly from Constantin's note on this point is Saussure's reluctance to endorse the common view of an ideogram. The term itself was invented by Champollion in connexion with the decipherment of Egyptian hieroglyphs. Given their etymological associations, *ideogram* and *ideograph(ic)* seem appropriate words for discussing a 'writing of ideas'.

This is evidently what Champollion thought. In his now celebrated *Lettre à M. Dacier* (1822), Champollion commented on the hieratic and demotic forms of Egyptian script:

> these two kinds of writing are, both of them, not alphabetic, as had generally been supposed, but *ideographic*, like the hieroglyphs themselves, that is to say depicting the *ideas* and not the *sounds* of a language.[3]

Brilliant Egyptologist as he was, Champollion had little interest in any general theory of writing: he merely took on trust a traditional distinction that goes back to the Greeks, who regarded hieroglyphs as a 'pictorial' form of script (unlike their own). That is precisely why Champollion thought he had made such an important discovery in demonstrating the existence of 'phonetic hieroglyphs' (as he called them). These were for him 'exceptions' to 'the general nature of the signs of this writing', because they could 'express the sounds of words' (*exprimer les sons des mots*).[4]

According to Saussure, however, the whole notion of being able

---

[3] Italicization reflects the original text as published in J-F. Champollion, *Lettre à M. Dacier*, Fontfroide, Bibliothèque Artistique et Littéraire, 1889, p.1. (Dacier was the secretary of the Académie Royale des Inscriptions et Belles-Lettres.)

[4] Champollion's lack of (modern) theoretical sophistication is evident throughout the *Lettre à M. Dacier*, which introduces the category of 'semi-alphabetic' alongside the notion of 'strictly alphabetic' (*proprement dit*), without giving any definition of the latter. Saussure, we must not forget, had an uphill struggle against this kind of muddle, which was still current in his day. (Champollion died in 1832, and his decipherment of Egyptian hieroglyphs was one of the monumental 'modern' achievements for linguists of Saussure's generation.)

to write down an idea is a misapprehension, due simply to the fact that ideographic writing is not phonetic. There is no 'writing of ideas', strictly speaking: there are only forms of writing which pay no attention to the *signifiant*, and this gives rise to the inference that the signs must somehow represent ideas instead. Ideographic writing, in Saussure's view, is also designed to record speech, but does so less effectively than phonetic writing because it has no way of indicating the structure of the *image acoustique*.

Here again we see how Saussure's typology of writing is determined in advance by his semiological assumptions. The bipartite division into 'phonetic' and 'ideographic' is a direct projection of the postulated relationship between written sign and vocal sign. In one case it is the vocal sign which is the *signifié* of the written sign, whereas in the other case it is not. We also see why syllabic writing has to fall together with alphabetic writing, in spite of failing to indicate the sequence of sounds in the word. And finally the unhappy terminology chosen for the two main divisions ('phonetic' versus 'ideographic') falls into place: 'phonetic' not because sounds as such are signified (Saussure takes some trouble to point out that this is not so) but because that kind of writing reflects the structure of the *image acoustique*; and 'ideographic' not because ideas as such are signified but because that kind of writing ignores the *image acoustique* altogether. In short, the essential difference for Saussure between the two categories of writing is that between (i) writing in which the minimal units signified are themselves signs and (ii) writing in which the minimal units signified are not signs. He would have done better to call them (i) *écriture sémique* and (ii) *écriture asémique* respectively.

* * *

Although Saussure's typology of writing systems is patently dictated by theoretical elegance rather than empirical observation, Saussure does not hesitate to draw psycholinguistic conclusions from it.

The written word [. . .] tends to become a substitute in our mind for the spoken word. That applies to both systems of writing, but the tendency is stronger in the case of ideographic writing. For a Chinese, the ideogram and the spoken word are of equal validity as signs for an idea. He treats writing as a second language, and when in conversation two words are identically pronounced, he sometimes refers to the written form in order to explain which he means. But this substitution, because it is a total substitution, does not give rise to the same objectionable consequences as in our Western systems of writing. Chinese words from different dialects which correspond to the same idea are represented by the same written sign.[5]

On the basis of this evidence, Saussure clearly qualifies for inclusion in H.L. Chang's list of Western scholars who betray their ignorance of the Chinese language by making rash generalizations about Chinese writing.[6] The list of guilty parties begins in the seventeenth century with John Wilkins and goes down to Derrida in the twentieth: it includes Leibniz, Descartes and Hegel.

Derrida describes Western views of Chinese writing as split between 'ethnocentric scorn' and 'hyperbolic admiration', and opines that we are dealing with a kind of 'European hallucination'. Chang agrees about the hallucination, but regards Derrida himself as a victim of it. Those under the spell of this hallucination see Chinese writing as having a quite different relationship with the spoken language than that which obtains between writing and speech in Western countries. They are fascinated on the one hand by the gap which they perceive between written and spoken forms in China, and on the other hand by the 'visible' connexion (in certain cases) between the Chinese character and its meaning. Leibniz thought this a great advantage for a writing system and predicted that it would become a universal means of communication. For Hegel, quite the opposite: this was a great disadvantage,

---

[5] Saussure, op.cit., p.48.
[6] Han-Liang Chang, 'Hallucinating the other: Derridean fantasies of Chinese script', *Center for Twentieth Century Studies*, Working Paper No.4, 1988.

because it made it impossible to indicate in writing all the nuances of speech. Derrida's illusion, according to Chang, follows in the same tradition; for Derrida cites Chinese as proof that Chinese culture has succeeded in avoiding the phonocentrism which dominates and distorts European thinking.

This is not the place to pursue Chang's interesting argument, but it raises an interesting question about the nature and extent of Saussure's 'hallucination' about Chinese writing. Although the distinction between phonetic and ideographic systems is fundamental to Saussure's semiology of writing, he admits that the difference is not always as clear in practice as it may appear in theory, because

Ideographic writing systems easily develop into mixed systems. Certain ideograms lose their original significance, and eventually come to represent isolated sounds.[7]

Thus although he admits the existence of 'mixed' systems of writing (i.e. systems which combine phonetic and ideographic signs), Saussure does not place Chinese writing in this class. For him, it remains the 'classic example' of the ideographic type. The admission that there are 'mixed' systems is nevertheless theoretically significant. It implies that the criteria which distinguish the various types apply in the first place at the level of the individual sign, and only consequentially at the level of the system.

There is a problem here on which Saussure does not comment; how, in the case of a mixed system, can the analyst determine – sign by sign – which are ideograms and which are not? This may seem a minor methodological point. Within a Saussurean framework, however, it is far from trivial. For what is under threat here is the entire Saussurean notion of a semiological 'system', i.e. a whole held together by an internal structure of oppositions. It is, in principle, easy to see how one phonetic sign contrasts with another or one ideogram with another; but in what sense a phonetic sign can contrast with an ideogram *within the same system* is by

---

[7] Saussure, op. cit., p.47.

no means evident. If it can do so, however, that raises far-reaching and (for Saussure) awkward questions. (For instance, why cannot written signs contrast with spoken signs within a single system? But then the whole edifice of Saussurean linguistics would collapse.)

* * *

Before pursuing Saussure's conception of Chinese writing any further, it is apposite to say something about the way in which Chinese characters are classified in the indigenous Chinese tradition. Six categories are usually recognized and the typology dates back to at least the second century. What is summarized below is the account given by Y.R. Chao: his translation equivalents are also adopted.[8]

The first category of characters are *shianqshyng* ('pictographs'), the second *jyyshyh* ('simple ideographs'), the third *hueyyih* ('compound ideographs'), the fourth *jeajieh* ('borrowed characters'), the fifth *shyngsheng* or *shyesheng* ('phonetic compounds') and the sixth *joanjuh* ('derivative characters'). It is interesting to note that Chinese authorities themselves do not always agree in which category a given character should be placed. However, Chao provides the following as typical examples.

1 *shianqshyng*: the character meaning 'sun' in early Chinese writing is a circle with a dot in the centre.
2 *jyyshyh*: the character meaning 'three' comprises three horizontal strokes.
3 *hueyyih*: the character meaning 'bright' is a compound of the characters for 'sun' and 'moon'.
4 *jeajieh*: the character meaning 'come' is a pictogram representing a kind of wheat. This cereal has a name that happens to be pronounced in the same way as the word for 'come'.
5 *shyngsheng* or *shyesheng*: the character meaning 'burn' is a com-

---

[8] Y.R. Chao, *Mandarin Primer*, Cambridge, Mass., Harvard University Press, 1948, Ch.4.

pound of the two characters 'burn' + 'fire', the former having been taken over as the character for the word 'thus', which happens to have the same pronunciation as 'burn'.

6 *joanjuh*: the character meaning 'enjoy' is formed by adding an extra stroke to the character meaning 'propitious', to which it is felt to be related in meaning.

It is not difficult to see how some of these categories might cut across one another. To make matters more difficult, some of the categories have alternative definitions. (For example, the second category is sometimes said to be the category of characters 'indicating an action'.) But without going any further it would seem that Chinese writing is rather more complicated than Saussure's cursory remarks allow for. If Chinese is indeed the 'classic example' of ideographic writing that Saussure claims, and if Chao's descriptions of the processes of character formation are correct, it begins to look as though ideographic writing is something of a disaster area for Saussurean semiology. In particular, it appears that not all ideographic signs are arbitrary.

Chao, however, like Saussure, insists that Chinese characters represent spoken words, not ideas:

[. . .] from very ancient times, the written characters have become so intimately associated with the words of the language that they have lost their functions as pictographs or ideographs in their own right and become conventionalized visual repre sentation of spoken words, or "logographs". They are no longer direct symbols of ideas, but only symbols of ideas in so far as the spoken words they represent are symbols of ideas.[9]

Chao goes on to say that this has been recognized by Sinologists since the first half of the nineteenth century, and he refers to the publication in 1838 of *A Dissertation on the Nature and Character of the Chinese System of Writing* by P.S. du Ponceau. (In which case, it is

---

[9] Chao, op. cit., pp.60–1.

possible to see Saussure's remarks about Chinese as merely sum-
marizing a *communis opinio* held by the scholars of his day.)

The matter can hardly be left there, however, even if all the
world's Sinologists spoke with one voice on this question, since it is
not at all clear what is meant by the claim that Chinese characters
represent spoken words 'directly' and ideas only 'indirectly'. Is this
a psychological claim or a semiological claim?

If it is a psychological claim, is it open to verification? If so,
how? Is it a matter of determining for *how many Chinese* the characters represent in the first instance spoken words and ideas only
secondarily, and for how many the priority is the other way round?
And would this be an investigation of Chinese people's opinions,
or of their neurolinguistic processes? Are all Chinese included, or
only those who can read and write? And Chinese fluent in several
dialects, or only monoglots? How, exactly, is the linguist or the psychologist to set about collecting evidence bearing on any of this?

As soon as these questions are posed it begins to emerge just
how obscure any psychological 'priority' claim is. The obscurity is
particularly problematic for Saussure, who champions the thesis
that it is *la langue* which furnishes speakers with their stock of ideas.
One wonders how to make psychological sense of the notion of
'indirect representation' of ideas, given that the linguistic sign
itself, according to Saussure, unites concept and *image acoustique* in
the mind, and that *the two are inseparable*.

Perhaps, on the other hand, it is a mistake to treat the claim as a
psychological thesis. Does it make any better showing as a semiological thesis? Hardly. For Saussure, an ideogram is a metasign: it
is the written sign of a vocal sign. But in that case, it is hard to see
any justification for 'indirect representation' of ideas, given that
the Saussurean vocal sign combines a concept with an *image acoustique*. Where in this analysis is there any room for a second level of
representation? The concept is already present in the vocal sign.

However, if we are to regard that state of affairs as constituting
eo ipso 'indirect representation', then by the same token it would
seem inevitable that the metasign also includes an indirect representation of the *image acoustique*. For that was also originally present

in the vocal sign. This conclusion would be entirely compatible with Saussure's admission that sometimes ideograms end up as representations of sounds. (It is difficult to see how that could happen unless the metasign began by signifying a combination which included an *image acoustique*.)

To that extent, the logic of the metasign seems consistent with the thesis of 'indirect representation'. That is to say, the metasign, in virtue of signifying a vocal sign, is held to 'represent indirectly' both the concept and the *image acoustique* associated with that vocal sign. So far, so good. The trouble is that this doctrine, although internally consistent, at one stroke destroys the basis of Saussure's taxonomy of writing systems. In other words, *every* writing system now emerges with the capacity to represent indirectly both the meaning and the pronunciation of vocal signs. The semiological *raison d'être* for distinguishing between 'phonetic writing' and 'ideographic writing' has vanished.

Is there any evidence that Saussure was aware of this theoretical *impasse?* Constantin's notes report an observation which did not survive into the published text of the *Cours*. In his lecture of 20 December 1910, Saussure remarked in connexion with orthography:

One must not forget that the written word eventually becomes, through force of habit, an ideographic sign. The word has a global value <independently of the letters of which it is formed>. We read in two ways: spelling out unfamiliar words and reading familiar words at a glance.[10]

This seems to confirm the conclusion that, for Saussure, the ideogram is defined negatively with respect to alphabetic writing, i.e. by its *failure* to give an analysis of the *image acoustique*. But it is nevertheless a surprising admission for someone wedded to Saussure's account of writing.

The notion of a gradual degeneration of alphabetic writing through habit is to be found in Hegel, as Derrida points out:

---

[10] Komatsu and Harris, op. cit., p.64.

Acquired habit also eventually suppresses the specificity of alphabetic writing, namely of taking the eye a roundabout way through the sense of hearing in order to reach what is represented, and turns it into a kind of hieroglyphics, so that we no longer need to be aware of the intermediary role of sounds when using it.[11]

But Derrida does not seem to notice that whereas this kind of admission poses no theoretical problems at all for Hegel, in Saussure's case it certainly does. Saussure is doubtless right to say that a reader does not need to 'spell out' words that are familiar. But if that means that all the familiar words in an alphabetic text have become ideograms, and only the unfamilar ones retain the status of phonetic writing, it follows that whether or not a written sign is an ideogram no longer has anything to do with its actual graphic form. And that, at one stroke, puts paid to Saussure's typology of writing. Theoretically even more damaging – if that were possible – is that the semiological status of the metasign becomes dependent on the competence of the reader, i.e. the individual; and that puts paid to any theory of writing *systems*. (It belongs to the graphic counterpart of a study of *parole*, not of *langue*.) In short, the remark reported by Constantin threatens to demolish the entire edifice of a Saussurean semiology of writing. (It confirms, however, albeit unwittingly, exactly what an integrational theorist would claim; namely, that the semiological status of any given graphic configuration depends on how it is contextualized in particular cases. The reader who has to 'spell out' unfamilar forms is engaged in a different integrational programme from the reader who has no need to do so.)

On first inspection it is not obvious how Saussure has come by this self-inflicted injury. Did he *have to* concede that alphabetic writing can 'become' ideographic? The explanation lies in his conception of the relation between alphabetic writing and speech. He needs to account somehow for the existence of cases like *oiseau*

---

[11] Cited by Derrida, op. cit., p.40.

and, more generally, for the fact that alphabetic forms are not altogether reliable evidence about pronunciation. As noted earlier, Saussure inveighs against the alleged 'immobility' of writing and holds it responsible for most of the 'discrepancies' between spelling and pronunciation. This in turn raises the question of what causes 'immobility' in writing.

Saussure's cryptic answer is contained in the observation Constantin reports: the written sign tends naturally to become an ideogram. This is an inevitable consequence of the social use of writing and hence familiarity with written forms. It supplies the reason why the French word for 'king' has been able to keep its medieval spelling in spite of all the sound changes that have occurred in the interim. The form *roi* has become in practice an ideogram and can be accommodated to any pronunciation, just as Chinese characters can. The history of phonetic writing is a constant struggle between establishing the orthographic analysis of the vocal *signifiant* at a given period and the countervailing tendency towards ideography. This latter tendency is inherent in writing and has nothing to do with diachrony: hence the term *conservatism* is inappropriate and *immobility* is preferable.

If this interpretation of Saussure's thinking is on the right lines, it suggests either that Saussure thought it more important in the end to explain the mismatch of alphabetic spelling with pronunciation, or else that he simply failed to distinguish at crucial points in his theorizing between the semiology of writing and the psychology of reading. In this connexion it is remarkable that Saussure had nothing to say about abbreviations. For it is in this area of writing that he would have found the most plausible examples of alphabetic signs being reduced to ideograms. Abbreviation, he could have argued, is the clearest indication that the word is so familiar that we can dispense with the usual representation of the *image acoustique*.

This, however, would have taken Saussure much closer to the integrationist position than he would (or should) have been willing to move. The whole phenomonenon of graphic reduction (in the sense of substituting a less complex for a more complex graphic form) is one which demonstrates the validity of the integrationist principle that signs articulate the co-ordination of activities. Graphic reduction starts from one written form and 'reduces' it to another: it essentially involves a comparison between the original and the substitute, seen as alternative ways of achieving the writer's purpose. The common methods of alphabetic abbreviation are well known; but theorists of writing have failed to realize their theoretical implications. Saussure must have been perfectly familiar with the practice of writing *Madame* as *Mme*; but seems never to have reflected on the circumstances in which this abbreviation is found, or on the significance of the fact that there is no corresponding oral form *[mm]. Had he done so, it might have led him to revise or qualify his view that the basic function of alphabetic letters is to 'represent' the *image acoustique*. For if that required *Madame* in the first place, it is hard to see how leaving out the three letters *ada* makes no difference. Here there is no question of appealing to the alleged 'immobility' of writing (as in the case of *oiseau*): for this is a case of deliberate contraction of the original orthographic form. In order to contruct a 'phonetic' explanation of the abbreviation, one would presumably need to make out a case for saying that some letters give more information about the *image acoustique* than others. But even if such a case could be made, only someone brainwashed by the phonocentricity of the Western tradition is likely to believe it.

For the integrationist, 'phonetic' explanations of alphabetic abbreviations simply obscure what is taking place in such cases. Once it is realized that the sole function of written signs (in glottic writing) is to integrate visual, manual and oral aspects of communication, one would in general expect simplification of the written form to occur when there is no risk of compromising the integrational function of the sign in question, *irrespective of the phonetic structure of the corresponding utterance.* The validity of this assumption is independently corroborated by numerous pieces of evidence. Among them the following might be mentioned: (i) the whole history of Western shorthand systems from Graeco-Roman antiquity down to the present day, (ii) the simplification of Chinese characters in writing reforms (aimed primarily at reducing the number of strokes without obscuring the visual identity of the character), (iii) the common European practice of using figures to replace corresponding number words (e.g. 'Louis XIV'), (iv) the 'borrowing' of alphabetic abbreviations from other languages (usually Latin in the case of English), such as 'cf.' for 'compare' and 'lb.' for 'pound', (v) the use of personal initials to substitute for a full name, *but only when the identity of the person in question is presumed known to the reader*, (vi) cases where abbreviations are treated as having a 'grammar' of their own, independently of the grammar of the words they 'stand for'[12], and (vii) the current proliferation of acronyms in newspapers and other printed publications. In this last category we find examples which would constitute yet another kind of 'monstrosity' for Saussure. These are instances like *GATT* (= *General Agreement on Tariffs and Trade*) which have actually given rise in the spoken language to a re-phoneticized form of the acronym (pronounced [gat]). Some of these new formations enter into circulation so rapidly (e.g. *AIDS*) that current speakers may have forgotten or not even know what they originally 'stood for'. All these cases illustrate various aspects of the integrational function of the written sign in a literate society.

Once further point calls for special comment here. The development of shorthand systems in the West, from Greek tachygraphy and Latin *notae Tironianae*[13] onwards, while presupposing an already established tradition of 'full' writing, is motivated by the need, as Peter Bayles put it in his *Arte of Brachigraphie* in the late sixteenth century, 'to write as fast as a man speaketh'. Modern shorthand systems actually enable experts to write considerably

---

[12] Quite common in Latin epigraphy. Sandys (*Latin Epigraphy*, 2nd rev ed., London, 1927, p.292) cites the remarkable example of DDDD NNNN FFFF LLLL for *dominis nostris Flaviis quattuor*, i.e. the *siglae* are not merely pluralized (by reduplication, which is a frequent practice) but 'quadruplized', because here there are four emperors in question.

[13] Traditionally named after Cicero's secretary Tiro, who supposedly invented the system or adapted an earlier one.

faster than that (up to about 250 words a minute). But the relevant point here is that writing 'as fast as a man speaketh' is a special integrational requirement based on the biomechanical factors involved in the two different activities. In other words, if we ignore the integrational function of the written sign, the invention of the scripts we call 'shorthand' becomes theoretically inexplicable. Writing is commonly discussed in the Western tradition as if both writing and speaking were 'timeless' activities. Shorthand is a reminder that they are not. Nor can we suppose that there are no temporal contraints at all on scripts other than shorthand systems. Had it taken the speediest scribe in antiquity an hour to write each letter of the alphabet, we can be fairly sure that, at the rate of approximately two-words-per-working-day, neither Cicero nor any other orator of antiquity would have bothered to dictate his speeches.

Would it not be possible for a theorist who outdid even Saussure in phonocentricity to dismiss these problems by roundly declaring all abbreviations to be ideograms? Yes, it would. Whether it is plausible to regard *Mme* (for *Madame*) as falling into the same semiological category as a Chinese character is another question. Both do indeed fail to offer any detailed 'phonetic analysis' of the *signifiant*. But that observation simply brings us back via another route to the original fault line in Saussure's typology, where ideographic writing was defined negatively with respect to phonetic writing.

* * *

Is there, then, a semiologically viable definition of the term *ideogram* – a definition of the kind that Saussure failed to provide? Theorists are far from unanimous.

There are some, like J.G. Février, who use this term for the symbols of a *Wortschrift* which designate objects but give no indication of how the words in question are pronounced.[14] This usage, although not coinciding with Saussure's, is not far removed from it. There are other authorities who reject the term altogether.

---

[14] Février, op.cit., p.103.

There are others again who admit the existence of ideograms but maintain that ideograms are devices that cannot serve as the basis for a system of writing. In other words, such theorists reject not the notion 'ideogram' but the notion of 'ideographic writing'. One of these is John DeFrancis, for whom an ideogram (or ideograph) is 'a symbol representing a meaning without indicating a pronunciation'.[15] In his view individual ideograms can serve certain communicational purposes (for example, an ideogram may mean 'No smoking') but cannot be used as the foundation of writing: the term 'ideographic writing' is simply a misnomer. Although this sounds like a challenging thesis, it turns out to be of no semiological interest whatever, being based on DeFrancis's refusal to count 'strictly' as writing any graphic system which lacks the capacity to record the totality of utterances in a spoken language. Having made this arbitrary decision, DeFrancis finds no difficulty in convincing himself that all traditional forms of writing are more or less phonetic, but some systems are phonetically better than others. Hence the title of his book: writing, as he understands it, is nothing other than 'visible speech'.

According to Geoffrey Sampson, the term *ideographic* is to be avoided because it is not clear what it means and, furthermore, it blurs a fundamental distinction between 'semasiographic' and 'logographic' writing.[16] What Sampson calls a 'logographic' symbol, however, seems to correspond to what other theorists call an 'ideogram'. Sampson sees no reason to deny the possibility of developing a logographic system for any spoken language. As an illustrative example, he proposes as a logographic rendering of the English sentence *The cat walked over the mat* the following sequence of seven logograms: (i) a finger pointing right, (ii) a cat's face, (iii) a pair of legs walking, (iv) a clock face with an arrow pointing anti-clockwise, (v) a rectangle with an arrow pointing right, (vi) another finger pointing right, and (vii) a mat. Sampson explains that 'the pointing hands in first and sixth place are being used to represent

---

[15] DeFrancis, op. cit., p.279.
[16] Sampson, op. cit., p.34.

the word *the*, the walking legs in third place represent the root *walk* and the clock with anticlockwise arrow in the fourth place represents the past-tense morpheme *-ed*.'[17]

A related issue over which authorities disagree is the distinction between ideograms and 'pictograms' (or 'pictographs'). This is another term that Sampson rejects.[18] Others, however, recognize pictography as one of the important stages in the history of writing, or at least as an important preliminary to the emergence of 'true' writing. Florian Coulmas claims that both Chinese writing and Mesopotamian cuneiform, quite independently of one another, went through a pictographic phase. 'Both systems started with pictographs which were interpreted as logograms.'[19] What Coulmas calls the 'pictographic principle' is the adoption of written characters based on the visual image of an object, as with the Chinese category of *shianqshyng*.

A related and no less controversial classification is 'picture-writing'. Leonard Bloomfield dismisses *picture-writing* as a misleading term on the ground that it confuses writing with something else.[20] Examples Bloomfield cites include graphic signs used by American Indians either for purposes of trade or as mnemonic aids in the recitation of sacred chants. But these Bloomfield does not accept as 'real writing'. Real writing, according to Bloomfield, requires a determinate relationship with the sounds of a spoken language and also a limited inventory of characters.

Marcel Cohen takes the view that pictography, although not actually writing, is nevertheless 'proto-writing' (*protoécriture*).[21] He refuses to accept it as writing on the ground that pictography is independent of any spoken language. He draws a distinction

---

[17] Sampson, op. cit., p.33.

[18] Sampson, op. cit., p.85.

[19] F. Coulmas, *The Writing Systems of the World*, Oxford, Blackwell, 1989, pp.99–100.

[20] Bloomfield, op. cit., p.284.

[21] M. Cohen, *La grande invention de l'écriture et son évolution*, Paris, Klincksieck, 1958, pp.27ff.

between 'pictographic signs' and 'pictographic signals'. The former provide a visual representation of what they signify, while the latter are merely aids to memory and presuppose a prior acquaintance with the message in question.

David Diringer, on the other hand, counts pictography among the categories of 'true writing'. He distinguishes it from 'embryonic writing', which lacks the capacity to represent continuous discourse. Pictography, in Diringer's view, makes it possible to represent a 'simple story': that the story could equally well be translated into several spoken languages makes no difference.[22]

* * *

A variant version of ideographic hallucination makes the status of the written form depend on the variety of possible vocalizations. Thus the hallmark of ideographic writing, according to some, is the possibility of different oral readings which nevertheless express the same 'content'. The case of Chinese has already been mentioned above. Another example often cited is that of mathematical notation: $2 + 2 = 4$ will be read aloud quite differently by an English child and a French child, but both readings express the same mathematical proposition.

For Coulmas, however, diverse oral renderings prove nothing about the ideographic character of the system.

It is noted with wonderment by many Westerners that what is written in Chinese characters can be read throughout China, in spite of the pronounced differences between the dialects which in speech are mutually unintelligible. For two reasons this argument is not very pertinent. First, until recently, mastery of the Chinese script was the prerogative of a very small elite, and this mastery was invariably acquired in conjunction with learning Mandarin. Second, to find mutually unintelligible dialects sharing a common written norm one does not have to restrict one's attention to non-alphabetically written languages; English is a perfect example. A speaker of Indian English from Bombay

---

[22] D. Diringer, *Writing*, New York, Praeger, 1962, p.21.

will be hard put to understand the broad drawl of a southern Texan, and the latter will find the dialect of Glasgow quite difficult to comprehend. Yet neither of them has any problems reading standard British or American English and relating it in some way to their own dialect. From this observation, no one would want to draw the conclusion that English orthography is ideographic.[23]

In spite of what Coulmas maintains, the conclusion that English writing has become (at least for some readers) ideographic is by no means absurd and would be fully in accord with the Saussurean thesis that 'the written word eventually becomes, through force of habit, an ideographic sign'. It is interesting to note in passing that the conclusion that English writing had become at least in part ideographic was reached many years ago by an eminent English philologist and lexicographer, Henry Bradley, who had never read Saussure.[24]

Any further examination of the diversity of opinion that reigns on the subject of ideographic writing would be superfluous here, since what has been noted above already makes it obvious that what are lacking in this controversial area are any well-founded semiological criteria. Experts select whatever suits their immediate purpose as a reason for accepting one view or rejecting another, but make little attempt to justify their choice within a broader semiological framework. The student thus gains the unfortunate impression that in the end all positions on the question are equally arbitrary, or else determined by considerations which have nothing to do with semiology at all.

Worse still, one rarely encounters any analysis of such basic notions as 'representation of ideas', 'representation of objects', 'representation of words', or 'representation of sounds'. Discus-

---

[23] Coulmas, op. cit, pp.106–7.

[24] H. Bradley, *On the Relations between Spoken and Written Language, with Special Reference to English*, Oxford, Clarendon, 1919. (The original paper dates from before the publication of the *Cours de linguistique générale*.)

sion is conducted as if all these notions were entirely perspicuous and mere inspection sufficed to determine whether or not they applied to a particular form of writing.

Such notions, on the contrary, are far from clear in semiological terms. In particular, the notion of 'representation' cannot be satisfactorily reduced to binary relations. In other words, we cannot explicate 'representation' within the framework of a dualist theory of signs. The Procrustean bed of dualism inevitably results in taxonomies of writing which attempt to classify a written sign by reference to a prior classification of possible candidates for 'what is represented'. The categories of written sign are thus determined by *what* the signs are deemed to signify. Signs signifying ideas will be placed in one class, signs signifying sounds in another, and so on. The problem with this programme is that it remains quite unclear how to determine what a sign signifies. Does, for instance, the written form & signify the letters *and*, or the sound [and], or the English word so pronounced, or the concept 'and', or the relation of conjunction, or some combination of these, or none of them? In spite of the definitions commonly given of such terms as *ideographic* and *phonographic*, in practice the determining factor is often the form of the written sign. That, indeed, is the basis of Saussure's paradoxical complaint about written forms like *oiseau*: they look as if they should be phonographic when in fact they ostensibly flout expected phonographic principles. (The complaint is paradoxical in that it is precisely the assumption that the alphabet is a phonetic system which gives rise to the problem.) Similarly, for non-alphabetic writing, if the written form looks anything like a schematic drawing of an object, and the object in question corresponds to what the sign is taken to mean, theorists are happy to claim without more ado that the written form 'represents' the object signified. If there is no recognizable object-image, they are equally happy to claim that the written form 'represents' something more abstract: the word or the idea signified.

This simplistic approach breaks down when dealing with cases like the ampersand (&), which historians tell us is the vestige of a former Latin abbreviation. Presumably only those with an education that includes the paleography of Western scripts can actually 'read' it in this way. The rest are left to make sense of it as best they can. Those with sufficient imagination might perhaps see the ampersand configuration as a looped knot and thus construe it as a metaphorical pictogram. ('Knot' = 'joined together' = 'and'.) Those with less imagination will perhaps construe it as an interlingual ideogram. Others, focussing on its occurrence in texts belonging to a particular language, may treat it as a logogram. Few will be tempted to classify it as a phonogram, since they will fail to see the shape as an alphabetic abbreviation. Now there is an element of rationale in all these possible interpretations, but nothing to tell us which is the 'right' one. And that is already an indication that we are trying to squeeze the ampersand into a taxonomy which is itself semiologically inadequate.

It may perhaps be objected that a sign like the ampersand is a marginal case, since it does not function as an intrinsic unit in any established system of writing. But similar problems arise with graphic signs which cannot be dismissed in this way. The Chinese character for the number 'three' consists of three horizontal strokes, arranged one above the other without ligature. It is impossible to say whether these are – or were originally – supposed to be three sticks, three planks, three fingers, three swords, etc. Three unidentified long thin objects? No matter, it will be said, since the important thing is that there are just three of them, and that is sufficient to make the numerical meaning clear. But that reply misses the point. The difficulty does not reside in counting the strokes, but in interpreting the fact that there are three of them. For it does not follow that a character with three strokes must mean 'three'. The Chinese character meaning 'forest' appears to show three schematic trees, each with its trunk, branches and roots. In both the character meaning 'three' and the character meaning 'forest' we see three units grouped together. But in the case of the trio of trees it looks as though three means 'many' not 'three' (nor even 'a few'). Analogously, it might have been supposed that the trio of horizontal strokes meant 'a pile' or 'a lot' (or perhaps 'a few'). In neither case does what the sign 'shows' automatically make clear what it signifies: it makes no difference whether we can recognize what is shown (as in the tree case) or whether we cannot (as in the numeral case).

In the traditional Chinese classification, the character meaning 'forest' belongs to the 'pictographic' category of *shianqshyng*, while the character meaning 'three' belongs to the 'ideographic' category of *jyyshyh*. Does this difference correspond to two different ways of 'reading' the marks? Can one say that in the former case we have a picture, but in a latter case merely an abstract representation of a number? The suggestion is not very convincing, given the way Chinese characters are distributed into these two categories. But the very possibility of envisaging different solutions depending on the visual interpretation of the marks illustrates the kind of problem that may arise even in apparently simple cases.

It is interesting to compare this case with that of the Arabic numeral *3*. Arabic numerals are often cited as typical examples of ideograms, and much is made of their 'international' character. They are said to represent not words but mathematical abstractions. As regards the individual shapes of the figures, opinions are divided. For Sampson, *0* represents an 'empty hole' and *1* a 'single stroke', whereas *6* and *7* are 'arbitrary' shapes.[25] But what about *3*? In angular writing it is not difficult to detect three horizontal strokes, linked by a vertical to the right. But the rounder the hand becomes, the more this image tends to disappear and be replaced by a curly figure not unlike *8*. So can the same notational character be 'ideographic' in one person's handwriting, but not in another's?

Those acquainted with the Saussurean notion of semiological 'motivation' may feel inclined, like Sampson, to say that written shapes can be more or less motivated; so that it is not always possible to give a clear 'yes' or 'no' to the question of whether or not we are dealing with a motivated shape. This concession manifestly fails to produce any solution to the more general problem of validating the (Western) categories of non-alphabetic writing

---

[25] Sampson, op. cit., p.35.

(even supposing there were any general agreement about what those categories were). More awkwardly still, it apparently leads straight to the conclusion that what for one individual may be a pictogram may for another be just an arbitrary shape. In short, the categories themselves are hallucinatory artifacts produced by the imaginative eye of the beholder.

CHAPTER SEVEN
On the Dotted Line

A test case for any semiology of writing is the signature. Signing one's name is a topic about which historians of writing have very little to say, possibly because they suppose that all there is to be said about it is already obvious to members of a literate community. But there is a great deal more to the signature than meets the eye. The signature has taken many different forms in different ages and cultures, including some (such as impressing one's thumbprint[1]) which are not traditionally regarded as forms of writing at all. But in many literate societies the signature involves signing one's name with one's own hand, and this is the institutionalized practice that will be the focal point of discussion here. The signature in this sense deserves a chapter of its own in any theoretical account of writing, since it utilizes the semiological resources of writing in a particularly revealing way. It also, as it happens, illustrates clearly the extent to which an integrational analysis of the written sign differs from traditional accounts.

---

[1] Although the thumbprint is ancient, fingerprinting as a general technique of identification, and the scientific evidence to back it, is relatively modern. It was introduced by the British in India in the late 19th century in order to provide a form of personal identification that was viable for a largely illiterate subject population. In that sense the fingerprint is not an ancestor of but a substitute for the signature.

Although written signs are often referred to as signs *used* by the writer, from an integrational point of view it would be less misleading to say that in writing the writer *creates* written signs. The signature provides a perspicuous example of this: each and every signature constitutes a new sign in its own right, uniquely created. A signature can be copied by someone else; but its status as a signature does not transfer to the copy. In this respect signing one's name exemplifies in an immediately obvious way a characteristic of all writing. Writing – at however humble a level – is a creative act in the same sense that a painter creates in the very act of applying each brush-stroke to the canvas. Not every text is signed, and many paintings are not signed either. But just as every painting is the potential bearer of a signature, so too is every text. The signature is the visible confirmation of its status as a creative act by a certain individual.

*   *   *

Within the domain of writing, the signature is the reflexive sign *par excellence*; it signifies by reference to its own making and the identity of its maker. That is the difference between A's signature and B's copy of A's signature, however indistinguishable to the eye the two sets of marks may be. The activities integrated in the production of the signature are not those integrated in the production of the copy, and the crucial difference is that in one case they are A's activities and in the other case not. Although this is a necessary condition for a mark to be A's signature, it is clearly not sufficient. What, then, are the linguistic requirements?

It might perhaps be argued that the signature as such is not strictly a linguistic phenomenon at all, even though in certain cultures it may require the writing of a certain linguistic form, i.e. a name. From an integrational point of view the exact linguistic status of the signature matters little. For integrational analysis is not exclusively concerned with linguistic phenomena; nor is it concerned with every aspect of communication. Its focus is on communication as a means of articulating human relations and human experience. The reason why it pays particular attention to language is that language is the area in which all matters pertinent to human affairs – questions of advantage, disadvantage, kinship, love, hate, work, play, duty, war, peace, etc. – come into the reckoning and affect communication. Language, in short, reflects human relations in all their complexity and, in turn, serves to establish and develop them. This applies at every level, from the interpersonal to the international, where human beings interact with one another. Language is something that no individual, alone and unaided, could ever have developed. From our birth, we are initiated into language by others, and it is through contact with others that, as individuals, we develop our own linguistic capacities and our own linguistic identity. Having a name and (in literate communities) the practice of signing one's name are interrelated as manifestations of one's linguistic identity. That, from an integrational point of view, is warrant enough for including the signature among the topics that fall within the scope of a theory of writing.

* * *

The point of departure for an integrational analysis of the signature (as of any other written form) is that in order to make sense of any episode of human communication we have to recognize an integration of activities being carried out by particular individuals in a particular set of circumstances. Signs are created in the course of this integrational process. They subserve understanding and negotiation within the limits imposed by that situation, both understanding and negotiation being efforts that human beings make to achieve a more satisfactory organization of their mental and social world.

Whatever activities are integrated in the course of human communication are always integrated into a temporal framework of some kind. Communication does not somehow lie outside the time-track of other events but is cotemporal with them. This cotemporality is not the theoretical fiction of Saussurean 'synchrony' but the cotemporality of human experience, in which there is always a past and a (possible) future. A past and a future are implicit in every semiological phenomenon. When we abstract from time, as Saussurean semiology does, we abstract from the process of communication altogether.

How does all this relate to the signature? Our semiological experience involves recognition of our own temporal existence. When we sign a document, we are (if in full command of what we are doing) aware of doing something that, formally and in accordance with established convention (as recognized by Austin and other speech-act theorists), integrates our past with our future. We may subsequently complain that we were acting under duress, the influence of drugs, that the balance of our mind was disturbed etc., in order to opt out of the consequences. But the very requirement that such justifications or excuses have to be made – and can be made – bears witness to the fact that in a literate society signing often involves signing *away* certain freedoms. It may also create certain entitlements (that we hope others will honour). In any case it integrates our lives into the life of society in a very special way that requires very special procedures to undo or retract. But if that were all, it would be no different in principle from taking a solemn spoken oath or going through certain kinds of initiation ritual. A satisfactory theory of the signature (or, at least, an integrational theory of the signature) requires something more.

A first clue to locating this 'something more' emerges if we reflect on why it is that whereas the rest of a signed document can be read aloud, when we come to the signature there is, strictly, no oral equivalent that can be produced. Reading out the name at the foot of the document is just that and nothing more: the reading of a name. But a name is not a signature. Names of all kinds can be appended to or included in documents without being *eo ipso* signatures. Reading aloud fails to distinguish phonetically between name and signature. This is a case of graphic heteronymy.[2] Or, to

---

[2] *Heteronymy* is a technical term usually applied to cases in which two words are pronounced the same but spelt differently, or pronounced differently but spelt the same. I here extend it to cover the case in which we have identical spelling and identical pronunciation but different written forms. For Pessoa (see below), heteronymic works are those written under a pseudonym which reflects a personality invented by the writer.

put the point another way, signatures have no pronunciation, other than the pronunciation of the name they exemplify. In this sense, the signature is essentially a phenomenon of writing: it cannot be 'transferred' into another medium.[3] Unless we grasp this, we shall fail to see what is *sui generis* about the semiology of the signature.

* * *

In order to clarify the relationship between the signature and the name of the signatory, it is first necessary to say something more about names. Inasmuch as one's name is a badge of social identity, we are here dealing with macrosocial factors. These may be very complex, since an individual may be known by various names, and not all of these are necessarily acceptable for all purposes as *the name one signs*. It would be odd, to say the least, to sign a love letter in the same form as one signs a cheque. Banks and businesses tend to be somewhat stricter than friends or casual acquaintances in the matter of what they will accept as one's signature. For certain purposes it may suffice to 'sign' with one's initials; but in those cases the initials are taken as 'standing for' one's name. However tenuous or specialized the macrosocial link between name and signature becomes, it is never severed entirely. Writers who decide to write under a *nom de plume* are regarded as deliberately concealing their identity. It is interesting to note that a writer like Fernando Pessoa, who writes under several pseudonyms, feels it necessary to apologize for this: he denies that it amounts to 'insincerity'.

I call 'insincere' anything done to impress, and also – please note, it is important – whatever does not harbour any fundamental metaphysical thought; that is, where there is no inkling, even fleetingly, of the mystery and seriousness of life. This is why I consider to be serious everything I have written under the names of Caeiro, Reis and Alvaro de Campos. Into each of

---

[3] When I read my own signature aloud, I am not *eo ipso* doing something orally equivalent to signing.

them I have put a profound concept of life, different in the
three cases, but always mindful of bearing witness to the
important mystery of existence.[4]

Such an apology would be inconceivable outside of tradition in
which the equation 'signature = name of signatory' was a standing assumption, and without a logic in which a signature is taken
to guarantee the *bona fides* of the signatory. (Compare giving a false
name and address, which is regarded by many as a *prima facie* case
of dishonesty.) The fact that a writer may be allowed by special
dispensation, as it were, to assume another name and 'sign' work
under it is not counterevidence to but confirmation of the unique
cultural role of the signature. A signature based on an alias is
intrinsically suspect. In short, we have no plausible semiology of
the signature at all unless we recognize and account for its *moral*
dimension. From an integrational point of view the morality of
the signature is not something adventitious or external to it, but
something that has to be explained in terms of what this particular written sign means. Sincerity is not just a personal quality that
individual writers choose to put into – or withhold from – what
they write (as one might choose to enter a competition 'seriously'
or 'for a lark'). It is something that is endemic to certain forms and
devices deployed in writing; and the linchpin to all of these is the
signature.

* * *

Although anthropologists tell us that in all societies children are
given names (often in accordance with very precise and elaborate
customs), and that in many societies one's personal name may
change during the course of one's lifetime (again, in conformity
with quite specific macrosocial criteria), they more rarely point
out that as literacy develops in a culture the very concept of a
personal name undergoes a significant change. Put briefly, the

---

[4] Letter to Armando Côrtes-Rodrigues, 19.1.15. F. Pessoa, *Sur les hétéronymes*, trans. R. Hourcade, Le Muy, Éditions Unes, 1985, pp.13–14.

change may be described as follows. The *written* form of the name comes to be regarded as its authentic form, at the expense of the oral form.

This is particularly noticeable in societies where the writing system makes available more than one possible way of rendering the spoken name. Thus even in announcing one's name orally it is sometimes advisable to refer to its spelling. (*White* 'with an *i*' is not the same family name as *Whyte* 'with a *y*'; nor is *Green* the same as *Greene* 'with an *e* on the end'.) This is not a merely occidental peculiarity. In Chinese, a family name is often given orally (to strangers) with an explanation that specifies the corresponding characters: 'My name is Li (as in 'wood' and 'son')'.[5]

Conceivably in some preliterate cultures (although the author knows no examples) it might be customary to announce one's name by giving a quasi-etymological explanation to avoid homonymic confusion. (Hypothetically: 'My name is Trog, after the sun god, not the crocodile spirit.' Or: 'My name is Sharp, meaning 'clever', not 'pointed'.) But this would be a quite different kind of onomastic elucidation from 'My name is *White*, not *Whyte*'.

The point of telling someone that your name is *White*, not *Whyte*, is to enable that person to integrate successfully a whole range of future activities that might involve correct identification of the name; including forwarding mail, making hotel bookings, charging expenses to your account, and so on. The whole problem of 'mistaken identity' in a literate culture is anchored to the notion that a name is a written form. It is only when personal identification needs to be pursued further that the name *qua* identification is superseded by the passport, the National Insurance number, the DNA test, etc. But even then the immediate evidence required in any particular case is usually documentary, backed by the signatures of experts; because a literate society cannot conceive of any better form of evidence.

* * *

[5] V. Alleton, *L'Écriture chinoise*, Paris, Presses Universitaires de France, 4th ed., 1990, pp.62–3.

If it is the *written* name which counts as the authentic designation of the individual in a literate society, then it is understandable that the signature – which involves that name being inscribed by the individual in person – should count for much more. It becomes not only the ultimate guarantee of authentication by the individual, but the most basic form of individual self-expression as well. We see manifestations of the latter at all levels of society and over many centuries. How many European potentates and noblemen have had their personal monograms decoratively incorporated into the architecture of their palaces, the wallpaper of their public and private rooms, the crockery on their dining tables, or the upholstery of their furniture? These are not, to be sure, instances of personal inscription, but only because the high and mighty do not stoop to manual labour. It is quite the opposite at the other end of the social scale, where countless otherwise undistinguished citizens have left the record of their initials personally carved or scratched on tree trunks, garden gates, school desks and lavatory doors; or, as is more fashionable nowadays, sprayed their 'tags' on walls and other public surfaces (Fig.5). One is reminded of the way in which certain animals spray-mark their 'territories'. Nor can it seriously be doubted that the princely monogram itself belongs to that vast class of signs which are sometimes called by historians of writing 'property marks'. What is interesting here is that, according to the same historians, property marks are among the important 'forerunners' of writing.

Diringer draws our attention to the widespread use of property marks among pre-literate peoples:

Property marks have been found amongst the Lapps in Sweden, the Votiaks, a Finnish people of north-eastern Russia, the Cherkessians, the Kadiuéo of South America, the Ainus of Yezo Island, on the Moresby archipelago, in Australia, amongst the Masai of eastern Africa [. . .][6]

As to how property marks originated (granted the relative

---

[6] Diringer, *The Alphabet*, p.29.

Figure 5

sophistication of the notion of 'property' itself), Gelb offers the following speculative explanation:

Suppose that a primitive man drew on his shield a picture of a panther. This drawing originally may have had the magic purpose of transmitting the strength or the swiftness of the panther to the man who owned the shield. But in the course of time the panther on the shield became also a symbol which communicated to everyone the fact that the shield was owned by a certain person. The symbol of the panther therefore became a property mark, whose aim was that of utilitarian writing. The drawing of a panther as a property mark is, of course, not yet real writing, even though it stands for a personal name and may be habitually associated with one certain person, because it does not yet form a part of a well-established and conventional system. But it is an important step in the direction of writing.[7]

---

[7] Gelb, op. cit., p.36.

There are points here on which an integrational theorist would disagree fundamentally with Gelb: it takes more than 'habitual association with one person' to transform a sign into a property mark. Associations count for little unless there are specific programmes of activity to be integrated. Nor does mere association explain how a panther-mark could 'stand for a personal name'. Nevertheless, what is of interest here is that if Gelb and Diringer are right in regarding the primitive property mark as an important forerunner of writing, what we see in the princely monogram of later centuries is writing returning to its origins. More exactly, we see the reinvention, within the framework of a literate society, of an extremely ancient semiological device. All that has altered is that literate property-owners not only have names but can spell them.

The case of the modern spray-gun signature is somewhat different, but intimately related – at least, from an integrational point of view – to the foregoing. Here we have a society in which many people own no property apart from a few personal effects. Yet they live in cities which are physically constituted by houses, cities, streets and factories owned by someone else. An integrationist will point out that part of what a sign means depends not just on where you put it but on whether you were authorized or entitled to put it there at all. The spray-gun signature is not only a form of self-expression but a form of social protest that both mimics and mocks the property mark from which it derives.

* * *

Consideration of the spray-gun signature leads on to another basic aspect of what a signature means. We nowadays find it natural to suppose that signatures are important because of what may follow – legally, financially, etc. – from our signing a document (or, as speech-act theorists would put it, from the 'perlocutionary' act[8]). Such considerations are not only important but

---

[8] J.L. Austin, *How to do things with Words*, Oxford, Clarendon, 1962, pp.101ff.

essential in any integrationist account of the signature. There is no doubt that by signing one document I may sign away my inheritance, by signing another I may pay my gas bill, and so on. The doctrine of perlocution is applicable to the signature, and fine as far as it goes. Nevertheless, like all speech-act theory, it misses out something more basic. To see what this is, we need to consider cases in which we have a *bona fide* signature, *but no legal contract entered into, no debt paid, no letter signed, etc.*

To begin with a trivial but nevertheless instructive example, there is the (relatively modern) practice of 'collecting autographs'. When the captain of the Australian cricket team signs the small boy's autograph book at Lord's he enters into no legally binding agreement. But he enters into a moral contract, nevertheless. If he signs 'Marilyn Monroe' (having had a bad day at the crease) he abuses a procedure, disappoints a hero-worshipper and renders himself liable to censure; for what he produces is neither Marilyn Monroe's signature nor his own. Every autograph-hunter knows enough to realize that. And every episode of autograph-hunting illustrates the integrationist lesson that in order to get the desired autograph in your book, you have to get your book to the signatory. Two potential progammes to be integrated (yours and the signatory's). That you have to know in order to be an autograph hunter in the first place.

So what bond exists between the captain of Australia and this small boy who, if lucky, comes away the proud – and potentially *permanent* – possessor of the autograph of a famous cricketer? What communicational 'rules' were tacitly invoked? The encounter itself lasts no more than a few seconds. One party knows who the other is, but the other has doubtless never seen the autograph-hunter in his life before and may never see him again. No word needs to be spoken. All is implicit in the book and the pencil thrust before the great man. The *cultural* bond is not just cricket but cricket plus minimal membership of a literate community.

What do we mean by 'minimal' here? If the signature occupies a very special position in the semiology of writing, this is in part because of one specific macrosocial implication attaching to it. In most literate societies, being able to sign one's name is recognized as the very least qualification for literacy. The signature, in itself, says: 'I belong to the literate community; and here is my membership card.' In the course of history there must have been millions of individuals for whom being able to sign their name was the only act of writing they could manage.

Among the chronicles of the 'wild child' family that have aroused so much interest on the part of educationists and psychologists doing research into language acquisition a place of honour is reserved for the well-known case of Kaspar Hauser.[9] In the sad story of this young man from Nuremberg, the detail worth noting here is that this hapless individual spent hour after hour filling pages with his signature. It is by no means absurd to see this, in the first instance, as a desperate attempt to establish his own identity, but also as an affirmation that he had the right to participate in the life of that society to which he had been denied access, and into which he so much wished to be integrated. The message of Kaspar Hauser's endlessly repeated signature can be read as: 'Here I am. This is my name. I am like you: look, I can write! What more do you want?'

But there is no need to appeal to pathological cases in order to make the point that signing one's name counts – and has always counted – among the most important rites of passage ever practised by the tribes of literacy.

* * *

The signature is subject, as far as the integrational theorist is concerned, to the usual circumstantial provisos that govern all acts of writing. One cannot write anything anywhere. *Where* do you sign (given the graphic space available)? That depends on *what* you are signing and the circumstances. But there are rather conspicuous

---

[9] First reported by von Feuerbach in 1832. For a bibliography covering similar cases, see L. Malson, *Les Enfants sauvages*, Paris, Union Générale d'Éditions, 1964.

regularities. For instance, the usual practice in Western letters, contracts, etc. is to sign at the foot of the text and either in the middle of the line or on the right-hand side. It is possible to find exceptions to this[10], but more significant than the exceptions is this tendency for the signature to gravitate towards a particular end-position. For instance, my cheque (a rectangular slip of paper measuring approximately 3″ by 6″) has a line reserved for my signature at the lower right-hand side. But why *there*? Why not in the top left hand corner? Or right in the centre of the rectangle? A plausible answer seems to be that in Western alphabetic scripts one reads from left to right along the lines and from top to bottom down the page. The position of the signature marks the conclusion of the document (the assumption being that the signatory has written it, or at least read it, before signing). This is important inasmuch as anything added below the signature line may be discounted as not belonging to what the signatory signed. So, again, there are potential programmes of activity implicit in the preferred place for putting one's signature, and these tie in with assumptions about *when* a document will be signed, i.e. *after* the text it contains has been settled to the satisfaction of the signatory or signatories. One can, to be sure, sign a blank cheque; but the risks one takes in so doing in themselves demonstrate that the signature is a sign which is subject, like all other signs, to integration into a temporal sequence. What distinguishes signing a blank cheque from the corresponding oral promise ('I will pay whatever sum you may subsequently decide') is precisely that the temporal logic is different in the two cases. The oral promise is only a promise: it remains to be seen whether you will pay up. But by signing the cheque you have *already* fulfilled the only biomechanical condition required (provided there is enough money in your

---

[10] In the U.S.A. there seems to be a preference for the left-hand side. I have been unable to find an explanation for this. It may have something to do with the fact that on the old manual typewriter it was difficult to centre type precisely, and rather inconvenient to go for right-hand justification along an otherwise blank line.

account: but that applies to all cheques, not just to blank cheques).

When what is signed is not a document but a painting, somewhat different considerations apply. In principle, the painter could sign anywhere on the canvas, and there are well-known examples of signatures being ingeniously inserted into the pictorial subject itself. Nevertheless, here too the tendency in Western art for the signature to gravitate towards the bottom right-hand corner is remarkable. Although art historians rarely comment on this, the *prima facie* explanation is that the practice is borrowed from written documents. It took many centuries in the West for painting to be recognized as an art form on a par with the verbal arts. The practice of signing a painting as one signs a document may be seen as an implicit affirmation of the painter's parity of status with the writer.

The usual explanation that is offered for the gradual extension in Europe of the custom of signing art works at all is one that appeals to social and commercial factors. According to Michel Butor:

> Previously (in the Middle Ages and the Renaissance) painters signed their work only when they were sufficiently proud of it to regard it as an advertisement for themselves or their studio. But the change in the situation of the painter within the economy of the West, whereby works were executed not at the behest of some church or prince but as objects for sale through commercial channels, objects needing a maker's mark or guarantee of authenticity, resulted in the signature becoming increasingly usual and increasingly important.[11]

This provides a classic example of semiological value derived from the way a certain type of written sign comes to be macrosocially *required* as the formal sign on which hinges the successful integration of various activities: in this case, those of painter, dealer and purchaser. It is not simply that the signature *identifies* the painter (that could be done in other ways) but that the unsigned

---

[11] M. Butor, *Les Mots dans la peinture*, Geneva, Skira, 1969, p.80.

picture is increasingly regarded as being rather like an unsigned document – of dubious value because no one is prepared to take responsibility for it. Here again we are dealing with the morality of the signature. The key question is no longer 'Why sign it?' but 'Why isn't it signed?' That shift is as important a landmark in the semiology of the signature as in the history of painting.

No such considerations, it is clear, weighed with the artist responsible for the celebrated medieval tympanum of the cathedral of Autun (Fig. 6), who nevertheless 'signed' his work (insofar as one can produce a signature with a chisel). The Latinized form of his name (*Gislebertus*) may even have been one unfamiliar to the artist in daily life, and the evidence provided by the words GISLEBERTUS HOC FECIT doubtless does not satisfy the usual modern criteria for signing. There may be sceptics who doubt whether Gislebertus (or Gilbert) held the chisel himself. They are welcome to their scepticism. Much more important than these irrecoverable historical details is the conclusion, which it is difficult to escape, that the whole conception of the Autun tympanum is that of a signed work. And the most persuasive detail is the position of the name *Gislebertus*. It is placed in the centre of the composition, right at the feet of the majestic figure of Christ. A coincidence?

* * *

The inescapable reflexivity of the signature is what makes it a magnet for modern graphologists. The graphologist sees the signature as an important source of information about the character of the signatory. What is of interest here to the semiologist is not the validity of graphological interpretation as such but, in the first place, the rise of graphology itself. The first published work in this field dates from the 17th century and graphology can reasonably claim to be one of the first forms of semiological inquiry bearing on some aspect of daily behaviour in Western civilization. Also of interest are the particular features of the signature that graphologists regard as significant.

The expansion of graphology in Europe during the 18th and

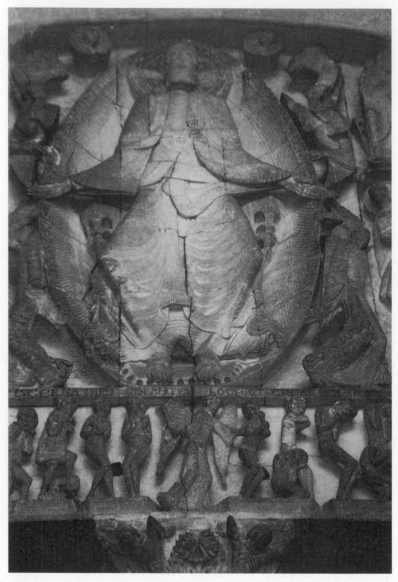

Figure 6

19th centuries may be regarded as in part a reaction against the 'impersonal' character of the printed word. Typography to a large extent suppresses the individual features of written forms in favour of uniform reproduction of copies. The notion of a 'printed signature' verges on self-contradiction. This emerges particularly clearly in cases where signatures are mechanically reproduced in order to 'authenticate' documents. A paradigm case is the 'signature' of the Chief Cashier of the Bank of England that appears (much reduced) on a five-pound note, alongside the picture of the head of the reigning monarch. The position of the signature suggests we are dealing with a signed document, for above it appear the words: 'I promise to pay the bearer on demand the sum of five pounds'. It is interesting to speculate what would happen if one confronted the Chief Cashier with this and demanded to be paid five pounds.

According to Michel Moracchini, no serious graphological study can be undertaken at all without taking the writer's signature into account. He warns us, however, that

the question of determining what the basic meaning of the signature is must be approached with great caution. For some, the signature reveals the depths of the personality, its most essential nature, including unconscious tendencies, insofar as it is the product of a spontaneous mark, free from any calligraphic constraint. For others, on the contrary, the signature is an advertisement, a social label carefully produced, which the writer inscribes as a 'representation' in Klages' sense; that is, in conformity with an anticipated image and quite the opposite of a spontaneous expression.[12]

There are obvious problems with the notion of 'spontaneity' in any form of activity that relies on habits inculcated by long training. But let us set those on one side. What is of interest here from a semiological point of view is that, even with a sign as reflexive as the signature, and in the course of a work which does not hesitate

---

[12] M. Moracchini, *ABC de graphologie*, Paris, Grancher, 1984, pp.148–9.

to treat writing as revealing the personality of the writer, there is recognition of a certain tension between the demands of the individual and those of the community. However idiosyncratic the signature, it never loses its social character. Like other written signs, it is meant to be recognized by the reader.

It is consequently no surprise to find that graphologists attach considerable importance to comparison between the signature and the signatory's 'normal' writing. According to Moracchini, if there are no divergences this indicates

a certain 'unity of the Self', or well-integrated personality. Hence indications of authenticity, genuineness, simplicity, self-possession, balance, constancy and equanimity. The writer accepts what he is, and entertains a good opinion of himself.

The situation is different when discrepancies between the signature and other writing appear. These indicate conflict or conflicting tendencies within the writer [. . .][13]

Among the discrepancies Moracchini lists are: (i) the signature written in larger letters than normal, indicating a tendency to pride, vanity, self-satisfaction, etc., (ii) the signature written in smaller letters than normal, indicating modesty, self-effacement, diffidence, etc., (iii) a sloping signature contrasting with upright normal writing, indicating concealed sensitivity and emotion, and (iv) an upright signature contrasting with normally sloping writing, indicating a tendency towards repression of feelings or adoption of a false cordiality.

Whether these supposed correlations have any empirical foundation is another matter. The same might be said of the graphological interpretation of flourishes and superfluous marks accompanying the signature: for example, a signature incorporating an underline is taken as indicating a tendency to self-promotion.

Such analyses are often supported by reference to the signatures of famous people. According to Moracchini, Napoleon's signa-

---

[13] Moracchini, op. cit., pp.158–9.

ture, with its emphatic crossed flourish, is indicative of a 'brusque, curt, aggressive' person, while Hitler's, with its short flourish crossing the final letter of the first name, indicates a 'high degree of pugnacity'. In fact, to the untrained eye, the signatures of Napoleon and Hitler do not look remotely alike (Fig.7); or at least by no means as similar as the accompanying psychological descriptive terms ('brusque', 'curt', 'aggressive', 'pugnacious') might lead one to expect. Sometimes graphologists see more direct pictorial analogies in the form the signature takes. For instance, in the signature of Marat with its prominent looped flourish descending from the final letter we are invited to see 'a rope and dagger', appropriate for 'the bood-stained hangman of the French Revolution'.[14]

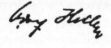

Figure 7

However, this is not the place to attempt a detailed criticism of the assignment of psychological descriptions on the basis of graphological evidence. What is more relevant to the present discussion is the fact that graphological analysis, from its very beginnings, adopted a structuralist methodology, and in so doing anticipated by some considerable time the 'official' emergence of structuralism in linguistics. That is to say, graphologists always sought to reduce handwriting to a relatively small number of presumably significant oppositions (letter size – large or small; letter angle – upright or sloping; pressure of writing instrument – heavy or light, etc.). Furthermore, these contrasts operated within and up to the limits imposed by the writing system itself. In this connexion it is worth recalling Saussure's observations on variations of handwriting discussed in an earlier chapter. According

---

[14] E. Singer, *Graphology for Everyman*, London, Duckworth, 1949, p.70.

to Saussure, it is the structure of the system which accounts *both* for the range of possible variants and for the limits beyond which variation cannot go. There are dozens of ways of writing a letter *t*: they are all valid provided that, under the pen of the same writer, *t* is always distinct from *l*, *d*, etc. That one writer's *t* may look like another's *l*, or like the *d* of a third, does not matter. All, provided they maintain the internal oppositions between the various letters, are using 'the same system'. Here we have structuralist principles pushed to their logical conclusion and applied at the level of the individual.

What Saussure seems to have overlooked is that the writer's own signature frequently violates these principles. These are the cases of what are commonly described in lay terms as 'illegible' signatures; or what graphologists would classify as extreme inconsistency between the writer's 'normal' hand and the signature. The point to note here is that whereas Saussure would presumably have had to dismiss such cases as random 'exceptions' to the observation of the writer's own structural rules, for an integrational theorist they are not exceptions at all but exactly what integrationist theory would predict. That is to say, the occurrence of such cases demonstrates that the written sign is identified in the first instance by 'global' contextualization, not by analysing its constituent units in terms of a postulated series of internal oppositions. In the case of the signature, its distinctive position in the graphic space available is usually sufficient to identify it *as a signature*. The issue of *whose* signature is a quite separate matter, from a semiological point of view; i.e. a question of the relationship between signature and name. That this is so is confirmed by the existence of graphic practices where the two functions are visibly divorced. A current example is the modern business letter, where the name of the signatory is typed out immediately below the signature. To suppose that this practice evolved because so many businessmen had bad handwriting would be putting the cart before the horse. On the contrary, what it demonstrates is recognition of two quite distinct semiological functions, each of which can be assigned to a separate written sign. The 'illegible' signature is not an 'exception' to the rules of writing, or to anything else: it is simply one more development in the functional differentiation of writing.

As to *why* this development should have followed this particular path, it is relevant to point out that there was always a tension, if not a contradiction, between the two macrosocial purposes that the signature was traditionally called upon to serve as an authenticating device. Needing to be recognized as belonging to the signatory alone, it needed also to be distinguishable from that of all other possible signatories: this precaution against forgery put a premium on developing unusual, idiosyncratic forms of signature. On the other hand, as a sign identifying a certain member of the community by name, it needed to be readable by readers who were not necessarily familiar with the signatory or the signatory's writing. These two requirements are in conflict inasmuch as the more idiosyncratic a signature becomes, the more it is likely to confound to the average reader's ability to decipher the name. (This relationship between idiosyncratic writing and readers' expectations applies not just to signatures but to handwriting in general.) The solution of adopting different signs for the two functions and juxtaposing them in graphic space is both a rational solution and one that fits a division of labour already in place: the secretary types the name (as well as the document), and the signatory supplies the signature in the appropriate place.

One further piece of evidence from the history of the signature corroborates the theory of semiological differentiation presented above. It is the development of procedures to enable even those who are totally illiterate to 'sign' a document. The classic device in Western culture is 'signing with a cross'. Thus even those who cannot write their own name (provided they can hold a pen) are admitted by graphic proxy to the benefits and disadvantages of literacy. The history of colonial expansion provides many examples of preliterate people who were duped into 'signing away' their lands and rights by a piece of graphic magic they never understood. But since one 'X' looks very much like another, such documents had to be validated (in Western eyes) by appending beside each cross a note identifying the signatory. Here we see the underlying logic of the signature laid bare. Marking a cross, even though it is totally undistinctive as a mark, counts as 'signing' simply in virtue of being made by a particular individual (who, supposedly, has the authority to do whatever the document in question requires to be done). The problem is that the cross itself defeats the purpose of the exercise by making the signatory anonymous. So this anonymity has to be counteracted by supplying the individual's name separately. Thus there is *de facto* recognition of two semiological functions and their formal separation.

* * *

The semiology of the signature has no counterpart in the domain of speech. Its uniqueness highlights in a particularly interesting way the semiological independence of writing. We sometimes have occasion to ask someone to repeat their name (because we did not catch it the first time). But this is not because they uttered it in some deliberately idiosyncratic way. There is no social or legal occasion in which protocol demands or allows an inarticulate grunt to substitute for the 'normal' pronunciation of one's name (which would be the equivalent of the 'illegible' – but proper – signature). Bank officials do not expect you to announce a specially distorted version of your name in order to identify yourself over the phone, but they may well expect something visually analogous to that on paper if you enter into correspondence with them. (The day may soon come when they will check your identity over the phone by means of a voiceprint, but it has not come yet.) But, as Béatrice Fraenkel points out, there is another paradox about the signature, which consists in requiring that it be not only distinctive but also recognizably uniform; and this as a legal requirement dates back at least to the Middle Ages.[15] If you keep changing your signature, your bank may well start returning your cheques. So although the signature is of all written signs the most ineradicably reflexive, nevertheless reflexivity cannot be carried to

---

[15] B. Fraenkel, *La Signature. Genèse d'un signe*, Paris, Gallimard, 1992, p.205.

the point where the individual is allowed totally idiosyncratic freedom of decision and action. Odd though it may sound, you are not in charge of your signature, even though no one else can sign in your place: there are powerful macrosocial constraints operative. The signature is the only written sign which has to meet both the requirement that it be written by one specific individual and at the same time the requirement that the individual, in so doing, conform to a previously established graphic habit. Only in respect of the signature does society expect its literate members to be consistent in their personal forms of writing. It makes no comparable demand in the case of speech. But in the case of the signature, in effect, the individual is expected to behave like a graphic replicating device. As Fraenkel notes:

> The use of seals allowed the production of impressions similar in every detail to their common matrix. In order to forge a seal, a false matrix must be made. The signatory is deemed to produce a signature as if he himself were a matrix capable of replicating a form.[16]

What the semiology of the signature tells us is something about the society responsible for its evolution as a graphic practice. It is evidently a society with great respect for the individual, and the gradual extension of the signature as a formal procedure goes hand in hand with the development of the rights of the individual, in both political and economic matters. At the same time, however, the individual is expected to respond by conforming to consistent behavioural patterns that will, by sacrificing a small amount of freedom on particular occasions, facilitate and safeguard greater freedoms in the long run. And, in order to lock both signatorial functions into place, the signature is made morally sacrosanct. The validity of your own signature is thus integrated with your not faking the signature of anyone else.

---

[16] Fraenkel, op. cit., p.206.

CHAPTER EIGHT
Beyond the Linguistic Pale

Is writing language? In modern linguistics, an intrinsically controversial discipline, this question rates as one of the most controversial. What is at issue, as often, is unfortunately obscured by uncertainties of terminology. According to some theorists, it is legitimate to apply the term *writing* in both a broad and a narrow sense. Writing, in the broad sense, is any visual and spatial semiotic system; in the narrow sense, it is a graphic system of linguistic notation.[1]

The trouble is that this 'narrow' sense itself depends on a no less narrow interpretation of the term *language*. For in a 'broader' sense, language too can be taken to include many forms of communication. It would beg the question to dismiss this by saying that the broader sense must involve metaphor (as in 'the language of architecture', 'the language of flowers', 'the language of bees', and so on); for 'metaphor' itself is a semiologically contentious concept.[2] In short, it would be naive to imagine that the relations

---

[1] O. Ducrot and T. Todorov, *Dictionnaire encyclopédique des sciences du langage*, Paris, Seuil, 1972, p.249.

[2] For a discussion of metaphor from an integrationist perspective, see M. Toolan, *Total Speech. An Integrational Linguistic Approach to Language*, Durham, Duke University Press, 1996, Chapter 2.

between writing and language can be elucidated by appeal to dictionary definitions or etymologies or supposedly 'literal' meanings of the terms in question. For this whole metalinguistic terrain is a quicksand.

Those writers who invoke a 'narrow' sense of *writing* and a correspondingly narrow sense of *language* seem to take for granted the legitimacy of equating language with speech. Histories of writing provide numerous examples of this. To take one at random, according to James Février writing is

a process used to immobilize, to fix articulated language, which is, in its very essence, ephemeral.[3]

Here, it has to be assumed, 'articulated language' must be speech, unless Février takes a more cosmic view of ephemerality than most of us. What Février is doing seems to be summed up by Julia Kristeva when she writes:

Writing is considered a *representation* of speech, its double; not a separate material form whose combinations give rise to linguistic functions different from those of sound. Thus the science of writing is trapped in a conception of *language* which equates language with *spoken language* [. . .].[4]

What Kristeva describes covers the whole Western tradition of assumptions about writing. These assumptions have their roots in pedagogic programmes developed for initiating children into the rudiments of alphabetic literacy, where a basic one-to-one correspondence between 'letters' and 'sounds' has been taught for many centuries, with cases of non-correspondence being dismissed as 'exceptions'. However effective such programmes may have been pedagogically, that does not make

---

[3] Février, op. cit., p.9.
[4] J. Kristeva, *Le Langage, cet inconnu*, Paris, Seuil, 1981, p.35. Italicization as in the original.

the assumptions Kristeva describes any more acceptable semiologically.[5]

As soon as one begins to probe the traditional 'representation' story at all insistently, both terminological and conceptual embarrassments are revealed. For if language is what writing represents, then writing can hardly be at the same time language. Unless we are being asked to accept that what writing represents is all language, including itself. Yet we hear not only of 'written language' but of 'written languages'. How could there be any such thing(s) if writing were no more than representation? If language is by nature audible and ephemeral, how could anything which is neither phonetic nor transient be a form or variety of language? And how could it, as Février claims, 'fix' the ephemeral flux of the spoken word? It is rather like maintaining in all seriousness that the meteorological chart fixes the weather; that, moreover, it makes the weather visible; and finally, for good measure – as some television weather-forecasters seem to believe – that the isobars actually *are* the weather (or at least a cause or manifestation of it). In the case of writing we find ourselves straight away plunged into similar semantic gobbledegook: the intrinsic ephemerality of language is contrasted with the non-ephemerality of writing which, nevertheless, allegedly 'fixes' the unfixable, while at the same time what started out only as a visible representation of language eventually emerges as a form of language itself.

Is this making too much of mere *façons de parler*? Hardly. For none of the accepted authorities in the Western tradition, from Plato onwards, has ever proposed a way of discussing writing that does not pitch one straight away into these contradictions.

Perhaps someone will object that it is perfectly reasonable to say that a painter 'fixes' on the canvas one fleeting visual impression of a landscape. If that example were at all pertinent, it would be

---

[5] Their pedagogic effectiveness has been, and continues to be, a debatable issue. But that is irrelevant to the point being made here. All kinds of effective training programmes may be based on simplifying assumptions which turn out to be or are known to be false.

an argument from analogy. Does the analogy hold for language and writing? Before we bother about that, there is a prior question to be addressed. Does this *façon de parler* even hold for a painting? Or for a photograph? Getting people to 'sit still' was indeed a major practical problem for early portrait photographers, who devised neck rests and other contraptions to ensure the (unnatural) immobility of the body. But does this paragraph on the printed page bear a relation *of that kind* to the sounds you might hear if someone read it aloud? It is very doubtful. At least a photograph of the landscape is (supposedly) a *visual* record of a *visible* subject. But does it make sense to talk in the same breath of a visual record of the invisible? For this is what is involved in the case of writing. When our comparisons cross the border between sense modalities, we risk talking nonsense. What would a photograph of a smell look like?

* * *

It is clear that if the traditional 'representational' account is to pass muster at all, it must be given a much more careful formulation than the muddled one which historians of writing are still evidently happy to perpetuate. Can this be done in such a way as to rescue the story from its own incoherences?

One strategy might be to maintain an absolute distinction between writing and language, and avoid as far as possible talking about 'written language(s)' altogether. For instance, the author of an influential linguistics textbook of the late 50s and 60s, C.F. Hockett, declares that the term *written language* 'is not desirable'.[6] But it has always been one of the pious frauds of modern linguistics to refuse writing admission at the front entrance while letting it slip in quietly by the back door. Thus we find the same linguist in the same book announcing that because what speakers actually say is often marked by hesitations, gaps and inconsistencies of various kinds, the scientific study of language should be

[6] C.F. Hockett, *A Course in Modern Linguistics*, New York, Macmillan, 1958, p.549.

based 'exclusively on edited speech'.[7] Where the notion of 'editing' speech comes from, unless from the forbidden 'written language', he does not explain. The casuistry is blatant: the linguist will study the spoken language 'scientifically', but only insofar as it approximates to standards of clarity and coherence expected in writing.

One of the best-known American linguists of the interwar period, Leonard Bloomfield, was particularly adamant on the non-linguistic status of writing. 'Writing is not language, but merely a way of recording language by means of visible marks.'[8] This still leaves unresolved the problem of how the ephemeral phonetic phenomena of language can be 'recorded' by means of written forms, i.e. static visible marks. The notion of 'recording' is explicated by Bloomfield in terms of 'symbols'. But Bloomfield's symbol is neither Aristotle's nor Peirce's, much less Saussure's. Symbols for Bloomfield are defined in terms of 'representation', which in turn is interpreted as follows.

A symbol "represents" a linguistic form in the sense that people write the symbol in situations where they utter the linguistic form, and respond to the symbol as they respond to the hearing of the linguistic form.[9]

This curiously unconvincing *a priori* account was presumably dictated by Bloomfield's intellectual commitment to behaviourism rather than by observation of the actual behaviour of writers. But at least it can be said in Bloomfield's favour that what he means by 'representation' is reasonably clear; which is an advance on those accounts where 'representation' is left in limbo as a theoretical mystery term. (In Bloomfield's account, the traditional notion that writing 'fixes' language has dropped out of the picture altogether.[10])

---

[7] Hockett, op. cit., p.144.
[8] Bloomfield, op. cit., p.21.
[9] Bloomfield, op. cit., p.285.
[10] It might even be argued that Bloomfield's account implicitly dismisses this as misconceived.

A different move from Bloomfield's would be to concede that writing *does* acquire linguistic status, but only insofar as it succeeds in 'representing' language. This would allow for writing including both linguistic and non-linguistic features. But does that help? It is hard to see that it does; for what now remains to be explained is the puzzle of how something which itself is 'not language' can nevertheless acquire linguistic status in virtue of merely 'representing' language. A map does not become a town or acquire the status of a town simply because it shows – however accurately – where the streets are. We drive along the streets, but not along the map. Furthermore, the notion that it is the representational function which confers on writing whatever linguistic status it has cannot be squared with the notion that writing somehow 'fixes' language. On the contrary, it would be the other way round: a case of language 'fixing' writing, i.e. determining the linguistic values of the letters or characters. (Likewise, it is the town which determines the accuracy of the map, not the map which determines the accuracy of the town.)

The belief that writing – or, at least, an ideal writing system, if one existed – *could* actually be an exact visual 'representation' of language, i.e. exhibit visually all and only the features present in the oral mode in language (whatever they might be) is a fantasy which has haunted the imagination of many modern theorists. It does not bear serious scrutiny. There is not – as is often supposed – a merely practical difficulty; that is, a difficulty that could be sorted out if linguists sat down and worked out a sufficiently minute 'transcription system', albeit one too complex to stand any chance of acceptance by the general public. What stands in the way of devising an ideal writing system in this sense is not any practical obstacle of detail but the requirements of the enterprise itself. There could be no complete isomorphism between any system of visible marks and any system of sounds for a quite fundamental reason already mentioned above; namely, the incommensurability of the sensory modalities involved. It is not merely that the choice of particular configurations to 'represent' particular sounds (as, for example, the letter *p* to represent the sound of a voiceless bilabial stop) will be arbitrary in the Saussurean sense, but that the basis on which visual configurations are identified and distinguished *has no phonetic counterpart at all.* In other words, saying that a certain shape 'represents' a certain sound is not like saying that on this diagram, drawn to scale, an inch 'represents' a foot. The sense in which an inch can represent a foot is explicable by reference to a common system of measurement and appeal to physical proportions. The sense in which the letter *p* can represent the sound of a voiceless bilabial stop (if indeed it can) is not. It is not that choosing *that* shape to correspond to *that* sound is odd, unmotivated, capricious, etc. but, much more fundamentally, that to ask what phonetic relationship is represented by the way the downstroke of the letter *p* joins the loop, or whether that is a correct representation, are questions that *do not make sense.*

C.E. Bazell pointed out more than forty years ago that linguists deceive themselves about the alleged correspondences between the structure of writing systems and the structure of phonological systems.[11] In the case of alphabetic writing, it is supposed that to the phoneme there must correspond a unit called the 'grapheme' (which always turns out to be a born-again version of what was traditionally called the 'letter'). But when one examines examples, blatant discrepancies appear. For example:

By definition the phoneme cannot contain smaller distinctive features unless these are simultaneous. The corresponding graphic unit should equally have no smaller features except such as are spatially superimposed. But letters are normally distinguished from each other by features (dots, curves, etc.) located in different positions, these positions themselves being relevant (e.g. b/d). Hence it is, for instance, the bar and the loop of *b* and *d*, not these whole letters, that answer to phonemes.[12]

Thus the prospect that one might *validate* the traditional notion of 'representation' by actually demonstrating isomorphisms

---

[11] C.E. Bazell, 'The grapheme', *Litera*, vol.3, 1956, pp.43–46.
[12] Bazell, op. cit.

between writing and what it is supposed to represent collapses almost as soon as investigation begins.

* * *

Bazell did not conclude from his analysis that writing systems are 'autonomous' (at least, as regards the areas of language structure falling under phonology). However, such a conclusion might be drawn. More generally, the thesis that writing is 'autonomous' with respect to language has been identified by Jacques Anis as one of three possible theoretical positions on the question of how writing and language are related.[13] This third position is important for the present discussion, because it dispenses with the notion of 'representation' altogether.

However, it is far from clear exactly what the 'autonomist' position is. The term seems to imply something radically different from the traditional view that writing merely 'reflects' speech. But does it? That depends on what *other* assumptions are being made at the same time.

To illustrate the problem, consider the following pronouncement:

Writing, as we have defined it, does not imply any unique, determinate relationship with language (*langage*); it can be placed at any level: a mere reflection of a linguistic system (*système linguistique*), or entirely autonomous with respect to the latter, even though the content of the signs (*signes*), as we have said, is necessarily the same in the two systems; that is to say, human experience (*l'expérience humaine*).[14]

---

[13] J. Anis (with J.L. Chiss and Ch. Puech), *L'Écriture: théories et descriptions*, Bruxelles, de Boeck, 1988, p.77. The other two possible positions are 'phonocentric' and 'phonographic'. The former treats writing as an imperfect representation of speech (but a representation nevertheless), while the latter treats writing as representing the structure of (spoken) language, but incorporating into this representation features of its own.

[14] E.A. Llorach, 'Communication orale et graphique'. In *Le langage*, ed. A. Martinet, Paris, Bibliothèque de la Pléiade, Gallimard, 1968, p.518.

This is Emilio Llorach, whose account of writing will be examined in more detail below. 'Autonomy' is patently here conceived of as one *possible* relationship between writing and language. For Llorach writing and language are separate semiological systems, but linked by having a common 'content'.

The two systems of communication, language and writing, share an identical content: general human experience. They are distinct in that their *signifiants* are different: writing uses graphic elements and language vocal elements.[15]

This appears neo-Saussurean, inasmuch as it adopts a Saussurean view of the sign as comprising a *signifiant* linked to a *signifié*; but it is otherwise quite unSaussurean, for it seems to imply the possibility that a spoken and a written sign could have the same *signifié*. Here Llorach begins to hedge his bets, admitting that in principle 'it is not essentially necessary that writing should be a graphic copy of language (*calque graphique du langage*)'. Exactly what a *calque graphique* would be he never explains, but his discussion seems to assume that the possibility of this copying is something that writing makes available.

It is difficult to know what to make of Llorach's concept of 'autonomy'. He insists on the notion that language and writing have a common 'content' (*contenu*). But in the sense in which a book or speech may be said to have a content, it is difficult to see that writing as such or language as such have any. The 'content' problem is complicated rather than simplified by appealing to 'general human experience'. Presumably human experience varies enormously, depending on the circumstances of individual human lives. If there is indeed a common residuum that might supply the 'content' of both language and writing, it would be interesting to know who has discovered this and how. And even if there is, Llorach offers no reason for supposing that language and writing necessarily relate to the same aspects or parts of that experience.

---

[15] Llorach, op.cit., p.518.

When we come to consider what Llorach proposes by way of the analysis of writing systems, it seems he assumes that for most practical purposes the writing system of a community will be employed for expressing the same range of messages as speech. Thus the 'autonomy' of writing which was admitted initially as a theoretical possibility remains just that: a theoretical possibility. Llorach even goes so far as to admit that any graphic system that organized the 'content' of human experience in a way that bore no relation to any form of language could not be counted as writing. In practice, then, we are left with analysing as 'writing' only those systems of marks which in some way or other reflect linguistic organization. Which is a roundabout – even tortuous – way of reasserting the dependency of writing on speech.

The autonomy of writing, as a semiotic system, would exist if, as we have seen, it were an immediate and direct expression of the content. In that case, we should have a system of signs each of which had a graphic expression and a content which could coincide, or not coincide, with each of the contents distinguished by the expressions of the linguistic system, since there would be an analysis independent of that made by language (*langage*).[16]

So now you see it, now you don't. The autonomy of writing exists as a theoretical possibility; but if that possibility were actually realized, then it would not actually count as glottic writing (i.e. would fall outside any enterprise of *linguistic* analysis).

* * *

The 'autonomy' option reappears in a different guise in the work of theorists of 'medium-transferability'. Their basic assumption is that semiological relations remain constant across material instantiations. This translates into such apparently 'commonsense' pronouncements as:

---

[16] Llorach, op. cit., pp.521–2.

Language, as we know it today in most parts of the world, exists in two main forms: speech and writing.[17]

Who – we are implicitly invited to ask – could possibly disagree? (Other than cantankerous academics like Bloomfield?) So straight away writing is accorded the linguistic status that others have denied. It is a 'form' of language. Furthermore, written language is immediately granted 'some degree of independence' (i.e. from other forms of language and communication).[18] This is not exactly full autonomy, but goes some way towards it. The basis on which this status is granted depends on (i) a theoretical decision and (ii) a piece of dubious metaphysics (not, it should be noted, on the mere fact that everyday parlance sanctions talk about 'spoken' and 'written' language). The theoretical decision is the decision not to treat sound as 'an essential feature of language'.[19] The metaphysics in question, introduced to prop up that decision, boils down to this:

> Sound (and more particularly that range of sound which can be produced by the human 'speech organs') is the 'natural' *medium* in which language is realised: written utterances or texts result from the transference of language from the *phonic* to the *graphic* medium.[20]

There are already various problems here, including the interpretation of 'natural' and the notion of 'transfer'. But even if we bypass those, there remains the question of *what* it is that is, allegedly, being 'transferred'. What could it possibly be? Manifestly, not sounds. A mark on paper is not a sound transferred. Or is it? ('See, my dear Watson, I have transferred that sound on to paper!' 'Really? You astound me, Holmes.')

---

[17] J. Lyons, 'Human language'. In R.A. Hinde (ed.), *Non-Verbal Communication*, Cambridge, Cambridge University Press, p.62.
[18] Lyons, op. cit., p.65.
[19] Lyons, op. cit., p.64.
[20] Lyons, op. cit., p.63.

No, it turns out to be not the sounds that are being transferred from one medium to another, but just 'the words', or at least most of them. Exactly what 'a word' is that makes it transferable is never explained, but we are reassured that

> people can learn, fairly easily and successfully for the most part, to transfer from one medium to another, holding invariant much of the verbal part of language.[21]

Here, at last, the metaphysical conjuring trick is revealed, and very disappointing it is too. All depends on the notion of 'invariance'. If I read this written sentence aloud, I am deemed to be holding 'the words' invariant. But it is difficult to see that I am doing anything of the kind: I am simply reading it aloud, i.e. engaging in a vocal performance of a kind I was laboriously trained in as a child. One might as well say that when I play the piano from a score I am 'holding the notes invariant' too. The alleged 'invariants' turn out to be theoretical abstractions derived from the correspondences they are invoked to explain, not actual items transferred at all. In short, a certain kind of linguistic analysis is being passed off as if language were a form of energy and the analyst were explaining the processes of energy conversion.

* * *

A more interesting version of the 'autonomy' thesis, which dispenses with the specious fiction of 'medium transferability', is proposed by glossematicians (notably Louis Hjelmslev and H.J. Uldall). Glossematic analysis is based on the assumption that linguistic units are independent of their expression in speech, writing, or any other material form. This is held to follow logically from accepting Saussure's dictum that a language is a form, not a substance.

> The system is independent of the specific substance in which it is expressed; a given system may be equally well expressed in

---

[21] Lyons, op. cit., p. 65.

any one of several substances, e.g. in writing as well as in sounds. [...] The fact that articulated sound is the most common means of expression is not a consequence of any particularity inherent in the system, but is due to the anatomic-physiological constitution of man.[22]

According to Uldall,

it is only through the concept of a difference between form and substance that we can explain the possibility of speech and writing existing at the same time as expressions of one and the same language. If either of these substances, the stream of air or the stream of ink, were an integral part of the language itself, it would not be possible to go from one to the other without changing the language. [...] ink may be substituted for air without any change in the language [...] When we write a phonetic or a phonemic transcription we substitute ink for air, but the form remains the same, because the functions of each component form have not been changed.[23]

More explicitly:

The system of speech and the system of writing are [...] only two realizations of an infinite number of possible systems, of which no one can be said to be more fundamental than any other.[24]

One objection sometimes raised against the glossematic position is that in fact the written language does not always correspond exactly to the spoken language: so it becomes implausible to treat both as equivalent manifestations of exactly the same underlying abstract system. There are often, for instance, words that are spelled alike but pronounced differently. Hjelmslev acknowledges

---

[22] B. Siertsema, *A Study of Glossematics*, 2nd ed., The Hague, Nijhoff, 1965, pp.111–112.

[23] Siertsema, op. cit., p.113.

[24] Siertsema, op. cit., p.118.

that 'not all orthographies are "phonetic"'.[25] But he claims that this is irrelevant: 'it does not alter the general fact that a linguistic form is manifested in the given substance.'[26] He goes on to add that

the task of the linguistic theoretician is not merely that of describing the actually present expression system, but of calculating what expression systems in general are possible as expression for a given content system, *and vice versa*.[27]

It is rather difficult to see how Hjelmslev proposes to deal with cases of heteronymy. For example, the fact that the English noun *entrance* and the English verb *entrance* are identically spelt does not automatically obliterate any difference of meaning. All that happens in such cases is that those familiar with written English learn – to put it in traditional terms – that there are quite different usages, grammatical constructions and pronunciations associated with a single written form. However, according to Hjelmslev, the fact that some orthographies are not phonetic shows that 'different systems of expression can correspond to one and the same system of content.'[28] The problem is that if cases like *entrance* are admitted as actual examples of this state of affairs, it becomes theoretically possible to imagine writing systems which economize on their inventory of orthographically distinct words by allowing homographs to proliferate. The *reductio ad absurdum* would be a writing system which had only one word.

The difficulty is compounded by Uldall, who claims:

If we keep the units of content constant, we shall have the same language whatever system is used to make up the corresponding units of expression. [...] a system of any internal structure

---

[25] L. Hjelmslev, *Prolegomena to a Theory of Language*, trans. F.J. Whitfield, rev. ed., Madison, University of Wisconsin Press., 1961, p.104.

[26] Hjelmslev, op. cit., p.105.

[27] Hjelmslev, op. cit., p.105.

[28] Hjelmslev, op. cit., p.105.

will do, provided that a sufficient number of units can be made up from it to express the units of content.[29]

This seems to imply that at least as many distinct units of expression are needed as there are units of content in the language. Which in turn means that any vocal or graphic systems which allow cases of homophony or homography automatically misrepresent the content system of the language. But that in turn leads to the paradoxical conclusion that neither English speech nor English writing properly expresses English. It is paradoxical because without English speech or English writing it is difficult to see what kind of existence the English language would have. Furthermore, if it is possible in principle that speech and writing may misrepresent the structure of a language, there seems to be no *a priori* reason to assume that we can with any assurance detect which elements of phonic or graphic manifestation correctly represent the structure of the language and which, on the other hand, do not. In brief, within the framework of glossematics, the 'autonomy' of writing turns out to be a direct consequence of the assumption that language systems can exist independently of any specific materialization whatsoever. Whether one can make any theoretical sense at all of that assumption is another matter.

* * *

The glossematic approach has been criticized by the Prague school theorist Josef Vachek for not bringing out sufficiently 'the autonomous character of written language, as opposed to spoken language'.[30] The basis of his criticism is that speech and writing fulfil quite different social functions. This, in his view, is 'more

---

[29] Siertsema, op. cit., p.118.

[30] J. Vachek, 'Some remarks on writing and phonetic transcription', *Acta Linguistica*, vol.5, 1945–9, pp.86–93. Reprinted in E.P. Hamp, F.W. Householder and R. Austerlitz (eds), *Readings in Linguistics II*, Chicago, University of Chicago Press, pp.152–7. The remark cited occurs on p.152, fn.2, of the latter.

profound and more essential' than the 'difference of material' between them. Here we have yet another interpretation of 'autonomy'; i.e. writing is regarded as an autonomous form of communication in that written messages are not merely duplications of or substitutes for spoken messages, but are employed by the linguistic community for quite different purposes.

Other Prague school linguists, concerned with practical problems of language teaching, have pointed out that the notion of written language representing spoken language is in any case illusory, inasmuch as the norms characteristic of each are recognizably different. Thus while it is possible to read aloud a leader article from *The Times* no native English speaker hearing this would mistake it for an oral discussion of the topic. Written composition has its own hallmarks, selecting a grammar and a vocabulary distinct from those of everyday speech. Written French, for example, uses tenses and modal forms of the verb that are never encountered orally *except* when a written passage is being read aloud. In some literate cultures, reading aloud a particular text may even be treated as calling for a particular form of expertise (as is the case in the recitation of the Koran in the Islamic tradition).[31]

For an integrationist, 'disparities' of this order are unsurprising. They reflect the fact that glottic writing is *not* based on any uniform set of correspondences with an independent mode of orality called 'speech'.

* * *

Possibly for this reason, the integrationist position is also sometimes regarded as 'autonomist'.[32] This characterization, however, is misleading on various counts.

---

[31] K. Nelson, *The Art of Reciting Qur'an*, Austin, University of Texas Press, 1985.

[32] J. Anis and C. Puech, 'Autonomie de l'écriture'. In J.G. Lapacherie (ed.), *Propriétés de l'écriture*, Pau, Publications de l'Université de Pau, 1998, pp.79–87.

For the integrationist, written communication of the kind that takes place if you read and understand this chapter is a form of communication in its own right. It does not become so simply in virtue of and insofar as written forms can be correlated with spoken forms, even though you are perfectly at liberty to read the chapter aloud if you so wish. In order to communicate in written English it is not essential that one should also know how to speak it, any more than reading or writing Latin requires one to know how Caesar, Cicero and their contemporaries pronounced it. As Vachek points out, those who suppose otherwise are conflating writing with phonetic transcription.

> That is to say, in deciphering a text put down in writing no detour by way of spoken language is necessary to make out its content, as is the case in deciphering a phonetically transcribed text. A clear proof of this assertion is the well-known fact that there are many people who can, for instance, read English without having any idea of how the written text should be pronounced.[33]

However, that this *can* be done does not alter the fact that there are also biomechanical and socially institutionalized practices known as 'reading aloud' and these are systematically integrated with optical scanning of the text. That form of integration, precisely, is one of the criteria available for distinguishing between 'glottic' and 'non-glottic' writing. Anyone who can read and understand an English text without, as Vachek says, 'having any idea' of how to pronounce it (and presumably having no co-relative idea of how to write down in English orthography an English utterance) has simply not mastered English as a form of glottic writing. It is fair to say, in short, that there is something important missing from such a person's grasp of communication-in-English. So to adduce the fact that written English *can* be treated as non-glottic as a reason for claiming it to be an autonomous form of communication would be rather beside the point.

---

[33] Vachek, op. cit., p.155.

Furthermore, from the fact that written English *can* be treated as non-glottic it does not follow that it could exist independently of *any* other form of communication, but simply that it could exist independently of spoken English. If that is all that being an 'autonomist' amounts to, then integrationists are autonomists. But then so are many other theorists – at least, all those who accept that there are forms of writing (e.g. musical notation) that have nothing to do with speech at all. The whole point of the term 'glottic' writing is to recognize that there *are* forms of writing intimately connected with spoken language. So if anyone wants to insist that glottic writing has to do with speech, they are merely – as far as the integrationist is concerned – harping on a tautology. The question of *what* exactly glottic writing has to do with speech is another matter, and here the integrationist proposes an account which is quite different from any 'representational' account.

If anyone should feel inclined to object that none of the above considerations provides a theoretical justification for including written English as a form of *linguistic* communication, the integrationist reply is that this is how its practitioners regard it (i.e. as a form of their language). This assimilation holds across all literate societies for which reliable evidence is available. The evidence in question is metalinguistic: i.e. the name of the spoken language is automatically transferred to the associated form of writing. This seems to be universal in societies that have reached the stage of utilitarian literacy. What stands in need of justification, on the contrary, is the position of those theorists who insist on equating language with speech and treating writing as 'a kind of highly unsatisfactory pseudotranscription'.[34]

It is a mistake to regard the integrationist position as 'autonomist' in any other than the respect already indicated above, since within an integrational framework there are no autonomous signs and no autonomous sign systems. Nor could there be. For signs exist only as contextualized products of particular communication situations. This applies as much to the written sign as to any other

---

[34] Vachek, op. cit., p.153.

kind of sign. In the case of glottic writing the debate about 'autonomy' is particularly futile, since the whole function of glottic writing is to act as an interface between biomechanically different
modes of communication.

*   *   *

Some of the points made above may be illustrated by reference to
one of the most curious episodes in the history of writing: the
attempt by Jean Itard, resident physician at the National Institute
for Deaf Mutes in Paris, to introduce the alphabet into the education of Victor, the languageless 'wild boy of Aveyron', whose case
aroused such interest in the early nineteenth century. Itard's own
account of this runs as follows.

> I had the twenty-four letters of the alphabet printed in large
> type, each on a piece of cardboard two inches square. I had an
> equal number of slots cut in a plank one-and-a-half feet square,
> into which I had the pieces of cardboard inserted, but without
> glueing them, so that they could be rearranged as required. An
> equal number of letters of the same size were made in metal.
> These were to be compared by the pupil with the printed let-
> ters, and placed in the corresponding slots. The first trial of this
> method was made in my absence by Mme Guérin. I was greatly
> surprised to learn from her on my return that Victor could
> distinguish all the letters and arrange them properly. This was
> straight away tested and he did it without the slightest mistake.
> Delighted with such rapid success, I was still far from being able
> to explain it; and it was only a few days later in my room that
> the way our pupil managed to sort the letters was revealed. To
> make it easier, he had devised a little trick which alleviated the
> work of memory, comparison and judgment. As soon as the
> board was in his hands, he did not wait for the metal letters to
> be removed from their slots; he took them out and piled them
> up on his hand in order; so that the last letter of the alphabet
> was on top of the pile when the board had been cleared. Then
> he started with this one and finished with the last in the pile,
> thus beginning at the foot of the board and proceeding always

from right to left. That is not all: he managed to perfect this procedure; for often the pile collapsed and the letters fell down; and then he had to sort it all out by paying careful attention to each one. The twenty-four letters were arranged in four rows of six; so it was simpler just to take out each row and put it back again, leaving the second row until the first had been dealt with.

I do not know if his reasoning was as I suggest; but he certainly carried out the operation as I have described. So it was indeed a routine, and one of his own invention, which perhaps did as much credit to his intelligence as a methodical classification was soon to do to his discrimination. It was not difficult to put him on the right track, by giving him the letters all jumbled up each time he was offered the board. Eventually, in spite of my frequently changing round the printed characters in their slots, and presenting tricky juxtapositions, such as puttting G next to C, E next to F, etc., his identification was impeccable. By this training in all the letters, my aim was to prepare Victor to make some, albeit elementary, use of them to express the needs he could not express by means of speech. Far from believing that I was already so close to that important stage in his education, more out of curioisity than hope of success, I tried the following experiment:

One morning when he was waiting impatiently for his daily milk at breakfast, I took the four letters L A I T from his set and arranged them on a board I had specially prepared. Mme Guérin, whom I had alerted, comes forward, looks at the letters and then gives me a cup full of milk, which I pretend to take for myself. A moment later I go to Victor and give him the four letters I have just taken from the board: I point to the board with one hand while offering him the jug of milk with the other. The letters were immediately replaced, but in exactly the reverse order, so that they read TIAL instead of LAIT. I showed him the corrections needed, pointing to each letter and where it should go. When these changes had produced the sign of the thing, I did not deprive him of it any longer.

It may be difficult to believe that five or six such trials sufficed not just to get him to arrange the four letters of the word *lait* systematically, but also, I would say, to give him the idea of the relation between the word and the thing. That is at least strongly suggested by what happened eight days after this first experiment. We noticed that while getting ready to leave one afternoon to go to the Observatory he took these four letters on his own initiative, put them in his pocket and, as soon as he arrived at citizen Lemeri's, where, as I said earlier, he goes for a drink of milk every day, arranged them on a table to form the word *lait*.[35]

It cannot be supposed that Itard was an integrationist seeking experimental confirmation for any hypothesis about the semiology of the alphabet; but if he had been, he could hardly have done better. Victor first of all treats the letters as units of a notation (in the sense of Chapter 4), because this is how they feature in his 'lessons'. At the beginning, the only activities to be integrated, as far as he is concerned, are those involved in matching the twenty-four letters visually with their exemplars and putting them in the right slots. What the letters signify, as far as he is concerned, is exhausted by their role in this matching game, which he soon learns to play. But this is no longer the case at the next stage, which concerns just four letters and their arrangement in a fixed order, this invariable combination being matched with access to a drink of milk. To assume, as Itard did, that this new performance is explained by Victor's having understood the relation between the word and the thing is already to impose a dualist psychological interpretation on the case, and quite unnecessarily so. The systematic integration of the activities involved is all that is required to account for the semiological value of the combination L-A-I-T in this new game. That is all Victor needed to grasp, just as he had previously done in the letter-matching game.

According to Harlan Lane, Victor's failure to make significant

[35] This passage from Itard's original text (1801) is reprinted in L. Malson, *Les Enfants sauvages*, Paris, Union Générale d'Éditions, 1964, pp.181–4.

linguistic progress at this stage in his education was due to 'misplaced stimulus control', and specifically to his inability to grasp the difference between 'tacting' and 'manding'.[36] (This, in Skinnerian jargon, is the difference in verbal behaviour between naming and requesting.[37]) But the behaviourist explanation hardly fits the evidence cited above. To suggest that 'the response may have been evoked by the many cues that accompany milk as presented in this setting' is hardly a convincing diagnosis of Victor's exploit at citizen Lemeri's. Carrying letters in your pocket in anticipation of the need to 'name' an object is not *prima facie* explicable as a response to a stimulus: it looks too suspiciously like conceiving a plan of action. Victor's initiative makes more sense if seen as an experiment in creative contextualization. Put in integrationist terms (although these are obviously not those Victor would or could have used), the question to be answered was whether the previously established value of the sign 'L-A-I-T' could be carried over to a new situation with new participants. Its outcome does not have to be interpreted in terms of any theoretical distinction between 'tacts' and 'mands', and in itself it neither proves nor disproves Victor's understanding of the concept of 'requesting'. We are reckoned to understand concepts like 'requesting' when we show we have grasped *by participation* the biomechanical, macrosocial and circumstantial limits within which integrational patterns of give-and-take operate over a whole range of situations.

Itard eventually taught Victor the rudiments of writing and reading, but never had any parallel success in teaching him to

---

[36] H. Lane, *The Wild Boy of Aveyron*, London, Allen & Unwin, 1977, p.124.

[37] The following definitions are given in A.R. Reber, *Penguin Dictionary of Psychology*, Harmondsworth, Penguin, 1985. 'Tacting is verbal behavior that is most clearly under the control of its antecedents; it results from or is linked with that which has gone before. Naming is the classic tact.' (p.757.) '[...] manding represents verbal behavior primarily under control of its consequences. Classic examples of mands are "Please pass the salt" and "Get me my book".' (p.416.)

speak. The reasons for this failure have been much debated. But clearly the case speaks to the question of writing as 'representation'. For Victor, writing never was – and never could have been – a 'representation' of speech. But here too the traditional view of the 'primacy of speech' prevailed – to Victor's irrecoverable disadvantage. As Lane observes:

> In teaching Victor to understand and produce written language, Itard inexplicably left off once Victor had mastered strings of verb plus noun. Small steps indeed lay between this performance and the control of elementary French sentences [. . .]. If Itard had been less committed to oral language, Victor might have realized Bonnaterre's ambition for him and gone on to master the written language and to become a Massieu after all.[38]

* * *

One of the most original thinkers of the nineteenth century, Wilhelm von Humboldt, recognized that in a literate society speech and writing cannot remain indefinitely in a state of developmental apartheid.

The needs, limitations, merits and peculiarities of both influence each other. Changes in writing may lead to changes in language; and even though we write as we do because that is the way we speak, it is also the case that we speak as we do because that is the way we write.[39]

It is interesting that it was not until more than a hundred and fifty years later that the latter part of Humboldt's observation was

---

[38] Lane, op. cit., p.170.

[39] W. von Humboldt, 'Über die Buchstabenschrift und ihren Zusammenhang mit dem Sprachbau', *Abhandlungen der königlichen Akademie der Wissenschaften zu Berlin*, 1826, pp.161–8. Quoted and translated by T.C. Christy, 'Humboldt on the semiotics of writing': in I. Rauch and G.F. Carr (eds), *The Semiotic Bridge*, Berlin / New York, Mouton de Gruyter, 1989, p.340.

taken up seriously by any academic linguist: this was done by F.W. Householder in his book *Linguistic Speculations*.[40] He argued that in (American) English cases in which pronunciation adapts to spelling are more numerous than the other way round and, furthermore, the 'rules' which relate written forms to their pronunciation are much simpler than the 'rules' which relate the pronunciation of words to their spellings. One way of explaining this would be to suppose that although American children learn to speak before they learn to write, the written forms, once learnt, serve to explain and regularize the spoken forms the child is already familiar with orally. In short, written English would, on this view, provide a first elementary metalanguage – the letters of the alphabet – which made it possible for the learners to describe, compare and analyse the oral forms they heard, and thus the continuous process of learning new spoken words would come to be guided by fitting them into the framework supplied by spelling. Householder called his thesis (provocatively, given the views then current in orthodox linguistics) 'the primacy of writing'.

This thesis was later developed and generalized by David Olson.[41] According to Olson, we are dealing with a universal process underlying the history of all literate societies. It is illusory to suppose that writing systems owe their origins to the need to 'represent' oral structures already recognized. On the contrary, it is the development of a writing system which facilitates conceptualization of a corresponding oral structure:

[. . .] writing systems provide the concepts and categories for thinking about the structure of spoken language, rather than the reverse. Awareness of linguistic structure is a product of a writing system, not a precondition for its development.[42]

---

[40] F.W. Householder, *Linguistic Speculations*, Cambridge, Cambridge University Press, 1971.
[41] D.R. Olson, 'How writing represents speech'. *Language & Communication*, Vol.13 No.1, 1993, and *The World on Paper*, Cambridge, Cambridge University Press, 1994.
[42] Olson 1994, p.68.

On this view of literacy, what it involves is remaking one's conception of speech in the image of the writing system one has been taught. Thus the alphabet would not have been invented in order to 'represent' the word as a sequence of sound units already recognized. The boot is on the other foot: acquaintance with alphabetic writing would have induced those familiar with it to regard the stream of speech (even when not 'written down') as comprising such a sequence of units. This relationship does not apply merely at the level of alphabetic literacy. In Olson's view, the word itself as a discrete linguistic unit is likewise a graphic conception.

If this is so, the relationship between speech and writing – as far as the lay members of the literate community are concerned – is exactly the reverse of what is assumed by orthodox theorists. The invention of writing gave birth to a new conception of the utterance, a projection of the graphic image on to the screen of oral awareness.

Evidence that can be mustered in support of this thesis is not wanting. Most obvious, perhaps, is the fact that the basic linguistic terminology of Western education, including the term *grammar*, presupposes acquaintance with writing. There is no vestigial vocabulary of speech analysis surviving from an earlier 'oral' tradition. On the contrary, as was noted in Chapter 1, from Plato onwards one is struck by the absence of any rigorous terminological distinction between letters and sounds. This is a conflation which lasts right down to the nineteenth century, as Saussure's critical remarks about the comparative grammarians remind us.

The 'failure', however, must not be overinterpreted. It does not mean, as was already noted in Chapter 1, that we have to attribute to Plato and his contemporaries the superstitious notion of 'armies of little black signs issuing forth from human mouths, like the diamonds or toads of fairy stories.'[43] Nor did Saussure imagine that Bopp thought this. It remains true, nevertheless, that

---

[43] F. Desbordes, 'La prétendue confusion de l'écrit et de l'oral dans les théories de l'antiquité'. In N. Catach (ed.), *Pour une théorie de la langue écrite*, Paris, CNRS Éditions, 1989, p.27.

for the Greeks as for Bopp the alphabetic letter was not only an important model for their conceptualization of the unit-structure of speech, but *the only model available.*

The whole problem of phonetic analysis, from antiquity down to the present day, turns on a supposed correlation between the letters of the alphabet on the one hand and 'sound segments' on the other. It is obvious that the former are far more clearly defined than the latter. In fact, the puzzle is how one would ever set about segmenting a continuous sound sequence at all without appeal to an independent series of discrete graphic marks. The task itself calls for projecting imaginary discontinuities on to a continuum.

The dangers (for linguistic analysis) of this projection were recognized by Saussure when he admitted that 'the written word is so intimately connected with the spoken word whose image it is that it manages to usurp the principal role.'[44] From this usurpation Saussure did not draw the same conclusion as Olson; namely, that to think of the relationship in these terms is to see it the wrong way round. Olson's conclusion is that for literate communities, it is not the written word which is the image of the spoken word, but the spoken word which is the image of its written counterpart.

Interesting support from this comes from an area where it would be least expected if the orthodox view were right. Debates have raged endlessly in twentieth-century phonology over the 'phoneme' and how to determine how many such units any given spoken language has. For instance, it has been pointed out that for 'standard French' the number of vowel phonemes has been reckoned by different linguists as being as low as eight and as high as twenty.[45] Such disparate totals evidently imply different methods of counting, but that is the point: no comparable debate has arisen among linguists over analysing the letters of the French alphabet (in spite of the complications caused by acute, grave and circumflex accents). What emerges as a theoretical problem in phonology

---

[44] Saussure, op. cit., p.45.
[45] T.B.W. Reid, *Historical Philology and Linguistic Science*, Oxford, Clarendon, 1960, p.12.

is generated by the assumption that just as any schoolboy can tell you how many letters there are in a given written word (provided his arithmetic is up to counting them), so the linguist should be able to tell you how many phonemes there are in its oral form. The answer to the second question turns out to be much more elusive than the answer to the first. But the point here is that the form of the problem is dictated by looking for a determinate number of segmental phonemes in the first place. That itself supports Olson's thesis: the phonological word is being conceptualized after the image of the written word, not vice versa.

Olson also draws attention to various research findings which suggest that, psychologically, writing systems serve as a model for speech or even determine the way in which speech is perceived. For example, studies of 'phonological awareness' indicate that ability to divide words into sub-syllabic segments depends on acquaintance with alphabetic writing. Chinese familiar with the (alphabetic) *pinyin* system show an ability to do this which is not matched by those Chinese who can read only traditional Chinese characters.[46] Similarly, Vai literates, familiar with the Vai syllabic script, were found to be much better than non-literate Vai people at putting together separate syllables into phrases and splitting up phrases into their constituent syllables. Olson comments:

> This suggests that the learning of a syllabary is a matter of coming to hear one's continuous speech *as if* it were composed of segmentable constituents.[47]

Olson's claims raise many intriguing questions which cannot be pursued here. And the issue on which Olson calls in question the traditional Western wisdom about writing as a 'representation' of speech must not be oversimplified. No one argues that, prior to the advent of writing, speakers were quite oblivious to features of

---

[46] C.A. Read, Y. Khang, H. Nie and B. Ding, 'The ability to manipulate speech sounds depends on knowing alphabetic reading', *Cognition*, vol.24, 1986, pp.31–44.

[47] Olson, op. cit., p.82.

oral language. This would be like supposing that musicians were tone deaf before the invention of musical scores. It is clear from the evidence of poetry in pre-literate cultures that awareness of quite subtle patterns of rhythm, rhyme and assonance did not escape either the pre-literate poet or the pre-literate audience. What is at issue, however, is the role of writing vis-à-vis speech in that symbiotic relationship which characterizes literate societies. Two hypotheses stand in confrontation. According to one, writing serves to record linguistic units and structures already recognized by speakers of the language in question. According to the other, writing itself serves as the model for the recognition of such units and structures.

What neither hypothesis offers is a direct answer to the question of *how* the written sign comes to play the role hypothetically assigned to it. Integrational theory is in a position to offer a semiologically motivated answer:

Any graphic configuration acquires a certain linguistic value insofar as it serves to articulate the integration of one form of verbal activity with another, or verbal activities with non-verbal activities.

In short, the very integration with speech that glottic writing affords in such practices as 'dictation' and 'reading aloud' is what, inevitably, leads the participants to treat these as alternative or correlative forms of linguistic expression. When this happens the linguistic units comprising such messages – whether previously recognized as such or not – can no longer be defined by purely oral criteria. The integration of speech with writing irreversibly transforms social conceptions of language. Language becomes subject to other conditions than those of orality. It becomes possible to ask for the identification of linguistic forms in visual as distinct from auditory terms, or even to demand, for particular purposes, that they shall be so expressed.

The cultural history of the signature (Chapter 7) provides a particularly clear illustration. In a pre-literate society, a personal name serves to identify an individual, enabling others to call or refer to that person: if A's name coincides phonetically with B's name, then A and B both have 'the same name'. In a literate society, on the other hand, the name can serve other purposes; for example, in signing a document. Here the name remains, as before, a means of identification. But, as Béatrice Fraenkel aptly remarks, through the signature recording one's name also becomes a form of action.[48] This extension in the functions of the name is bought at a certain price: its phonetic characteristics become secondary. What is important is no longer how it sounds but how it is written. So Mr White and Mr Whyte are no longer counted as having the same name. This change is a change in the concept of the name. And for so long as that change is supported by the social and legal practices of a literate society, there is no prospect of reverting to the old oral concept of what a name is. Nor can it be supposed that the old oral concept survives alongside the new concept. When someone asks your name, you do not say: 'Which one? My written name or my spoken name?' In a literate society you have only one name, even though it has both an oral and a written form.

That, in a literate society, goes not only for names but for words, phrases, sentences and for language in general. What distinguishes a literate culture from a pre-literate culture is not so much the *addition* of a quite separate mode of verbal communication as the *incorporation* of oral communication into a higher-order semiological synthesis involving the written sign. In that synthesis, however, it is increasingly the graphic element which dominates.

Something similar can be observed in the history of Western music. The crucial development is not the invention of new instruments with new 'sounds', or new ways of playing old instruments, important though these may be, but the introduction of systematic and detailed forms of music notation. Originally an aid to performance, written notation made possible compositions of an extent and complexity that could not be undertaken before. Just as in the case of language, the price paid for this is a change in

---

[48] Fraenkel, op. cit., p.12.

the conception of the musical work. The score becomes its 'authentic' form.

In both the linguistic and the musical case, the underlying reasons are not difficult to see. The integration of writing with both speech and music produces a new material object: the document. From the moment of its creation, the document leads an independent material existence. It thus provides an effective means of controlling the future of whatever text or composition it contains. It supplies a basis for replication, analysis and verification which did not exist in the pre-documentary era.

The macrosocial advantages of writing appear no less evident. Documentary records facilitate forms of control over individuals and whole populations that are impossible in a pre-literate society. These do not appear overnight. (It took, for example, several centuries in Anglo-Saxon England to establish the validity of written wills.[49]) But once the effectiveness of these forms of control is recognized, it is only a matter of time before they are extended. We are destined to live in an ever more minutely documented society, even though the documentation will be electronic documentation, not paper documentation.

* * *

For societies that have reached this historical turning point, the choice is between an 'old' semiology of writing in which writing is treated simply as one possible form for the expression of a message and a 'new' semiology in which writing is treated as the creation of textualized objects. For reasons indicated in the preceding chapters, only an integrational approach can do justice to the latter. The essential difference between the two is that in one case semiological values will depend on the 'adequacy' of the written form to express the given message, whereas the other will see semiological values as derived from the role of the textualized

---

[49] B. Danet and B. Bogoch, 'From oral ceremony to written document: the transitional language of Anglo-Saxon wills', *Language & Communication*, Vol.12 No.2, 1992.

object in integrating the activities of those who participate in its making and interpretation. These are two quite different conceptions. The first leads to a reification of 'the message' as something which exists in a prior form, either physical or mental, needing to be reconciled with the exigencies of a particular writing system. The second leads to recognizing 'the message' not as something given in advance – or given at all – but as something created by interaction between writers and readers as participants in a particular communication situation.

But if we are to envisage how this may affect the future of a literate society, it is important not to go on thinking of 'writer' and 'reader' as occupying sempiternally the fixed roles that were allotted to them under the old regime of utilitarian literacy.

CHAPTER NINE

Mightier than the Word

Even before the publication of Saussure's *Cours de linguistique générale* in 1916, a far more revolutionary rethinking of writing was already under way. The revolutionary forum was not linguistics but literature, and its most spectacular early manifestation was Mallarmé's poem *Un coup de dés*. At first sight it might appear that its novelty consists merely in being a work in which 'the type is an integral part of the enterprise'.[1] In his brief preface, Mallarmé admits that perhaps the most upsetting aspect of the work for the average reader is likely to be the absence of the regular lines that define the visual form of poetry (Fig. 8). Mallarmé's meticulous concern with the exact positions of the words on the page is revealed in the proofs he corrected shortly before his death for the (subsequently unpublished) Lahure edition, which was to have been illustrated by Odilon Redon.[2]

A recent critic describes Mallarmé's engagement with typography as follows:

> So as to indicate the structure of this fairly lengthy and extremely complex piece of prose made up of some 650 words

---

[1] R.G. Cohen, *Mallarmé's Masterwork. New Findings*, The Hague/Paris, Mouton, 1966, p.78.

[2] Cohen, op. cit, reproduces Mallarmé's corrected proofs and also Redon's lithographs.

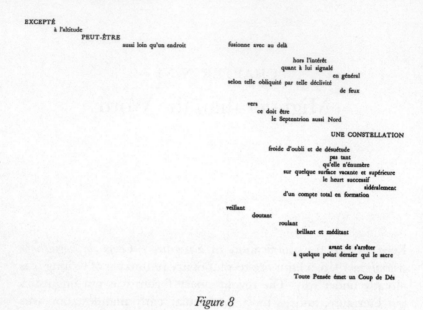

EXCEPTÉ
à l'altitude
PEUT-ÊTRE
aussi loin qu'un endroit   fusionne avec au delà

hors l'intérêt
quant à lui signalé
en général
selon telle obliquité par telle déclivité
de feux

vers
ce doit être
le Septentrion aussi Nord

UNE CONSTELLATION

froide d'oubli et de désuétude
pas tant
qu'elle n'énumère
sur quelque surface vacante et supérieure
le heurt successif
sidéralement
d'un compte total en formation

veillant
doutant
roulant
brillant et méditant

avant de s'arrêter
à quelque point dernier qui le sacre

Toute Pensée émet un Coup de Dés

Figure 8

covering 21 pages Mallarmé uses different kinds of lettering.
The main clause, printed in bold capitals, is interrupted after
'jamais' by a subordinate clause in smaller capitals which, in
turn, is interrupted by a long and intricate passage in ordinary
roman type. Only after these two parentheses does the verb
'n'abolira' appear and it too is followed by a long parenthesis in
italics before the object of the verb, 'le hasard', makes its
appearance. A final qualifying clause is then introduced, at first
in italics and then in roman type, to bring the work to a close.[3]

If that were all, it would already suffice to show that at least one
poet in the nineteenth century had grasped the fact that writing
has a potential for going beyond the resources of oral poetry, and
beyond the resources of conventional speech altogether. For on
Mallarmé's page the reader sees the visual articulation of a syntax

---

[3] C. Chadwick, *The Meaning of Mallarmé*, Aberdeen, Scottish Cultural
Press, 1996, p.12.

that is orally 'impossible'. (To call it 'ungrammatical' would be on a par with saying that Picasso's *Les Demoiselles d'Avignon* shows a poor grasp of perspective.) But there is more to the typography than that.

The words and sentences are sparingly distributed across the comparatively large area of the double page, which Mallarmé uses as his 'frame' instead of the single page, so that the lines of print, sometimes trailing across the paper like a drawing of the wake of a ship, sometimes grouped together like black dots on white ice, and sometimes more widely scattered like black stars in a white sky, reinforce the three kinds of imagery which dominate *Un coup de dés* [. . .]

It is interesting and no doubt significant that the concluding lines of *Un coup de dés* are set out not only in the shape of two dice which have finally been thrown and have fallen to reveal three and four dots respectively, but also in the shape of the constellation of the Great Bear with its slanting line of three stars and its rectangle of four stars.[4]

But when in his preface Mallarmé explains what he is trying to do, he has to fall back on comparing blank spaces with silences – a comparison which immediately reinstates the assumptions underlying the phonoptic tradition that *Un coup de dés* deliberately subverts. He speaks of 'this copied distance which mentally separates groups of words or one word from another' and how this sometimes accelerates and sometimes slows down the movement of the text.[5] What else can the 'copied distance' refer to, if not the interval which may separate two words or phrases in the spoken

---

[4] Chadwick, op. cit., pp.12–13, p.165.

[5] 'L'avantage, si j'ai droit à le dire, littéraire, de cette distance copiée qui mentalement sépare des groupes de mots ou les mots entre eux, semble d'accélérer tantôt et de ralentir le mouvement, le scandant, l'intimant même selon une vision simultanée de la Page.' S. Mallarmé, *Œuvres complètes*, ed. H. Mondor and G. Jean-Aubry, Paris, Gallimard (Bibliothèque de la Pléiade), 1945, p.455.

sentence? Unexpected spaces in the text correspond to unexpected pauses in speech. Here is a striking example of how difficult it is even for the iconoclast, within a phonoptic tradition, to conceive of writing as anything other than a substitute for speech.

It is even more striking that when Mallarmé addresses the semiological status of his poem as writing, he appeals to a musical analogy and says that his text is, for anyone willing to read it aloud, a score.[6] To suppose that Mallarmé is seriously thinking here of an oral delivery of his poem would miss the point of the metaphor. The score, for Mallarmé, is the paragon of a written text which presents directly, without ambiguity, what it signifies – the musical work, the composer's thoughts; whereas poets, on the contrary, are perpetually obliged to struggle against the constraints of language through which they must express themselves. Dualist theories of communication feed all forms of artistic schizophrenia. Mallarmé's schizophrenia takes the form of wanting to make poetry an artistic medium that can render ideas in all their pristine purity, uncontaminated by the words employed to express them. Saussure, who died just before the *ne varietur* edition of Mallarmé's revolutionary graphic work was published, would have regarded that ambition as a kind of linguistic dementia resulting from a total failure to understand the mechanism of *la langue*.

* * *

It is even more difficult to imagine what Saussure would have made of Guillaume Apollinaire's poem *Lettre-Océan*, published in 1914 (Fig. 9). Mallarme's *Un coup de dés* at least has a beginning a middle and an end, a sequential order of some kind, but with Apollinaire's poem the problem is 'where to start reading'; for the work

imposes no point of entry and offers no consistent order of

---

[6] 'Ajouter que de cet emploi à nu de la pensée avec retraits, prolongements, fuites, ou son dessin même, résulte, pour qui veut le lire à haute voix, une partition.' Mallarmé, op. cit., p.455.

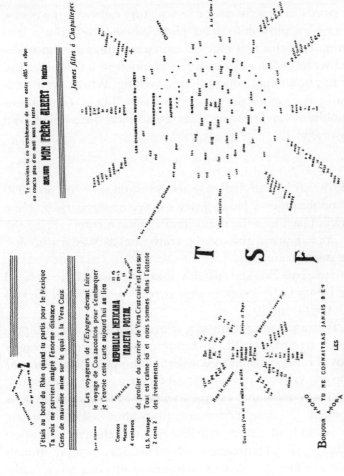

Figure 9

reading. It even undermines conventions of figure and ground, surface and depth, frame and canvas that traditional easel painting in the West has made second nature for most of us.[7]

In other words, even if we treat it as a picture rather than a poem, we find it no less difficult to 'read' pictorially than verbally.

The impact of this first modern calligram underlines just how restricted writers of the eighteenth and nineteenth centuries had been by the traditional conception of writing. Where even Mallarmé had paid a modicum of respect to the 'linear' conventions dear to publishers and printers, *Lettre-Océan* flouts them openly and enthusiastically.

* * *

A less obviously visual challenge to the tradition came in 1939 with the publication of James Joyce's novel *Finnegans Wake*. Here the attack is taken into the opposition's home territory: since the external appearance is that of the conventional Western book – until one starts reading.

riverrun, past Eve and Adam's, from swerve of shore to bend of bay, brings us by a commodius vicus of recirculation back to Howth Castle and Environs.

Sir Tristram, violer d'amores, fr'over the short sea, has passencore rearrived from North Armorica on this side the scraggy isthmus of Europe Minor to wielderfight his penisolate war: nor had topsawyer's rocks by the stream Oconee exaggerated themselse to Laurens County's gorgios while they went doublin their mumper all the time: nor avoice from afire bellowsed mishe mishe to tauftauf thuartpeatrick: not yet, though venissoon after, had a kidscad buttended a bland old isaac: not yet, though all's fair in vanessy, were sosie sesthers wroth with twone nathandjoe. Rot a peck of pa's malt had Jhem or Shen brewed by

---

[7] R. Shattuck, *The Innocent Eye*, New York, Washington Square Press, 1986, pp.296–7.

arclight and rory end to the regginbow was to be seen ringsome on the aquaface.

The fall (bababadalgharaghtakamminarronnkonnbronnton nerronntuonnthunntrovarrhounawnskawntoohoohoordenenth urnuk!) of a once wallstrait oldparr is retaled early in bed and later on life down through all christian minstrelsy. The great fall of the offwall entailed at such short notice the pftjschute of Finnegan, erse solid man, that the humptyhillhead of humself prumptly sends an unquiring one well to the west in quest of his tumptytumtoes: and their upturnpikepointandplace is at the knock out in the park where oranges have been laid to rust upon the green since devlinsfirst loved livvy.

And so on, for six hundred pages and more.

It has been said that the writing of *Finnegans Wake* marked the end of English.[8] Manifestly untrue. But doubtless *Finnegans Wake* was one of the events that marked the end – or the beginning of the end – for a theory of writing that had gone virtually unchallenged in Western literature since the days of Aristotle. Before Joyce produced his contentious masterpiece, it still seemed superficially plausible to maintain that all literary prose works were, in the final analysis, surrogates for speech; not because they were transcriptions of what the author had actually at one time said, but in the sense that they had been written in such a way as to suggest or invite a reconstruction of what the author or the author's characters would have said, had they spoken. But this traditional view was hard put to it to explain a work like *Finnegans Wake*, peppered with orthographic forms corresponding to no known words of anyone's spoken language. Joyce's text was – and is – a form of writing which defies oral rendition (which, as might have been expected, did not prevent the author from recording his own 'readings' from it). But, leaving such isolated virtuoso vocal performances on one side, for most readers the most salient fact about the book is, as one recent editor notes, that it is 'unreadable'.

---

[8] Philippe Sollers, *Théorie des exceptions*, Paris, Gallimard, 1986, p.80.

In order to pay it the attention it so impertinently and endlessly demands, the reader must forego most of the conventions about reading and about language that constitute him/her as a reader. The advantage to be gained from doing so is considerable; the conventions survive but they are less likely thereafter to dwindle into assumptions about what reading or writing is.[9]

Whatever doubts about the 'advantage' sceptics may entertain, there can be no doubt about the perspicacity of the remark in the latter part of the sentence. That the book is 'unreadable', as the same commentator remarks, is 'the first thing to say about' it. And perhaps not only the first thing – since it is obvious from the opening pages – but the last thing too. For those who survive the gruelling exercise of grappling with *Finnegans Wake*, there can be no doubt that the 'normal' process of reading will never seem the same again. This is not just a shock tactic that the author has decided to employ for attention-grabbing purposes. The 'unreadability' of the book is a focal point of the author's message *about language and about literature*. Line by line, we have to guess at – or ignore – the pronunciation of words we have never seen before. And yet, behind this mish-mash of neologisms, derived etymologically from everywhere and nowhere, we seem to hear – sometimes very clearly – the lilt of an Irish accent. This alone should suffice to convince us that 'unreadability' is, after all, only a relative term.

It was not English that failed to survive the earthquake of *Finnegans Wake* but the conception of written English as the accredited graphic transcription, however imperfect, however conventional, of a pre-existing oral English, a form of speech with which one was already acquainted. What cannot be said, in the case of Joyce, is that 'the language had always been there'. It had not. Joyce is the first writer in the Western tradition to reject the doctrine of 'linguistic priority' in its totality. Joyce's language is

---

[9] J. Joyce, *Finnegans Wake*, ed. Seamus Deane, London, Penguin, 1992, p.vii.

created by Joyce, and created *on the basis of resources offered by writing.* What would Saussure have made of that? Conceivably, he might have dismissed it as a playful attempt to create an imaginary language. But that would have been to miss the point. The language of *Finnegans Wake* is not an extended exercise on the model of More's Utopian.[10] Since, for Saussure, languages as systems are entirely autonomous systems of arbitrary signs, the resemblances between Joyce's language and English would have had to be entirely fortuitous. Furthermore, since writing systems, in Saussure's view, exist only as systems of metasigns, a language (*langue*) created on the basis of writing would be tantamount to the miracle of the tail wagging the dog.

This has not prevented French critics from foisting Saussurean interpretations on the language of *Finnegans Wake*. In what Joyce writes, claims Sollers, deliberately echoing a well-known Saussurean dictum, 'there are only differences'. The comment would have been more apposite if 'differences' had been replaced by 'analogies'. Sollers himself provides the following etymology for the Joycian word *traumscrapt*.

TRAUMSCRAPT. *Traum* ('dream'), *trauma* ('trauma'), *script* ('script'), *rapt* ('abduction'). Development: what's an *écrit* ('written work')? the rapt of a *trauma*; what's a *trauma* ? the *rapt* of an *écrit*, what's a *rapt* ? the *script* of a *trauma*. [. . .]

This is what Joyce calls his 'trifid tongue' – an expression in which you can hear *terrific* (terrible) but also *trifle* (joking).[11]

The chains of lexical analogy stretch out in all directions, ignoring linguistic boundaries. What emerges is the profound semiological originality of writing. Only writing is in a position to

---

[10] Appended to Thomas More's *Utopia* (1516) are four lines of verse 'in the Utopian tongue', together with a 'translation'. The printer apologizes for printing the passage transliterated in the conventional European manner, explaining that he does not have available 'the Utopian alphabet'.

[11] Sollers, op.cit., pp.87–8.

orchestrate, simultaneously and with equal resonance, this combination of phonetic, syntactic and etymological images, across a
whole range of languages and dialects. And that is the basis of
Joycian language-making. Words are still, apparently, its means of
articulation; but they are words freed from the constraints of any
fixed code.

It would be beside the point to dismiss *Finnegans Wake* as showing a bizarre, perverse, experimental approach to writing, just as it
would be beside the point to dismiss analytic cubism as showing a
bizarre, perverse, experimental approach to painting. If the analytic cubists accomplished nothing else, they demonstrated once
and for all that the semiological limits of painting do not coincide
with the representation of the visible world. Joyce did the same for
the semiology of writing and the representation of the spoken
word.

* * *

The lessons of *Un coup de dés*, *Lettre-Océan* and *Finnegans Wake* were
not easy to assimilate for a public educated to respect the norms
of the Western literary tradition. What exactly was going on here?
What was going on – and many commentators on the modernist
movement still have not realized it – was that the long-lived Western concept of glottic writing was being tested to the limit. It was
being deliberately subjected to intellectual and aesthetic pressures
under which it was bound to fracture, as did the 'representational'
conventions of academic painting when challenged by the avant-
garde of the *école de Paris*. The historical irony is that this was
happening at the very time when Saussure was mounting his
structuralist defence of the old phonoptic view of writing. Structuralism here emerges as the reactionary wing of modernism,
committed to a rearguard action that was already doomed to
failure.

Once it becomes obvious – by practical demonstration – that
written communication does not depend either on the existence
of an oral language which it transcribes, or on the existence of
orthographic conventions which govern it, only the persistence

of earlier and more rigid ways of thinking can prevent recognition of the conclusion that *writing can create its own forms of expression*. It took the genius of Mallarmé, Apollinaire and Joyce, as it had taken the genius of Picasso and Braque, to turn theoretical possibilities into semiological realities.

These bold innovations must also be seen as symptoms of a deeper malaise that makes itself felt during the nineteenth century in a society increasingly unhappy with – but nevertheless educationally committed to – the assumptions of utilitarian literacy. One of the striking differences between eastern and western attitudes to writing and writers is the far higher awareness in the east of the artistic dimension of the visual text. The same utilitarian logic which sees writing as no more than a convenient way of recording speech relegates the written text itself to a fairly low position in the hierarchy of artistic endeavour. It is not without significance that the art of calligraphy never attained in Europe the importance accorded to it in oriental and Islamic cultures. Western aesthetics clung on for centuries to the notion that what is written is merely a substitute for the author's voice. This idea survives long after the introduction of printing. We find a remarkable example in Hegel, who says of poetry:

> Now if we ask where we are to look, so to say, for the *material* basis of this mode of expression, the answer is that, since speaking does not exist, like a work of visual art, on its own account apart from the artist, it is the living man himself, the individual speaker, who alone is the support for the perceptible presence and actuality of a poetic production. Poetic works must be spoken, sung, declaimed, presented by living persons themselves, just as musical works have to be performed. We are of course accustomed to read epic and lyric poetry, and it is only dramatic poetry that we are accustomed to hear spoken and to see accompanied by gestures; but poetry is by nature essentially musical, and if it is to emerge as fully art it must not lack this resonance, all the more because this is the one aspect in virtue of which it really comes into connection with external existence. For printed or written letters, it is true, are also existent

externally but they are only arbitrary signs for sounds and words. Earlier we did regard words as likewise means for indicating ideas, but poetry imposes a form, at least on the timing and sound of these signs; in this way it gives them the higher status of a material penetrated by the spiritual life of what they signify. Print, on the other hand, transforms this animation into a mere visibility which, taken by itself, is a matter of indifference and has no longer any connection with the spiritual meaning; moreover, instead of actually giving us the sound and timing of the word, it leaves to our usual practice the transformation of what is seen into sound and temporal duration.[12]

Here we have repeated emphasis on the oral nature of poetry combined with manifest disparagement of the printed word – evidently not a coincidence. What lies behind it? No one would wish to argue against Hegel that European poetic forms do not spring from a tradition of song and recital, based on rhythms, rhymes, assonances and other auditory – even musical – patterns. But that hardly explains Hegel's appeal to a mysticism of orality which credits the poet with the ability to confer on mere sounds 'the higher status of a material penetrated by the spiritual life of what they signify'. This is not just another manifestation of Aristotelian dualism, nor a resuscitation of Platonic scepticism about writing, but the backward-looking polemic one might expect to find in an age when the poets have in fact lost touch with their bardic heritage and are increasingly concerned with words on the page. The writer-poet is for Hegel, it would seem, a fallen creature, if not a traitor to the cause of poetry.

It is a far cry from this to the oriental perspective, in which poetry has always been seen as closer to painting than to music. Chinese characters are not the inert marks that Hegel evidently regards alphabetic letters are being. Nor is it an accident that Chinese civilization never developed its own system of phonetic

---

[12] G.W.F. Hegel, *Aesthetics*, trans. T.M. Knox, Oxford, Clarendon, 1975, p.1036.

writing (in the sense in which Western historians understand that term). The semiology of writing in Chinese has a pictorial dimension that is altogether lacking in the west.

Hegel's refusal to recognize a visual aesthetics of poetry has something obscurantist about it; for in the European tradition the poem on the page always adopted a visual form that echoes its oral structure. (That is why Mallarmé feared that his readers would find *Un coup de dés* difficult.) The line of verse, as it appears in western manuscripts, has never been anything other than a graphic unit mimicking an auditory unit. It is the work of writers who can hear what they write and see what they hear: a monument to glottic writing.

But by Hegel's time all literature except for drama was increasingly being confined to expression in written form.[13] This sits uncomfortably within a literary tradition which has deep roots in orality. The result is a crisis in which all relations between sound and written form are called in question, as is the authorial 'voice' itself. The nineteenth century sees the beginnings of 'free verse', a term which to some extent sums up the problems at issue. For the 'freedom' was a question of breaking the bondage which kept the line of poetry tied to the traditional metrical conventions, rather than being at liberty to follow the (alleged) cadences of speech. These cadences, in fact, were from the outset a graphic mirage, which never corresponded to those of everyday talk. The rhythms of free verse were always those of an imaginary language, constructed by poets. We are dealing with a kind of literary illusion, in which the resources of writing are deployed to install and authenticate an orality that never existed (except for the poets concerned and their poetry-readings). It is an interesting example of a cultural narcissism that has – and could have – no analogue in a pre-literate society: a phenomenon entirely generated by writing.

A related development, associated with Romanticism, is that those who adopt the literary role of 'writer' suddenly begin to

---

[13] Hegel even complains that 'no play should really be printed'. (Hegel, op. cit., p.1184.)

realize that they are 'free' to write in a so-called 'oral style': hence the linguistic aesthetics of Wordsworth and his school. This new interest in orality is in part prompted by the fear that, in a society still largely illiterate, the writer – unlike the bard of old – risks losing touch with the majority of the population. The category 'oral style' still survives today in odd corners of contemporary stylistics. A curious example is François Richardeau's analysis of the style of Marguerite Duras.[14] Richardeau's so-called 'rhythmo-typographic' analyses of texts adapt a technique borrowed from Marcel Jousse in his work on Arabic and Hebrew material.[15] Jousse, an anthropologist of note, regarded writing as a 'bastard' and 'parasitic' variant of natural language (i.e. speech), causing cerebral fatigue and exhaustion of thought. A precursor of Marshall McLuhan, Jousse was already in the 1920s accusing the ancient Greeks of 'ocular hypertrophy' and predicting the day when the page would be replaced by the disc. All these are manifestations of the same literacy crisis. Its history can be traced from the beginning of the nineteenth century down to the spread of radio and television, which simultaneously mask and accentuate it.

* * *

In retrospect, Mallarmé, Apollinaire and Joyce appear as visionaries who had glimpsed the future of writing, but lacked the appropriate writing instrument to put what they knew into practice. The instrument in question arrived in the second half of the twentieth century: the computer.

There is an old chestnut about how long it would take a monkey with a typewriter to produce, serendipitously, the complete text of a Shakespeare sonnet. Perhaps one reason why it has dropped out of circulation is that computers have now taken over from monkeys. We no longer have to imagine the bizarre occurrence of texts produced independently of the operation of human intentions.

---

[14] F. Richardeau, *Ce que révèlent leurs phrases*, Paris, Retz, 1988, p.40.
[15] M. Jousse, *L'Anthropologie du geste*, Paris, Gallimard, 1974.

The point of the monkey example was to raise the question of literary value. Would the sonnet have been any the worse for having been produced fortuitously by a chimpanzee? Is it not the product that matters, rather than the process of production? Is not value conferred by the reader, rather than being intrinsic to the activities of the author?

According to current gipsies' warnings, the computer is a technological innovation that threatens to undermine the educational virtues that literacy formerly stood for. This undermining is not peripheral, but apparently threatens the expertise of professional writers themselves. We hear that, because of the computer, news reporters are no longer learning how to rewrite their copy, or, more alarmist still, that 'the word processor is erasing literature'.[16] We are invited to contemplate a future in which our descendants will be counted 'illiterate' if they cannot operate a word processor; but, at the same time, becoming slaves to the word processor is just what will rob them of the benefits of the ('old-fashioned') literate classes. So on either count, the future of literacy is doomed.

Before we succumb to pessimism of this kind, we should stop to consider more carefully what the role of technology in the spread of literacy has been hitherto. Is it clear that the 'literate' values that are now held to be threatened depend on writing at all? Where exactly does literacy begin and end?

In his book entitled *On Literacy* Robert Pattison argues eloquently against what he regards as the misleading equation of literacy with the practical skills of reading and writing, and against what he sees as a consequential series of educational fallacies based on that equation. For Pattison, it is obvious that Homer was a paragon of literacy, and yet Homer could neither read nor write. Therefore those who define literacy in terms of the ability to read and write, and thus by implication relegate Homer to the ranks of the world's illiterate masses, merely demonstrate their own cultural myopia and a complete failure to understand what it is that makes literacy worth having.

---

[16] Gore Vidal.

It might perhaps be objected to Pattison that Homer would never have become a paragon of literacy had his poems not been reproduced in written form by a later generation of Greeks; and consequently Pattison's prime historical example proves the very opposite of what he takes it to demonstrate. Nevertheless Pattison's argument, even if we do not agree with it, is sufficiently provocative to compel attention. In effect, what he is saying is that it makes no more sense to dismiss Homer as illiterate than to judge musicianship by whether a player can play by sight from a musical score. If that were the test, then there could be no blind musicians. The mistake in both cases is to erect what is only a secondary, ancillary technique into the primary criterion of a complex ability which that technique happens to serve. Just as it makes no sense to suppose that playing from a score is the only kind of musical performance, likewise it makes no sense to suppose that reading and writing are the only kinds of activity that manifest literacy.

It is interesting to consider how Pattison's argument fares when applied to the specific form of literacy which is sometimes called 'numeracy'. The modern concept of numeracy treats it as essentially involving the manipulation of quantification symbols according to principles and patterns which have to be studied and learnt. When we come across examples of early civilizations capable of undertaking the building of large temples and palaces and engaging in extensive enterprises of irrigation or town planning we are reluctant to accept that they could have done all this on the basis of a purely oral culture, even if they have left behind no record of their writing system. We prefer to think that they must have developed a written mathematics and a geometry now lost, because we cannot otherwise imagine how they could have managed the complex calculations apparently required by their feats of planning and construction. But let us hypothesize for a moment that somehow they did manage precisely that. Would we then dismiss them as having failed to achieve numeracy, on the same ground that some people would describe Homer as illiterate? Or would we not rather be forced to conclude that they must have been so highly numerate that they did not *need* to commit their calculations to papyrus or to clay tablets?

In *The Domestication of the Savage Mind*, Jack Goody recalls that he found he could not count cowrie shells as quickly or as accurately as boys of the LoDagaa in Northern Ghana who had had no schooling at all. And this was because, in the manner of Western literates, he counted the shells one by one. The native boys, on the other hand, counted them according to a traditional method in successive groups of three and two, which was both faster and easier to check. Furthermore, they had different methods of counting different objects. Counting cowrie shells had its own special technique. When it came to multiplication, however, Goody found that he could easily manage calculations that were beyond the expertise of the local cowrie counters. And this superiority Goody attributes to the fact that multiplication, as distinct from addition, is essentially a literate operation. The native boys, he says, 'had no ready-made table in their minds' which they could use for purposes of calculation.

What might be questioned about Goody's explanation, however, is precisely what the connexion between multiplication and literacy is. In some cultures an illiterate can use an abacus to calculate at a speed which will match any literate mathematician's pencil and paper. Perhaps Goody would reply that using an abacus involves an operational technology which is in all respects equivalent to that of manipulating figures on paper. But that simply brings us back to Pattison's argument about what literacy is. For however we may describe using an abacus, we certainly do not call it 'writing'.

A conclusion similar to Pattison's might perhaps be reached by a different argumentative strategy. Suppose the first explorers from Earth to arrive on Mars reported the existence of a curious reversal of the familiar terrestrial relationship between speech and writing. In other words, let us suppose it was discovered that Martians communicated primarily for everyday purposes by means of making visible marks on surfaces, and were biologically equipped to do this because their fingers constantly exuded a coloured liquid which they used in much the same manner as we use ink. With this coloured liquid Martians from their earliest years were used to tracing graphic symbols on any convenient surface that came to hand. But only few Martians ever learnt to make sounds corresponding to these graphic symbols, because this involved learning to use a special piece of equipment invented for the purpose, which looked like a small box and was worn strapped round the throat. This box was known in Martian as the 'vocal apparatus', but very few Martians could afford to buy one, and in any case this apparatus could be used effectively only after years of special training in the correspondences between Martian graphic symbols and the sounds that the box could produce. Perhaps the first question that might occur to an anthropologist on the mission from Earth is: 'Why do these Martians bother with this clumsy vocal apparatus at all?' Taking this science-fiction story one stage further, let us suppose that the Martian answer to this question turned out to be that whereas any fool on Mars could write, using the vocal box required a special form of intelligence, and furthermore conferred certain advantages on speakers over writers. For instance, speakers could communicate to one another by means of sound even in the absence of a writing surface. Furthermore, speakers could communicate even when doing something else with their hands and eyes, whereas writers could not. Third, speakers could communicate with one another audibly in ways that those who could only write were quite unable to understand. Fourth, vocalization had the inestimable practicality of leaving no trace, so that it was impossible for anyone subsequently to prove what had been said. It thus required mental alertness to engage in vocal communication, and quick reactions of an order quite beyond the average slow-witted writer. In short, speaking was a privileged form of communication shared by an elite, but beyond the grasp of the masses. Any sensible Martian, therefore, could see that it was well worth buying a vocal apparatus and learning to use it, because being able to use a vocal apparatus brought with it all kinds of communicational superiority.

This allegory, it will be self-evident, is constructed so as to reverse, on every crucial point, the usual terrestrial assumptions about the relationship between speech and writing. The lessons to be drawn from it do not need to be spelled out in laborious detail. Whether writing is judged to be a better form of communication than speech depends on one's point of view, and that point of view will be shaped by certain biological and cultural presuppositions. But in one sense it does not matter at what point and in what precise form technology enters the picture. As the allegory illustrates, it is possible to imagine a culture in which speech depends on the availability of certain tools, just as in our more familiar case writing depends on the availability of certain tools. What matters in both cases is the use made of those tools. And the utility of the tools is always measured against what could be done without them. This, at least as one reader understands it, is precisely Pattison's point about Homer.

In brief, the identification of intellectual progress with mastery of the technology of writing is an error typical of utilitarian literacy; in fact, a double error. The first mistake is to have confused a merely contingent use of artifacts with the cognitive consequences of their use. The second mistake is a failure to see that the technology would be pointless unless subserving other goals, which are not set by the technology itself. Both of these are essential points to grasp if we hope to discuss the future of human communication without falling into the pitfalls of nonsense.

Unfortunately, this is an area of speculation where prestigious nonsense abounds. Much of it derives from two sources. One of these sources is the endemic scriptism of the Western tradition; that is, the tendency to analyse spoken language as if it were written language *avant la lettre*. How deeply scriptism is entrenched in Western thinking about language emerges in various paradoxes. Perhaps the most striking is that linguistic theorists who subscribe to the doctrine of the primacy of speech as the characteristic form of human communication (Saussure is the classic example) nevertheless feel constrained to analyse speech in such a way that its units correspond in a quasi-miraculous fashion to the units of writing, even while proclaiming that writing practices are quite extrinsic to language. This may even carry over to meta-linguistic terminology. A quite remarkable case is the paper published by Leonard Bloomfield in 1927, in which he applied the distinction between 'literate' and 'illiterate' speech to a pre-literate speech community, the Menomini of Wisconsin.[17] The so-called 'International Phonetic Alphabet' is another example of scriptism disguised as linguistic analysis, based as it is on one culturally localized system of writing. Scriptism in all its forms encourages the view that literacy involves some kind of transference of linguistic skills from a natural medium (namely, that of speech) into an artificial medium (namely, writing).

Scriptism is defined by Florian Coulmas as:

the tendency of linguists to base their analyses on writing-induced concepts such as phoneme, word, literal meaning and 'sentence', while at the same time subscribing to the principle of the primacy of speech for linguistic inquiry.[18]

Linguists do indeed provide egregious examples. They have even proposed that human beings are equipped by their vocal apparatus with what Max Müller called a 'physiological alphabet' and A.J. Ellis 'the alphabet of nature'. One could hardly imagine more blatant cases of projecting the concepts of (one system of) writing on to the analysis of speech.[19] The underlying rationale is clearly: alphabets distinguish one sound from another – *ergo* such distinctions must exist already in Nature. ('How else could humans have recognized them?') But it is not simply linguists who are

---

[17] L. Bloomfield, 'Literate and illiterate speech', *American Speech*, 1927, Vol.2 No.10, pp.432–39.

[18] F. Coulmas, *The Blackwell Encyclopedia of Writing Systems*, Oxford, Blackwell, 1996, p. 455.

[19] Max Müller's chapter on 'The physiological alphabet' is to be found in his Second Series of *Lectures on the Science of Language* (London, Longman, Green, Longman, Roberts and Green, 1864). A.J. Ellis's 'The alphabet of nature' was published in the *Phonotypic Journal* (1844–5).

guilty of such *non sequiturs*: in this respect they simply follow – although indeed they have contributed to – the phonoptic bias that has prevailed in Western culture for many centuries.

The other principal source of nonsense about literacy can be traced to a body of pronouncements from what may be termed the *anti-scriptist* school. The members of this school include Walter J. Ong, Eric Havelock and Marshall McLuhan. Their major thesis is that writing, far from being merely speech made visible in the guise of inscriptions, constitutes a radically different cognitive enterprise. In their account, writing is not just a convenient way of recording speech, but involves a restructuring of thought. Anti-scriptism in its various forms encourages the view that literacy is a profoundly different mental condition from that of pre-literate humanity. Adherents to the anti-scriptist school often emphasize this radical change by speaking of the 'literacy revolution'.

As the terms *scriptist* and *anti-scriptist* suggest, there is certainly a deep divergence of views here. While accepting this, one may nevertheless wish to argue that the conflict between these views is often presented as a conflict over the wrong issue. The important difference between before and after the advent of utilitarian literacy is not essentially a difference between typical ways of thinking about the world, of classifying and ordering, of overcoming memory limitations, or of strategies for acquiring knowledge, although all these differences doubtless correlate with the spread of writing. But they are all manifestations of something more fundamental; and this something more fundamental is a shift in conceptions of language itself.

The change comes about for two reasons. One is that the introduction of writing destroys, once and for all, the former equation between language and speech. McLuhan was overstating the case when he claimed that 'until writing was invented, man lived in acoustic space'. What he should have said was that until writing was invented, language lived in acoustic space. In a preliterate culture the world of language is the world of sound. Writing changes all that. With writing, language invades the world of visual communication. It enters into competition – and partnership – with pictorial images of all kinds. The integration of writing with speech is what ushers in the misguided concept of language as something that is medium-transferable: words, it is supposed, can be spoken, 'transferred' into a different form where they are visible but no longer audible, and then 'transferred' back again into speech. This is what sometimes appears to preliterate communities, on their initial acquaintance with writing, as a form of 'magic'; but it does so only because their preliterate conception of language cannot immediately cope with the forms of integration involved.

The second reason is no less important. By making it possible to divorce the message both from its sender and from the original circumstances of its formulation, writing cognitively relocates language in an 'autoglottic' space. That is to say, the text takes on a life of its own, which is ultimately independent of the life – or intentions – of its author. It becomes an 'unsponsored' linguistic object, to which there is no parallel in a preliterate culture. And with this etiolation of personal sponsorship comes a fundamental change in the notion of meaning. Instead of tracing back meaning to the speaker or writer, as the authenticating source of the message, people come to regard meaning *as residing in the words themselves*. Plato's worries about writing are based on his recognition of this fallacy. But exactly what he feared came about. A culture in which writing has become 'internalized' has already prised open a conceptual gap between the sentence, on the one hand, and its utterance or inscription on the other. The sentence, being what lies behind and 'guarantees' *both* utterance *and* inscription, is itself neither. And this requires a conception of language which is necessarily more abstract than any that is required in a preliterate culture. Once this view of language is adopted, it is hard not to slide into adopting a parallel view of literature. Derrida's championship of the autonomy of the text is not just a philosophical aberration but the logical terminus of a questionable view of literacy that has become progressively established in Western culture over the centuries since Plato first objected to it.

* * *

The currently popular scenario for the future of writing gives pride of place to the development of techniques of word processing. It has already been claimed that our traditional concept of reading has been outdated by the advent of 'dynamic text' and 'hypertext'. The basis of this claim is a transformation in the role of the reader from passive recipient to active participant in the process of information transmission. Instead of merely receiving a message pre-determined by the sender in respect of both form and content, the reader is now able to control and access whatever information and information-sequences are deemed relevant for particular communicational purposes. Text is presented not in a traditional monolinear format, but as a simultaneous configuration of choices, from which the reader must make a selection. Depending on that selection, further selections become available, as the reader explores possible ways through the maze of information available. In this process of exploration, individual readers construct their own text instead of accepting a text dictated to them.

But this is not all. If it were, one might object that what it amounts to is simply a formalization and mechanization of reading strategies that have been available to the traditional reader for centuries. Western culture developed a special form of book and a special form of verbal deixis based precisely on such reading strategies. (The book is known as an *encyclopedia*, and the deictic device is known as *cross-referencing*.) So a stronger claim must be made if we are to be convinced that there is anything new here other than the technological format.

This stronger claim is based on the fact that programs may be set up in such a way that it may not be possible for the reader to retrieve a previously selected portion of text in exactly the same form as the first time: thus it may not be possible for the reader to turn back the page and find everything that was written on it before. Likewise, it may be impossible for the writer to foresee exactly the sequences and contextualizations that may arise as the result of selections made by different readers. Jay David Bolter sums it up as follows:

> Unlike printing, which lends fixity and monumentality to the text, electronic writing is a radically unstable and impermanent form, in which the text exists only from moment to moment . . .[20]

Under these conditions, we may ask, what exactly is the status of the text? Is it any longer a text at all?

Whatever it may be, it is clearly no longer a static object; and in that sense it may be claimed that we are dealing with a genuinely new form which actually requires us to rethink writing, whether we like it or not. For the primary characteristic of the writing process, as traditionally understood, was precisely that it produced a fixed form of words, available for inspection, re-inspection, interpretation and discussion as required. It was this fixity and quasi-permanence which was seen as contrasting with the ephemerality of speech. These non-ephemeral qualities were what made writing suitable for the recording of information and its transmission over space and time. It removed verbal communication from intrinsic dependence on the particular circumstances of a face-to-face situation or the vagaries of memory and uncheckable repetition. Hence, from Biblical times onwards, not only the Ten Commandments but edicts and laws of all kinds were set down in writing. Writing became the guarantee of authenticity because and insofar as it guaranteed in turn the invariance of the text. While it was true that a written text was only as durable as the material surface on which it had been inscribed, and on some surfaces writing is easily erased or altered, nevertheless it was also true that until altered by material decay or human interference the text remained static.

---

[20] J.D. Bolter, 'Beyond word processing: the computer as a new writing space', *Language & Communication*, 1989, Vol.8 Nos.2/3, p.129.

Again, however, if this were all, it might appear that what electronic writing has done is simply reintroduce via technology a *rapprochement* between writing and speech; or rather has endowed writing with the ephemerality which was formerly treated as characteristic of speech. And a sceptic might well ask what the point is of employing the latest technological innovations in order to revert to a more primitive type of communication.

A text which is not a static object not only defeats the storage function generally regarded as one of the primary utilitarian purposes of writing, but introduces something radically novel into our whole model of verbal communication, whether spoken or written; namely a discontinuity between the initial act of verbalization and its end product. And this discontinuity is of a different order from the material transformations which a message may undergo in its journey from, say, oral dictation to printed page. Simultaneously, it casts the text of Shakespeare's sonnets (as established by pre-computational editors) as merely an arbitrary reification within a range of possibilities. Compare the tedious dispute about the A-sharp in the first movement of Beethoven's *Hammerklavier* Sonata, opus 106. Did Beethoven 'intend' this? And does it matter?

*   *   *

Word processors, as everyone agrees, and as the term itself indicates, are essentially machines for manipulating verbal signs. Yet most of our current theories of verbal signs were formulated long before the advent of the computer. A serious question to be addressed is: are those theories now out of date? Has the semiology of the pre-computer era now been superseded?

A preview of how writing by machine may alter our concept of literacy is already offered by the pocket calculator. What is expected of students in a three-hour mathematics examination has changed dramatically since the days when all calculations had to be done by human brainpower. One can foresee analogous changes in the assessment of language skills when word processors automatically correct errors of spelling, grammar and punctuation. What is interesting about the word processor is that it provides a machine which enables the user to exploit *systematically* the potentialities afforded by the indeterminacy of the linguistic sign and the open-endedness of sign systems. Traditional writing does not do this because traditional writing is constrained by the writer's personal network of word associations, plus the orthological legacy of generations of educational convention. The word processor, on the other hand, is a piece of equipment for linguistic engineering. It can systematically invent new words, new paradigms, new constructions, new meanings and new languages if we wish. We can easily imagine a future in which 'Write a poem' is a standard examination question in the 'English' examination. (The vocabulary will be specified in the examination paper, and the test will be one of imagination in the deployment of the student's word processor's resources.) But this cannot go without repercussions on such concepts as 'style', 'text' and 'literature'.

* * *

What has passed almost unnoticed is that a tool with the power and ubiquity of the computer has the potential of reversing the twentieth century's received wisdom on the basic relationship between language, speech and writing. There are various reasons for this.

One is quite simply the sheer increase in the amount of written material generated. It is now confidently predicted that, with the internet explosion, written communication will quantitatively outstrip oral communication in the foreseeable future. If it does, that will certainly be a landmark in human history: speech will for the first time be the 'minor' form of communication.

But there are more important reasons which have to do with our grasp of the basic processes of verbal communication. As a writing machine, the word processor is already redefining our concept of what a 'word' is. The word is no longer a static lexical unit belonging to an inventory pre-registered in a dictionary. Implicitly, for a word processor, the word can be any symbol or symbolic unit which plays a role in the processing and can be controlled by well-defined keyboard operations. It is important to note that that role is not confined by the syntagmatic and para-digmatic relations which govern what we now recognize as the conventional words of ordinary language. Nor is it restricted by the conventional boundary lines which treat iconic symbols as non-words. Furthermore, such units and combinations can be invented by the writer as needed. The constraints on their invention are not conventions in the outside world, but constraints internal to the machine. The basic operational units are no longer, as in traditional scripts, either the word or the letter, but the separate keys provided by the keyboard; and the operational syntax is the combinatorial logic of pressing them in sequence or simultaneously. Thus far that logic is heavily indebted historically to the Roman alphabet (as one might expect in a transitional stage between forms of literacy); but there is nothing at all that requires it to remain so in the future. The alphabetic letter, like the Egyptian hieroglyph, is not indispensable.

Today, technology puts us in the position of projecting 'writing' as something altogether different from the ancillary system for recording, which was its traditional basic role. It opens up the possibility of treating writing as the essential creative process and speech as a marginal commentary on what has been written. That radical reversal of roles, we may reasonably speculate, will hold the key to the psychology of education in the next century. At the same time, it holds the key to what literature will be 'seen as'. Not a spontaneous linguistic expression of the writer's thought or emotion (which, arguably, it never was anyway, *pace* certain eminent theorists) but an exploration of verbal possibilities made universally available by the electronic writing machine. Electronic music is the relevant analogy here. In the computerized world of music, composers are less and less required to be able to play any instrument at all (including the human larynx).

* * *

It is within this perspective that it becomes relevant to return to Pattison's argument about Homer. Pattison may be right in insisting that traditional literacy had to be defined in terms of pre-existing goals or models, which were not set by the technology of writing itself but were already in place before the technology became available. Even if this was true in the past, however, will it be true in the future? Arguably not: and this is where the word processor not only makes a crucial difference, but turns Pattison's proposition upside down. The limits of literacy will be set by the technology, not in the sense of restricting the title 'literate' to those who read and write electronically, but by the exploitation of new linguistic possibilities which would not have been available without the technology to hand. And there is no way those limits can be set in advance; for we have as yet only an inkling of what computers of the future may make possible or even render commonplace.

The computer is the most powerful contextualization device ever known. Its capacity for creating and developing new contexts, visual and verbal, far outstrips that of the human mind. That is a far more important fact about the computer than its superhuman capacity for information storage. We are dealing with a machine which offers not only the possibility of integrating a simultaneous presentation of written, auditory and pictorial information, but of linking that information across languages and cultures as well. When future generations are quite accustomed to sitting at a keyboard and 'typing' an audio-visual product that incorporates sounds, letter-forms and pictures systematically interrelated, they will have acquired a new concept of writing, a new concept of literature, a new concept of language.

Bibliography

Abercrombie, D., *Elements of General Phonetics*, Edinburgh, Edinburgh University Press, 1967.

Alleton, V., *L'Écriture chinoise*, Paris, Presses Universitaires de France, 4th ed., 1990.

André-Salvini, B., *L'Écriture cunéiforme*, Paris, Éditions de la Réunion des musées nationaux, 1991.

Anis, J. (with Chiss, J.L. and Puech, C.), *L'Écriture: théories et descriptions*, Bruxelles, de Boeck, 1988.

Anis, J. and Puech, C., 'Autonomie de l'écriture'. In Lapacherie, J-G. (ed.), *Propriétés de l'écriture*, Pau, Publications de l'Université de Pau, 1998, pp.79-87.

Apollinaire, G., *Alcools et Calligrammes*, ed. C. Debon, Paris, Imprimerie Nationale, 1991.

Aristotle, *De Interpretatione*, ed. and trans. H.P. Cook, London, Heinemann (Loeb Classical Library), 1938.

Arnauld, A. and Lancelot, C., *Grammaire générale et raisonnée*, Paris, 1660.

Austin, J.L., *How to do things with Words*, Oxford, Clarendon, 1962.

Barr, J., 'Reading a script without vowels'. In Haas, W. (ed.), *Writing Without Letters*, Manchester, Manchester University Press, 1976, pp.71-100.

Barthes, R., *Le degré zéro de l'écriture*, Paris, Seuil, 1953.

Basso, K.H., 'The ethnography of writing'. In Bauman, R. and Sherzer, J., *Explorations in the Ethnography of Speaking*, Cambridge, Cambridge University Press, 1974, pp.425-32.

Bazell, C.E., 'The grapheme', *Litera*, vol.3, 1956, pp.43-46.

Bloomfield, L., 'Literate and illiterate speech', *American Speech*, 1927, Vol.2 No.10, pp.432–9.

—— *Language*, London, Allen & Unwin, 1935.

Bolter, J.D., 'Beyond word processing: the computer as a new writing space', *Language & Communication*, 1989, Vol.8 Nos.2/3, pp.129–42.

Bradley, H., *On the Relations between Spoken and Written Language, with Special Reference to English*, Oxford, Clarendon, 1919.

Buchler, J. (ed.), *Philosophical Writings of Peirce*, New York, Dover, 1955.

Butler, S., *Essays on Life and Science*, ed. R.A. Streatfield, London, Fifield, 1908.

Butor, M., *Les Mots dans la peinture*, Geneva, Skira, 1969.

Buyssens, E., *La Communication et l'articulation linguistique*, Paris/Brussels, Presses Universitaires de France, 1967.

Chadwick, C., *The Meaning of Mallarmé*, Aberdeen, Scottish Cultural Press, 1996.

Champollion, J-F., *Lettre à M. Dacier*, Fontfroide, Bibliothèque Artistique et Littéraire, 1889.

Chang, H-L., 'Hallucinating the other: Derridean fantasies of Chinese script', *Center for Twentieth Century Studies*, Working Paper No.4, 1988.

Chao, Y.R., *Mandarin Primer*, Cambridge, Mass., Harvard University Press, 1948.

Christy, T.C., 'Humboldt on the semiotics of writing'. In Rauch, I. and Carr, G.F. (eds), *The Semiotic Bridge*, Berlin/New York, Mouton de Gruyter, 1989, pp.339–45.

Cohen, M., *La grande invention de l'écriture et son évolution*, Paris, Klincksieck, 1958.

Cohen, R.G., *Mallarmé's Masterwork. New Findings*, The Hague/Paris, Mouton, 1966.

Coulmas, F., *The Writing Systems of the World*, Oxford, Blackwell, 1989.

—— *The Blackwell Encyclopedia of Writing Systems*, Oxford, Blackwell, 1996.

Danet, B. and Bogoch, B., 'From oral ceremony to written document: the transitional language of Anglo-Saxon wills', *Language & Communication*, Vol.12 No.2, 1992, pp.95–122.

DeFrancis, J., *Visible Speech. The Diverse Oneness of Writing Systems*, Honolulu, University of Hawaii Press, 1989.

Derrida, J., *De la grammatologie*, Paris, Minuit, 1967.

Desbordes, F., 'La prétendue confusion de l'écrit et de l'oral dans les théories de l'antiquité'. In Catach, N. (ed.), *Pour une théorie de la langue écrite*, Paris, CNRS, 1989, pp.27–33.

—— *Idées romaines sur l'écriture*, Lille, Presses Universitaires de Lille, 1990.

Diringer, D., *The Alphabet*, 2nd ed., London, Hutchinson, 1949.

—— *Writing*, New York, Praeger, 1962.

Ducrot, O. and Todorov, T., *Dictionnaire encyclopédique des sciences du langage*, Paris, Seuil, 1972.

Eco, U., *A Theory of Semiotics*, Bloomington, Indiana University Press, 1976.

Eiseman, F.B. Jr., *Bali: Sekala and Nisakala. Vol.1. Essays on Religion, Ritual and Art*, Berkeley / Singapore, Periplus, 1989.

Février, J.G., *Histoire de l'écriture*, 2nd ed., Paris, Payot, 1984.

Foucault, M., *Les mots et les choses*, Paris, Gallimard, 1966.

Fraenkel, B., *La Signature. Genèse d'un signe*, Paris, Gallimard, 1992.

Gelb, I.J., *A Study of Writing*, 2nd ed., Chicago, University of Chicago Press, 1963.

Goody, J., *The Domestication of the Savage Mind*, Cambridge, Cambridge University Press, 1977.

Gray, B., 'Language as knowledge: the concept of style', *Forum Linguisticum*, Vol.3 No.1, 1978, pp.29–45.

Harris, R., *The Origin of Writing*, London, Duckworth, 1986.

—— *Reading Saussure*, London, Duckworth, 1987.

—— *Signs of Writing*, London, Routledge, 1995.

—— *Signs, Language and Communication*, London, Routledge, 1996.

—— *The Language Connection*, Bristol, Thoemmes, 1996.

—— 'The integrationist critique of orthodox linguistics'. In Harris, R. and Wolf, G. (eds), *Integrational Linguistics: a First Reader*, Oxford, Pergamon, 1998, pp.15–26.

—— 'Making sense of communicative competence'. In Harris, R. and Wolf, G. (eds), *Integrational Linguistics: a First Reader*, Oxford, Pergamon, 1998, pp.27–45.

—— 'Three models of signification'. In Harris, R. and Wolf, G. (eds), *Integrational Linguistics: a First Reader*, Oxford, Pergamon, 1998, pp.113–25.

Harris, R., *Introduction to Integrational Linguistics*, Oxford, Pergamon, 1998.

Havelock, E.A., *The Literate Revolution in Greece and its Cultural Consequences*, Princeton N.J., Princeton University Press, 1982.

Hegel, G.W.F., *Aesthetics*, trans. T.M. Knox, Oxford, Clarendon, 1975.

Higounet, Ch., *L'Écriture*, 7th ed., Paris, Presses Universitaires de France, 1986.

Hjelmslev, L., *Prolegomena to a Theory of Language*, trans. F.J. Whitfield, rev. ed., Madison, University of Wisconsin Press., 1961.

Hockett, C.F., *A Course in Modern Linguistics*, New York, Macmillan, 1958.

Householder, F.W., *Linguistic Speculations*, Cambridge, Cambridge University Press, 1971.

Humboldt, W. von, 'Über die Buchstabenschrift und ihren Zusammenhang mit dem Sprachbau', *Abhandlungen der königlichen Akademie der Wissenschaften zu Berlin*, 1826, pp.161–8.

Jousse, M., *L'Anthropologie du geste*, Paris, Gallimard, 1974.

Joyce, J., *Finnegans Wake*, ed. Seamus Deane, London, Penguin, 1992.

Komatsu, E. and Harris, R. (eds), *Ferdinand de Saussure, Troisième Cours de linguistique générale (1910–1911)*, Oxford, Pergamon, 1993.

Komatsu, E and Wolf, G. (eds), *Ferdinand de Saussure, Deuxième Cours de linguistique générale (1908–1909)*, Oxford, Pergamon, 1997.

Kristeva, J., *Le Langage, cet inconnu*, Paris, Seuil, 1981.

Lallot, J., *La Grammaire de Denys le Thrace*, Paris, CNRS, 1989.

Lane, H., *The Wild Boy of Aveyron*, London, Allen & Unwin, 1977.

Larsen, S.E., 'Semiotics', *Concise Encyclopedia of Philosophy of Language*, ed. P.V. Lamarque, Oxford, Pergamon, 1997, pp.177–90.

Lee, S., *A History of Korean Alphabet and Movable Types*, Seoul, Ministry of Culture and Information, Republic of Korea, 1970.

Leroi-Gourhan, A., *Le Geste et la Parole*, I. *Technique et Langage*, Paris, Albin Michel, 1964.

Liddell, H.G. and Scott, R., *Greek-English Lexicon*, rev. ed., Oxford, Clarendon, 1996.

Llorach, E.A., 'Communication orale et graphique'. In Martinet, A. (ed.), *Le langage*, Paris, Bibliothèque de la Pléiade, Gallimard, 1968.

Locke, J., *An Essay Concerning Human Understanding*, 5th ed., London, 1706, ed. A.C. Fraser, 1894, repr. New York, Dover, 1969.

Logan, R.K., *The Alphabet Effect*, New York, Morrow, 1986.

Love, N., 'The fixed-code theory'. In Harris, R. and Wolf, G. (eds), *Integrational Linguistics: a First Reader*, Oxford, Pergamon, 1998, pp.49–67.

Lussu, G., *La lettera uccide*, Viterbo, Nuovi Equilibri, 1999.

Lyons, J., 'Human language'. In Hinde, R.A, (ed.), *Non-Verbal Communication*, Cambridge, Cambridge University Press, 1972.

Mallarmé, S., *Œuvres complètes*, ed. H. Mondor and G. Jean-Aubry, Paris, Gallimard (Bibliothèque de la Pléiade), 1945.

Malson, L., *Les Enfants sauvages*, Paris, Union Générale d'Éditions, 1964.

McLuhan, M., *The Gutenberg Galaxy*, Toronto, University of Toronto Press, 1962.

Moracchini, M., *ABC de graphologie*, Paris, Grancher, 1984.

Müller, F.M., *Lectures on the Science of Language. Second Series*, London, Longman, Green, Longman, Roberts & Green, 1864.

—— *Chips from a German Workshop*, Vol.IV, London, Longmans, Green, 1875.

Murdoch, I., *The Fire and the Sun*, Oxford, Oxford University Press, 1977.

Naville, A., *Nouvelle Classification des sciences. Étude philosophique*, Paris, 1901.

Nelson, K., *The Art of Reciting Qur'an*, Austin, University of Texas Press, 1985.

Ogden, C.K. and Richards, I.A., *The Meaning of Meaning*, London, Routledge & Kegan Paul, 1923.

Olson, D.R., 'How writing represents speech', *Language & Communication*, Vol.13 No.1, 1993, pp.1–17.

—— *The World on Paper*, Cambridge, Cambridge University Press, 1994.

Ong, W.J., *Orality and Literacy*, London, Methuen, 1982.

Pattison, R., *On Literacy*, Oxford, Oxford University Press, 1982.

Paul, H., *Principien der Sprachgeschichte*, 2nd ed., Halle, Niemeyer, 1886.

Pedersen, H., *Linguistic Science in the Nineteenth Century. Methods and Results*, trans. J.W. Spargo, Cambridge, Mass., Harvard University Press, 1931.

Pellat, J-C., 'La conception de l'écriture à Port-Royal'. In Lapacherie, J-G. (ed.), *Propriétés de l'écriture*, Pau, Publications de l'Université de Pau, 1998, pp.153–60.

Perec, G., *La Disparition*, Paris, Denoël, 1969.

Pessoa, F., *Sur les hétéronymes*, trans. R. Hourcade, Le Muy, Éditions Unes, 1985.

Plato, *Phaedrus and Letters VII and VIII*, trans. W. Hamilton, London, Penguin, 1973.

Potter, R.K., Kopp, G.A. and Green, H.C., *Visible Speech*, New York, Van Nostrand, 1947.

Pound, E., *ABC of Reading*, New York, New Directions, 1960 [1934].

Priestley, J., *A Course of Lectures on the Theory of Language and Universal Grammar*, Warrington, 1762.

Quintilian, *Institutio Oratoria*, ed. and trans. H.E. Butler, London, Heinemann (Loeb Classical Library), 1920.

Read, C.A., Khang, Y., Nie, H., and Ding, B., 'The ability to manipulate speech sounds depends on knowing alphabetic reading', Cognition, Vol.24, 1986, pp.31–44.

Reber, A.R., *Penguin Dictionary of Psychology*, Harmondsworth, Penguin, 1985.

Reid, T.B.W., *Historical Philology and Linguistic Science*, Oxford, Clarendon, 1960.

Richardeau, F., *Ce que révèlent leurs phrases*, Paris, Retz, 1988.

Richards, I.A., *How to Read a Page*, London, Kegan Paul, Trench, Trubner, 1943.

Rousseau, J-J., *Essay on the Origin of Languages*, trans. J.H. Moran, Chicago, University of Chicago Press, 1966.

Sampson, G., *Writing Systems*, London, Hutchinson, 1985.

Sandys, J.E, *Latin Epigraphy*, 2nd rev ed., London, 1927.

Saussure, F. de, *Cours de linguistique générale*, 2nd ed., Paris, Payot, 1922. All page references are to this edition. Translated passages are from F. de Saussure, *Course in General Linguistics*, trans. R. Harris, London, Duckworth, 1983.

Searle, J., *Speech Acts*, Cambridge, Cambridge University Press, 1969.

Shattuck, R., *The Innocent Eye*, New York, Washington Square Press, 1986.

Siertsema, B., *A Study of Glossematics*, 2nd ed., The Hague, Nijhoff, 1965.

Singer, E., *Graphology for Everyman*, London, Duckworth, 1949.

Smalley, W.A., Vang, C.K. and Yang, G.Y., *Mother of Writing: the Origin and*

Development of a Hmong Messianic Script, Chicago, University of Chicago Press, 1990.

Smith, D.E., (ed.), *A Source Book in Mathematics*, New York, McGraw-Hill, 1929.

Sollers, P., *Théorie des exceptions*, Paris, Gallimard, 1986.

Taylor, T.J., *Mutual Misunderstanding*, Durham, Duke University Press, 1992.

—— 'Do you understand? Criteria of understanding in verbal interaction'. In Harris, R., and Wolf, G., (eds), *Integrational Linguistics: a First Reader*, Oxford, Pergamon, 1998, pp.198–208.

Toolan, M., *Total Speech. An Integrational Linguistic Approach to Language*, Durham, Duke University Press, 1996.

—— 'A few words on telementation'. In Harris, R. and Wolf, G. (eds), *Integrational Linguistics: a First Reader*, Oxford, Pergamon, 1998, pp.68–82.

Trench, R.C., *English Past and Present*, London, Parker, 1855. Repr. Everyman's Library, London, Dent, 1927.

Tylor, E.B., *Anthropology*, London, Macmillan, 1881.

Vachek, J., 'Some remarks on writing and phonetic transcription', *Acta Linguistica*, vol.5, 1945–9, pp.86–93. Reprinted in Hamp, E.P., Householder, F.W. and Austerlitz, R. (eds), *Readings in Linguistics II*, Chicago, University of Chicago Press, 1966, pp.152–7.

Vendryes, J., *Le Langage*, Paris, Renaissance du Livre, 1923.

Wells, H.G., *The Time Machine*, London, 1895.

Whitaker, C.W.A., *Aristotle's De Interpretatione*, Oxford, Clarendon, 1996.

Whitney, W.D., *The Life and Growth of Language*, New York, Appleton, 1875.

Index